TONGUES

TONGUES

A Theological History of Christian Glossolalia

RICHARD HOGUE

TATE PUBLISHING & *Enterprises*

Published by Tate Publishing & Enterprises, LLC
127 E. Trade Center Terrace | Mustang, Oklahoma 73064 USA
1.888.361.9473 | www.tatepublishing.com

Tate Publishing is committed to excellence in the publishing industry. The company reflects the philosophy established by the founders, based on Psalm 68:11,
"The Lord gave the word and great was the company of those who published it."

Book design copyright © 2010 by Tate Publishing, LLC. All rights reserved.
Cover design by Tyler Evans
Interior design by Blake Brasor

Published in the United States of America

ISBN: 978-1-61566-674-4
1. Religion, Biblical Studies, History & Culture
2. Religion, Christian Theology, Pneumatology
2010.1.04

Table of Contents

Dedication

This book is gratefully dedicated to the courageous Charismatic men and women who through the centuries of Christianity endured hostility and ridicule while faithfully seeking and walking in the supernatural work and ministry of the Holy Spirit.

Acknowledgements

Like any significant writing, this book stands on the shoulders of several highly gifted men and women who have labored to produce materials in the same field. I am indebted to each one of them but feel it is important to name some who significantly impacted me throughout this work. I have been deeply challenged by the wealth of scholarship Professor James D. G. Dunn has brought to the understanding of the ministry of the Holy Spirit in his works, *The Baptism of the Holy Spirit* and *Jesus and the Spirit*. The monumental work of Professor Stanley M. Burgess in his trilogy, *The Holy Spirit,* proved a treasure field of historic knowledge along with Michael P. Hamilton in *The Charismatic Movement* and Dr. Eddie L. Hyatt and his *2000 Years of Charismatic Christianity*. Dean Vinson Synan in his many writings, including *The Holiness-Pentecostal Movement*, and Professor Cecil Robeck in *The Azusa Street Mission and Revival* opened for me the historic progressions that ultimately manifested in the outpouring of the Spirit at Azusa Street and the power of its continuing impact.

There are scores of others scholars, church leaders, popular teachers, and historic writers upon whom I have drawn during this writing. I have attempted to scrupulously notate each use of their writings and thoughts and sincerely pray this work can add to the enormity of their contributions.

I am very grateful to Harvard Divinity School and Oral Roberts University for the use of their libraries during this project, especially Dr. Mark Roberts and his staff at the Holy Spirit Research Center at ORU.

In addition, there are several close allies who have tirelessly assisted me in this undertaking with research, layers of editing, and countless ideas to sharpen my thoughts. I must mention Pastor Caszie Bennett, Dr. Bryan Frank, Pastor David Frank, Pastor Karen and Terrance Green, Pastor John Jewell, Pastors Roger and Sarah Lance, Pastors Greg and Kim Pierce, Jason and Ashley Taylor, and Pastor Glenda Baca. Blessings on each of you.

I must also acknowledge the faithful members of Citychurch in Oklahoma City. They are radical charismatic Christians who are committed to the full outpouring of the Holy Spirit in their individual lives and the life of our Church, and they are living in the power and authority of the gifts of the Spirit. They stood with me as I was away completing my graduate work at Harvard; they granted me time out of a hectic pastoral schedule to write and continually serve as my experiential laboratory as we move deeper and deeper into the miraculous demonstrations of the Spirit that challenge and change our lives continually.

Most importantly, I thank my precious wife, Marilyn, for encouraging me to study and write and partnering with me in countless hours discussing the theological and historic significance of speaking, singing, and praying in tongues. As always, she was the first and last to speak into each page.

Introduction

In 1975, Marilyn and I started MetroChurch in Edmond, Oklahoma, in the living room of our home. We had completed seven
years conducting major evangelistic meetings as a part of the
Jesus Movement and had seen thousands of young people accept
Jesus as Lord and Savior. The Jesus Movement was a remarkable time. Great freedom of the Holy Spirit permeated the entire
movement. As the emerging generation of Americans was exper-
imenting with drugs, demonstrating in the streets in opposition
to an unpopular war, delving into free love, getting high with
Janis Joplin and Jimi Hendrix, and learning to create tie-dye, etc.,
hundreds of thousands were committing their lives to Jesus. The
Movement was alive with the presence of the Spirit that produced a genuine hunger to know Jesus more fully and experience
His power and anointing. This hunger was a major motivating
factor with our evangelistic team. We loved Jesus and had seen a
scattering of incredible miracles, including the creative miracle of
a young girl born with no eyeballs who immediately received her
eyes and sight. Touching the supernatural deepened our commitment to the Lord Jesus and His Gospel, and produced an overwhelming desire to walk in the power of the Spirit.

The explosion of new converts in the Jesus Movement caught
most American churches ill-prepared and unwilling to deal with
their radical lives, faith, and music. Church after church refused to
accept this new generation of believers and turned back into them-

selves and the comfort of their traditions. Over a period of several months, we became convinced that a new kind of church had to be formed that would speak with a strong, uncompromising Christian message, yet be geared to reach and disciple new believers. Out of that climate and concern, MetroChurch was born.

MetroChurch became one of the great American churches and launched an era of large non-denominational works throughout the country. Even though we were not including the word Baptist in the name, we founded MetroChurch, fully expecting it would be a Southern Baptist church, but we soon knew God had other plans. I was asked by the head of Oklahoma Baptists to wait a year before petitioning the local Baptist Association for membership, which of course, I did. That was a critical decision for us. During that first year, MetroChurch grew quickly, and part of the growth was a number of very wonderful charismatic, tongue-talking Christians. They approached me about their practice of tongues and wanted to know my position regarding speaking and praying in tongues and with what freedom or restriction they could operate. In response to them, I developed a "don't ask, don't tell policy." They faithfully followed my request and never violated the guidelines I had established.

Throughout the first year of the church, these committed charismatic Christians became our most loyal and faithful workers. They took on the burden of building a new church with joy and fervor, and proved to be ones I could turn to for prayer. It was obvious that they possessed an unusual power and confidence in prayer and an inordinate faith. I enjoyed my time with them, listening to their experiences of prayer and miracles, and their remarkable love for the Lord Jesus.

Ultimately, I could not simply ignore the questions surrounding the charismatic, especially speaking in tongues. But finding legitimate theological answers was difficult. What I discovered were anecdotal writings on both sides of the issue, but very little theological insight. Those who opposed tongues wrote of the horrors of the practice: how tongues divided churches, caused feelings of spiritual superiority among those who spoke in tongues, and of course, the old evangelical contention that speaking in tongues could actually cause demon possession. The writings of those who favored speaking in tongues were just as vacant of theological insight. They spoke of great experiences of miracles, the supernatural, and the power they discovered in tongues. But I was a young pastor who needed Biblical answers for my people, not good or bad examples.

Unable to find the Scriptural rationale I desired, I set out to prove, at least to myself, what the New Testament taught regarding the question of tongues. To commit myself to the task, I announced to my church that I was undertaking this quest and would report to them in detail what I discovered. I honestly expected to find, as I had been taught for years, that tongues had ceased, that the New Testament presented a strong case against the use of tongues, that those who spoke in tongues inevitably misused the gift, caused problems in the church, and had to be corrected for their enthusiasm. Most significantly, I was confident I could discover historic grounds for the cessation of tongues tied to the coming of the New Testament canon.

My journey for answers took a full year.

What I discovered was not what I had expected. I announced to MetroChurch I had reached several decisions concerning speaking in tongues and that I would give my answers the following Sunday. When Sunday arrived, I shared with them that although I had never spoken in tongues, it was a legitimate New Testament experience that was to be a part of each believer's walk with the Lord Jesus. I presented the church with a series of questions regarding tongues and gave clear Biblical and historic answers to each inquiry. Much of the material I presented to MetroChurch thirty years ago is throughout this work.

The response I received was phenomenal. Remember, we were Baptists who had been taught and believed tongues had ceased with the original Apostles. But I believe because of the strong Biblical answers the Holy Spirit led me to discover and the anointing of the Spirit upon the truth of Scripture, MetroChurch embraced speaking, praying, and singing in tongues as a natural and desired aspect of the life of the Church of Jesus Christ. We had entered a new, exciting, supernatural world. Within a few weeks, our entire pastoral team, along with many of our people, were praying in tongues. During the ten years I pastored Metro-Church, the life and ministry of the Spirit grew as the Lord led us into greater understanding and experience of the supernatural.

When I went through the greatest challenge of my life and left the ministry in 1985, it was the reality of my relationship with the Lord Jesus and the undeniable supernatural experience of the Holy Spirit that drew me back from defeat. The ability to pray in tongues and know the Holy Spirit was praying the will of the Lord over my life when I did not have the courage or faith to do so was life changing.

In 1991, Marilyn and I returned to Oklahoma and launched Citychurch in downtown Oklahoma City. We committed ourselves to build, based upon the truth of the present reign of Jesus as King of kings, a truly multi-racial, multi-ethnic, multi-cultural church that is unapologetically charismatic. Citychurch is not huge. It is an inner-city work serving folks who desperately need the power and presence of the Spirit for their very survival; it is also the most radically committed group of people I have ever encountered. I have taught the principles in this book to City-church, and they have produced a people who expect the super-natural presence of the Spirit to manifest in their individual lives each time we meet, and it all begins with singing, praying, and speaking in tongues. I join with our pastoral team each evening to pray. We usually start lying face down on the floor praying in tongues for a prolonged period. We have found that by doing so the Holy Spirit quickly propels us into the presence of the Lord and into manifestations of His supernatural glory. What we experience in these times is phenomenal.

My decision to write this book came as the result of a television program I hosted on the Trinity Broadcasting Network. For some time, Southern Baptists have been experiencing a real controversy regarding speaking or praying in tongues. The controversy is not coming from Southern Baptists who speak in tongues, but those who are in ravage opposition. Southern Baptists have decided not to allow any of their missionaries, seminary professors, or other denominational leaders to pray in tongues even in their own private devotional life. Many Southern Baptist pastors have lost their pastorates because they pray in tongues, yet hundreds of Southern Baptist pastors continue to utilize the gift of tongues. When I learned of this controversy, and that over four hundred pastors had left the SBC because they spoke in tongues, I received permission to do a program on *Baptists Who Speak in Tongues*. The response to the program was remarkable. I received many responses from the program across the denominational spectrum. Several were Southern Baptists who desperately desired a Biblical understanding on which they could release their tongues, while others were Pentecostal-Charismatic pastors and laypeople who challenged me to put in writing the things I had discussed on the program. I realized, once again, that there is a great body of misinformation, distortions, and misunderstandings regarding the Biblical teaching and historic experiences of tongues, and as a result, I felt compelled to present this material.

My hope for this book is that it serves to help establish a clear Biblical teaching of the strategic place speaking, praying, and singing in tongues must always have in Christianity and the historic truth of the use of tongues in every century throughout the history of the church. As a result, I pray every Christian, regardless of their denominational background or affiliation, will receive the truth of this work and release this powerful super-natural manifestation. I join with the Apostle Paul and deeply desire, "That you all speak in tongues."

1

The Initiation of Jesus

The upper room stood prepared for history. The room, which may have belonged to a wealthy follower of Jesus, was highlighted by stately pillars supporting a high-vaulted ceiling illuminated by flickering candelabras. Couches surrounded the walls with tapestries occupying spaces between ornate windows and doors leading to the balcony overlooking one of the many narrow winding streets in the midst of ancient Jerusalem. Few rooms of its size existed in the city. Customarily, upper rooms were reserved for significant events. They served as quiet retreats away from the noise of busy, crowded streets, space for personal devotion, a place of honor for those who had died and awaited burial, or the site of special gatherings.[1] Most importantly for the Disciples, this chosen upper room was large enough to house one hundred and twenty men and women comprising the inner circle of those who believed Jesus to be the Messiah and was private enough to keep them safe. Even at this early moment in what would become Christianity, those devoted to Jesus were enemies to the Jewish

---

1 Acts 9:37–39; 20:8

authorities, who only forty days earlier had manipulated the crucifixion of Jesus.

Each man and woman entered the room ten days before the celebration of Pentecost, full of obedient expectation. Immediately prior to His ascension, the Lord Jesus explicitly instructed them not to leave the city: "But to wait for what the Father had promised, 'Which,' He said, 'you heard of from Me; for John baptized with water, but you will be baptized with the Holy Spirit not many days from now.'"[2]

Exactly how this spectacular baptism of the Holy Spirit was to unfold, none of them knew, but following the resurrection and ascension, they were confident of one thing: it would be *radically supernatural*.

The Pattern of the Spirit

The significant pattern of Pentecost was unveiled three years earlier at the time of the baptism of Jesus by John the Baptist, but it had very little to do with water. John the Baptist entered Israel declaring the coming of the Kingdom of God and preaching a baptism of repentance in preparation for the imminent appearance of the Messiah, who would establish the Kingdom.[3] For John, the kingdom was near but still future, and he awaited the appearance of the Eschaton,[4] the Messiah. The Baptist was thoroughly an Old Covenant character still operating in the "epoch of old salvation."[5] Jewish men and women flocked to the wilderness to be immersed by John in the waters of the Jordan River.

As would be expected, Jewish officials were curious, if not contemptuous, of John's ministry and sent a delegation to investigate this strange camel-skin-covered baptizer. "Who are you?"

2 Acts 1:1–4
3 Luke 3:3
4 Eschaton means the last thing. Jesus is the last thing.
5 James D.G. Dunn, *Baptism of the Holy Spirit*, (Philadelphia: Westminster Press, 1970), p. 25

they asked. "I am not the Christ," the Baptist returned. "Are you Elijah? Are you the Prophet?" "No," he emphatically replied. "Who are you then?" the delegation demanded.[6] John declared,

> "I am a Voice of one crying in the wilderness, 'Make straight the way of the Lord, as Isaiah the prophet said.'"[7] Now they had been sent from the Pharisees. They asked him, and said to him, "Why then are you baptizing, if you are not the Christ, nor Elijah, nor the Prophet?" John answered them saying, "I baptize in water, but among you stands One whom you do not know. It is He who comes after me, the thong of whose sandal I am not worthy to untie."[8]

Jesus was there at that moment in the crowd, yet remained unidentified, awaiting his messianic presentation by John. It seems Jesus was with John for several days surrounding his water baptism, for the following day after the departure of the delegation of Pharisees, John saw Jesus and declared,

> "Behold, the Lamb of God who takes away the sin of the world! This is He on behalf of whom I said, 'After me comes a Man who has a higher rank than I, for He existed before me.'"[9]

The messianic introduction of Jesus by John the Baptist pinpointed the salvific purpose of the Messiah. John exclaimed, "Behold, the Lamb of God!" Clearly, the Baptist reached back to Isaiah for this messianic moniker, speaking of the suffering servant of Isaiah. "He was oppressed and He was afflicted, yet He did not open His mouth; like a lamb led to slaughter ... He would

---

6 John 1:19–21
7 Isaiah 40:3
8 John 1:23–27
9 John 1:29–30

render Himself as a guilt offering."[10] This prophetically promised Lamb of God would be slaughtered for the "sins of the world," not just Jewish sins. His sacrifice would open messianic salvation to the world without distinction of race, religion, gender, or culture.[11]

Initially, the Baptist failed to recognize Jesus as the Messiah. He insisted, "I did not recognize Him," but at some point God gave John a prophetic vision identifying Jesus as the Anointed One. John demanded,

> "I have seen the Spirit descending as a dove out of heaven, and He remained upon Him. I did not recognize Him, but He who sent me to baptize in water said to me, 'He upon whom you see the Spirit descending and remaining upon Him, this is the One who baptizes in the Holy Spirit.'"[12]

From that point forward, John the Baptist understood the sole purpose of his baptism was the identification of the Messiah: "But in order that He might be manifest to Israel, I came baptizing in water."[13]

The Holy Spirit would descend and remain. That was the sign, the Messianic indicator. It would be the signal from heaven, the witness of the Father, that Jesus was indeed the Savior of the world. When it occurred, it was so powerful and overwhelmingly obvious that John the Baptist immediately declared Jesus was the

---

10 Isaiah 53:7, 10. The lamb could be used as a sin offering (Leviticus 4:32–35), but here John employs the term to bring clarity to the entire messianic mission. The New Testament identification of the Messiah as the Lamb of God only occurs in the Gospel of John and the Revelation.
11 F. F. Bruce, *The Gospel of John*, Grand Rapids: Eerdmans Publishing, 1983, p. 53
12 John 1:33
13 John 1:31

Messiah, the Son of God. "I myself have seen, and have testified that this is the Son of God."[14]

The Initiation of Jesus

The Baptist was under no illusion. He clearly recognized the limited significance of his baptism and the greater baptism of the Messiah. John understood he was the prophetically promised Voice, preparing the people.[15]

> "As for me, I baptize you with water; but One is coming who is mightier than I ... He will baptize you with the Holy Spirit and fire."[16]

Messianic baptism would surpass water baptism. Yet, the Messiah, Jesus, the mightier One, entered into the Jordan River to be baptized in water by John. By doing so, Jesus was not coming to repent or make a renewed commitment to the will of the Father; after all, He was sinless. Rather, Jesus entered the water of the Jordan to fulfill the prophetic ministry and baptism of John by being introduced as the Messiah. When the Lord came to John, the Baptist was hesitant to baptize Him, insisting he needed to be baptized by Jesus. Jesus assured John, "Permit it at this time; for in this way it is fitting for us to fulfill all righteousness."[17]

The Baptist obeyed. For Jesus, John's baptism was "an appointment of divine righteousness which was proper for Jesus to accept; it was from heaven ... to fulfill all righteousness apparently means to leave nothing undone that had been revealed as the righteous will of God."[18] As important as the water baptism of Jesus by John the Baptist was, it was not paramount. "John's

14 John 1:34
15 Luke 3:4
16 Luke 3:16
17 Matthew 3:15
18 R.E.O. White, *The Biblical Doctrine of Initiation*, (Grand Rapids: Eerdmans, 1960), p. 95

baptism was essentially preparatory, not initiatory."[19] Rather, it was the events immediately following His water baptism that were initiatory, historically pivotal,[20] and proved to be the pattern for the Church of Jesus Christ. Nothing approaching the importance of those events had ever occurred.

> Now when all the people were baptized, Jesus was also baptized, and while He was praying, heaven was opened, and the Holy Spirit descended upon Him in bodily form like a dove, and a voice came out of heaven, "You are My beloved Son, in You I am well-pleased."[21]

When the Holy Spirit came upon Jesus, Jesus experienced the initial baptism of the Holy Spirit. The ramifications were staggering. At *that* precise moment, the man Jesus, the incarnate Son of God, left the old covenant age into which He was born and entered into the new covenant. Though the new covenant age would require Jesus' death, resurrection, and ascension to be fulfilled for the church, Jesus alone entered the new covenant and would spend the remainder of His earthly life as a new covenant man baptized by the Holy Spirit.[22]

Saint Luke described three very distinct moments in the baptism of the Holy Spirit of Jesus, and the Apostle John adds a fourth. First, heaven opened. Properly understood, heaven entered earth. On the basis of His baptism by the Holy Spirit, from that moment forward, Jesus the man would operate with an open heaven. All the power of heaven would be available to

---

19 Dunn, ibid, p. 17
20 Dunn, ibid, p. 24: "There are only a handful of events in all this history which can be called pivotal. Jesus' reception of the Spirit at the Jordon is one of them."
21 Luke 3:21–22
22 Dunn, ibid, p. 27: "It is only then that he can properly be called Messiah (the Anointed One), only then that he takes up the function of Messiah, and only then that the messianic age can be said to have begun."

Jesus by the presence of the Holy Spirit in His life. Through the ministry of the Spirit, as the incarnate man, Jesus would live with the ability to know the will of His Father. Nothing was impossible to Him as long as He knew it was something His Father was doing.[23] The supernatural nature of the new covenant was revealed. Empowered by the presence and personal ministry of the Holy Spirit, the man Jesus and all those who follow Him as Lord and Savior would live as supernatural beings with an open heaven.[24]

Second, the Holy Spirit descended in bodily form like a dove. This event had never occurred in salvation history. It was in complete contradistinction to the normal coming of the Holy Spirit during the old covenant period.[25] Rather, the Holy Spirit descended upon Jesus in order to baptize Him with the Spirit. This alone was the messianic marker. The coming of the dove signalized that Jesus the man had entered the new covenant and from that position would live out His incarnation baptized and anointed by the Holy Spirit.[26]

Third, a voice came out of heaven. God the Father witnessed of His Son, Jesus, the second person of the Trinity; however, in His humanity He was incarnate, and by His Spirit baptism He was anointed as Messiah. [27] God spoke, "You are My beloved

---

23 John 5:19
24 Jesus described an open heaven as: "Whatever you bind on earth will be bond in heaven, whatever you loose on earth will be loosed in heaven "(Matthew 16:19.)"
25 There is no Old Testament reference to the Holy Spirit descending, or coming in bodily form, or coming as a dove. The Spirit is always transitory in OT references, "the Spirit of God came upon ... " *Judges 3:10; 6:34; 11:29; 14: 6; 19; 15:14; 1 Samuel 10:10; 11:6; 16: 13; 18:10; 2 Chronicles 15:1; "the Spirit of the Lord moved ... " Judges 13:25; "the Spirit of the Lord departed ... " 1 Samuel 16:14; "the Spirit of the Lord was upon ... " 1 Samuel 19:20, 23.*
26 Dunn, ibid, p. 27. Dunn sees Luke's emphasis on the dove as symbolizing the beginning of a new era of grace.
27 Hebrews 2:4. The Father testifies of the validity of the Son by sending the Holy Spirit.

Son, in You I am well-pleased."[28] The voice of God reached back to the great messianic Second Psalm, "You are My Son,"[29] and to the prophetic declaration of Isaiah, "Behold My Servant ... I have put My Spirit upon Him."[30] No question remained. Jesus was the Spirit-baptized Messiah sent to introduce a new salvation covenant with His new people, the Church.

Fourth, the Apostle John added the most unique, critical, and profound phrase to these events as he focused on the Spirit. He quoted the Baptist as saying, "I have beheld the Spirit descending as a dove out of heaven, and He remained upon Him."[31]

The Spirit came and remained. This was the ultimate messianic indicator. Until that moment, the Holy Spirit had come upon individuals to empower them for a specific task, but then the Spirit departed. This was the mode of operation for the Holy Spirit in the old covenant. But when Jesus was baptized with the Spirit, for the first time ever, the Holy Spirit remained, and the Lord entered the new covenant as a "representative man."[32] None of His followers, not even His closest disciples, would know this new covenant reality until Pentecost, but Jesus did. He was baptized in the Holy Spirit. "Only then could He properly be called Messiah (the Anointed One), only then did He take up the function of Messiah, and only then the messianic age can be said to have begun."[33]

---

28 Luke 3:22
29 Psalm 2 Jesus is the anointed of God for he has been baptized with the Holy Spirit.
30 Isaiah 42:1
31 John 1:32
32 Dunn, ibid, p. 32. Dunn correctly contends that the baptism of the Spirit was essentially an initiatory experience. "It is not something that merely accompanies the beginning of the New Age, it is that which effects it." Howard Ervin vehemently disagrees with Dunn. See Ervin, *Conversion-Initiation and the Baptism in the Holy Spirit* (Peabody MA: Hendrickson, 1984), p. 5. Like some other Pentecostals, Ervin saw the Baptism of the Spirit solely as an endowment of power.
33 Dunn, ibid, p. 27 parenthesis included. See, Psalm 2, Isaiah 42:1; Acts 10:38

Why? Why would Jesus need or desire to be baptized with the Holy Spirit? First, it is critical to state that the baptism of Jesus in the Spirit does not indicate Jesus lacked anything in His person that needed to be completed by the baptism of the Holy Spirit or that Jesus was ever at any time less than absolute God. Second, by receiving the baptism of the Holy Spirit, it initiated Jesus into the new covenant. He lived, taught, healed, and confronted the demonic and death from that point forward as a man baptized in the Holy Spirit. Third, Jesus established the model that each Christian would be baptized with the Holy Spirit, and that baptism of the Holy Spirit was initiatory. Fourth, and perhaps most importantly, it does speak of the state of His incarnation and the necessity of the baptism of the Spirit to fulfill His messianic mission.

The Apostle Paul wrote of the nature of the incarnation of Jesus: "Although He existed in the form of God, did not regard equality with God a thing to be grasped, but emptied Himself, taking the form of a bond-servant, and being made in the likeness of men."[34]

As the second person of the godhead, the Son of God was always God and always will be God.[35] From the moment of the conception of Mary with the Holy Son of God, the Son of God yielded to incarnation and restricted Himself to the form of the human Jesus. As such, He then entered the earth as an old covenant person and lived humbly, faithfully, and sinlessly the first thirty years serving the will of God the Father. In the fullness of time, the Son of God, incarnate as Jesus of Nazareth, began His messianic ministry. To prepare Him for this work and officially announce His messianic arrival, Jesus entered the waters of the Jordon to be baptized by John. This was the primary moment.

When Jesus entered His earthly work as Messiah, He did not become more God or more divine. His task was to live and die

---

34 Philippians 2:6–7
35 John 1:1

as the incarnate Son of God restricted to the form of a man. But not just a man, rather, as a man baptized with the Holy Spirit. This baptism of the Holy Spirit did not change Jesus as far as His status or person, but it anointed Jesus as the Messiah and thrust Him into the new covenant. "The thought is not so much of Jesus becoming what He was not before, but of Jesus entering where He was not before—a new epoch in God's redemption plan."[36]

But Jesus did change. From that point forward, Jesus operated in the power of the Holy Spirit. He overcame temptation by the power of the Spirit, [37] preached at Nazareth with the Spirit upon Him, [38] taught with unparalleled authority, [39] cast out demons by the power of the Spirit, [40] forgave sin, [41] and rejoiced greatly in the Holy Spirit because of His relationship to and knowledge of God. [42] Later, the Apostle Peter would explain, "You know of Jesus of Nazareth, how God anointed Him with the Holy Spirit and with power, and how He went about doing good, and healing all who were oppressed by the devil, for God was with Him."[43]

Jesus did not heal or perform supernatural miracles by the power of His divinity, but in His humanity that was baptized with the Spirit. Jesus' baptism in the Holy Spirit was "an official endowment and seal upon His divine commission as Messiah, a solemn anointing, becoming increasingly evident in the authority of His teaching, the unshakable assurance of His divine self-consciousness, the clarity of His purpose, the singleness of His

---

36 Dunn, ibid, p. 28
37 Luke 4:1–13. The newly Spirit baptized, messianically anointed Jesus, the second Adam, is led forth by the Spirit to do battle against Satan by refusing temptation Himself and by delivering the creation from the fall of the first Adam. He does so only in the power of the Holy Spirit.
38 Luke 4:18
39 Mark 1:22
40 Matthew 12:28
41 Mark 2:5
42 Luke 10:21–22
43 Acts 10:38

devotion to it, the transcendence of His claims, the power of His deeds, and the absoluteness of His demands."[44]

That was Jesus' messianic anointing; His baptism with the Holy Spirit, and it was the pattern that would be lived out by all those who follow Him as Lord and Savior, "the means by which God brings each to follow in Jesus' footsteps."[45] The new covenant was in the Spirit, and Christianity could not and cannot be experienced without the baptism of the Spirit.

Was Jesus a Charismatic?

The new age and covenant came, but only in Jesus. With His entrance into the age of the Spirit, Jesus was anointed with the Spirit as Messiah and stood alone as one baptized with the Spirit.[46] Since Jesus was obviously baptized in the Holy Spirit, the logical question must be asked: was Jesus a Charismatic? Without question, the Lord was certainly a charismatic personality, but the question does not concern His personality but His spiritual experience as a man. He did have great supernatural encounters, such as the episode of transfiguration, when He met with and talked to Elijah and Moses.[47] Dunn describes Jesus as a charismatic in terms of His power and authority. "He was charismatic in the sense that He manifested a power and authority which was not His own, which He had neither achieved nor conjured up, but which was given Him, His by virtue of the Spirit/power upon Him."[48]

The follow-up question must also be asked: did Jesus speak in

---

44 White, ibid, p. 98 "Henceforth, true baptism is inseparable from the gift of the Spirit." White goes on to demand, "Christian baptism proclaimed that the baptized had found the Savior, and the New Age had begun. The baptized were in the kingdom." p. 107
45 Dunn, ibid, p. 32
46 Luke 3:22; 4:18; Acts 4:27
47 Mark 9:2–8
48 James G.D. Dunn, *Jesus and the Spirit* (Grand Rapids: Eerdmans, 1975), p. 87

tongues? The answer seems to be no, for at least there is no specific record that He did so. However, there are three very interesting verses that could, repeat *could*, indicate Jesus experienced tongues. First, as He healed the deaf man at Decapolis, Jesus looked up to heaven "with a deep sigh" and commanded His ears to be opened.[49] The verse is easily compared to the tongue speech, "groanings too deep for words" in Romans 8:26. A second instance occurred as the Pharisees were arguing with Jesus and He is depicted as "sighing deeply in his spirit."[50] The argument can correctly be made that the Holy Spirit was sighing through Jesus' human spirit. If that is true, it parallels the words of the Apostle Paul when he speaks of tongues and declares, "For if I pray in a tongue, my spirit prays."[51] It seems as though Jesus was praying, *sighing deeply*, in His spirit, and it most definitely could have been in tongues. The third verse is in Luke. It is even more direct. Luke documents a moment in which Jesus "rejoiced greatly in the Holy Spirit," as He was beginning to pray and praise God.[52] Obviously, something supernatural was taking place. Luke, the author of the Acts of the Apostles, described Jesus as praying *in the Holy Spirit*. The similarities between these words and those describing speaking, singing, and praying in tongues down through the centuries of the church are remarkable. If Jesus was not praying in tongues, what was He doing? If the Scripture is allowed to define these moments, He seems to be speaking or praying in tongues.

The Essential Holy Spirit

Throughout their years with Jesus, the Lord led His disciples deeper and deeper into the supernatural, preparing the disciples for their ultimate baptism with the Holy Spirit. It was from that

---

49 Mark 7:34: It is very common for those exercising a gift of healing to pray in tongues as they pray for healing.
50 Mark 8:12
51 1Corinthians 14:14
52 Luke 10:21

empowering the disciples would build the church. They had seen firsthand the miracles of Jesus and His constant, victorious confrontation of the kingdom of darkness, but when they encountered the resurrection of Jesus, their entire concept of who Jesus was, and subsequently who they were, forever changed.

Immediately following the resurrection, Jesus appeared to His followers and "presented Himself alive after His suffering, by many convincing proofs."[53] It was during that period of forty days He "opened their minds to understand the Scriptures."[54] Up to this point, they had yet to fully comprehend some of the most fundamental teachings of Jesus, especially the supernatural nature of His kingdom, and as a result, they were still expecting a physical kingdom to be the purpose of His messianic ministry.[55] However, throughout those days following the resurrection, Jesus removed their confusion and unraveled the mysteries concerning the kingdom of God.[56]

His kingdom was to be a kingdom of power that would be released through them by the Holy Spirit. Everything the Lord Jesus would do as King, He would do through His Church by the power of the Holy Spirit: "You will receive power when the Holy Spirit has come upon you; and you shall be My witnesses both in Jerusalem, and in all Judea and Samaria, and even to the remotest part of the earth" (Acts 1:8).

The premier event marking the inauguration of His messianic kingdom would be His pouring forth the Holy Spirit into the earth. The power of His kingdom, the work of the Spirit, would destroy the kingdom of darkness, and through His Church His kingdom would victoriously cover the earth with righteousness and justice. The fulfillment of these deeds would take place through His disciples as they entered the supernatural and became

---

53 Acts 1:3
54 Luke 24:45
55 Acts 1:6
56 Acts 1:3

the Church of the Lord Jesus Christ, empowered by the presence of the Holy Spirit.

The Promised Paraclete

Initially, the idea of the coming Holy Spirit was not well received by the disciples. Jesus declared:

> I will ask the Father, and He will give you another Helper, that He may be with you forever; that is the Spirit of truth, whom the world cannot receive, because it does not see Him or know Him, but you know Him because He abides with you and will be in you.[57]

The disciples were not impressed. In fact, they were confused, angry, and not at all sympathetic or excited about a new helper. "What is He saying," they demanded to one another, and understandably so. [58] The thought of Jesus being replaced, even by the Holy Spirit, was not what they expected or desired. His strong assurances that He would never leave them "as orphans" [59] and that "their sorrow would turn to joy" [60] failed to satisfy them. Only following the resurrection did the teaching of Jesus concerning the coming Holy Spirit become palatable. "But I tell you the truth, it is to your advantage that I go away; for if I do not go away, the Helper will not come to you; but if I go, I will send Him to you."[61]

It was essential that Jesus ascend into heaven, receive His kingdom, take His place on the throne of His father David, and reign as King of kings and Lord of lords over everything on the earth, above the earth, and under the earth. In order for His will as king to be accomplished, Jesus would send the Holy Spirit to

---

57 John 14:16–17
58 John 16:18
59 John 14:18
60 John 16:20
61 John 16:7

empower His church and lead them by faith into the supernatural world of God. Jesus could not complete His work incarnate, and they could not receive all He had for them in the natural; their humanity restrained them just as the humanity of Jesus had restricted Him. Jesus told His disciples:

> I have many more things to say to you, but you cannot bear them now. But when He, the Spirit of truth, comes, He will guide you into all the truth; for He will not speak on His own initiative, but whatever He hears, He will speak; and He will disclose to you what is to come. He will glorify Me, for He will take of Mine and will disclose it to you.[62]

Jesus laid out His demands. His work in history, the church of Jesus Christ, could not exist apart from active ministry of the Holy Spirit. Throughout the church age, the Holy Spirit would take the will of King Jesus, all truth, and deliver it to His church in the lives of individual Christians and then fill the church with faith and the supernatural power to miraculously and supernaturally fulfill the will of King Jesus to His church and over His enemies.

---

62 John 16:12–14

2

The Initiation of the Church

Resurrection Sunday night was filled with anticipation and raw fear for the disciples. Mary Magdalene and the other women had told them of their encounter with the resurrected Jesus and His promise to visit the disciples that evening. [63] Even though several rejected her report, they nevertheless obediently gathered behind closed, locked doors, fearful of the Jews, but anxious to see Jesus. Miraculously, Jesus entered the room. "Peace to you," the Lord said as He showed them His hands and side to settle their questions and fears. [64] Immediately, the room changed. What had been an atmosphere of apprehension filled with gloom spontaneously erupted with rejoicing and celebration. Jesus was alive again! As the room settled, Jesus spoke again, "'Peace be with you; as the Father has sent Me, I also send you.' And when He

---

63 Obviously, there was a significant group of women with Mary Magdalene as she went to the tomb, encountered the resurrected Jesus, and talked to the disciples. Matthew 28:1 records Mary Magdalene and the other Mary; Mark 16:1 identifies Mary Magdalene, Mary the mother of James, and Salome; Luke 24:10 states Mary Magdalene, Joanna and Mary the Mother of James; also other women were present; John 20:1 singles out Mary Magdalene alone.
64 John 20:19

had said this, He breathed on them and said to them, 'Receive the Holy Spirit.'"[65]

This was a critical imperative from the Lord Jesus. Until that point, all of Jesus' promises regarding the coming of the Holy Spirit and His ministry to the disciples were future.[66] But then, following His resurrection, Jesus breathed upon them and brought the command into the present. What did this mean? What was the significance of this moment with Jesus and His men and women? What did they experience?

A plethora of answers exists to explain these events found in John 20. Some insist that the followers of Jesus were born again at this event and that the Spirit they received was an act of salvation bestowed by Jesus.[67] Others believe this to be a description by the Apostle John of Pentecost, the Johannine Pentecost.[68] Some imagine this event as a partial limited gift of knowledge, understanding, and empowerment until Pentecost.[69] Still others see the command as a pre-Pentecost empowerment for ministry.[70] Some insist the disciples began a process of salvation that would culminate at Pentecost.[71]

However, it seems the clearest meaning of this event lies in the totality of what Jesus did and said. First, the Lord began by saying, "Peace to all of you." It was a corporate greeting. His

---

65 John 20:21–22
66 John 7:39; 14:18–23, 28; 16:7–24, 28
67 Howard Ervin, *These Are Not Drunken As Ye Suppose* (Plainfield, NJ: Logos International, 1968), p. 89 While at Cornelius' house the Apostle Peter made it clear that the disciples did not receive the Holy Spirit and were therefore not saved until Pentecost. He demanded that those Gentiles had received the Holy Spirit, "just like we did (Acts 10:47)." By doing so, the Apostle recognized the legitimacy of Gentile salvation experience because it mirrored that of the disciple on Pentecost. They both spoke in tongues.
68 Donald G. Bloesch, *The Holy Spirit* (Downers Grove, IL: Inter-Varsity Press, 2000), p. 305
69 John F. Walvoord and Roy B. Zuck, *Bible Knowledge Commentary* (US: Victor Books, 1983), 343
70 F. F. Bruce, *The Gospel of John* (Grand Rapids: Eerdmans, 1983), p. 392
71 Dunn, *Baptism of the Holy Spirit* ibid, p. 182

directive was to all of them. Second, Jesus insisted, "As the Father has sent Me, I also send you." Whatever was about to occur was based upon the need of the disciples to be equipped like Jesus for the task they were about to undertake. Just as the Father had sent Jesus into the world, Jesus himself was now sending these chosen men and women. They were now to be His sent ones.

Third, Jesus "breathed on them." John used the Greek pharse, ἐνεφύσησεν καὶ λέγει αὐτοῖς, Λάβετε πνεῦμα ἅγιον, for the first time in the New Testament. It is the same word used in the *Septuagint* in Genesis 2:7 when God breathed into the face of His created being and he became a living soul and in Ezekiel 37:9 when Ezekiel prophesied over the dry bones that the breath of life would enter. Following His resurrection and ascension, it would be Jesus who breathed life into His church.

Fourth, Jesus demanded, "Receive the Holy Spirit." Literally, the phrase is "Take the Holy Spirit." The Greek verb is aorist, active, imperative, and second person plural. It was not an offer; it was a command. Take the Holy Spirit! Jesus did not circle the room, laying His hands on each one and breathing over them individually. It was a corporate prophetic command; *take the Holy Spirit*. It was as though the Lord Jesus said, "You will not receive the Spirit until Pentecost, but do everything that is necessary to take the Spirit." Everything the disciples would do as they birthed and built the church would require the Holy Spirit. Just as Jesus had first commanded, they were to take the gospel of the kingdom to their world: preach, heal the sick, raise the dead, cleanse the lepers, cast out demons, and they would not be successful without the power and presence of the Holy Spirit. [72]

Fifth, Jesus instructed them, "If you forgive the sins of any, their sins have been forgiven them; if you retain the sins of any, they have been retained."[73] The same power and authority Jesus had as a man baptized with the Holy Spirit, the disciples, and the

---

72 Matthew 10:8
73 John 20:23

Church of Jesus Christ would possess, even the power to forgive sins. The enormity of the mission of the Church would require that they obey the prophetic command of Jesus to take the Holy Spirit!

Forty Days with Jesus

In the afterglow of the resurrection and the forty post-resurrection days spent with Jesus, the expectation of the disciples concerning the coming of the Holy Spirit and His place in their lives and ministry radically changed. These were days of rebuke, instruction, challenge, and promise. As a result, the disciples understood they would be living in the supernatural by the power of the Holy Spirit. The resurrected Jesus was with them, teaching them about the kingdom of God, answering their questions concerning who they would be, the roles they were to play in the kingdom, and prepared them for the coming Holy Spirit. They would no longer be under the Law, not even a new law. Never again would they expect to fulfill their work in the natural.

> Afterward He appeared to the eleven themselves as they were reclining at the table; and He reproached them for their unbelief and hardness of heart, because they had not believed those who had seen Him after He had risen. [74]

Despite the enormous task before them, they were no longer fearful. It was then Jesus opened the work they would complete in the kingdom. He said to them, "Go into all the world and preach the gospel to all creation. He who has believed and has been baptized shall be saved; but he who has disbelieved shall be condemned."[75] However, they would not go alone. As Jesus

---

74 Mark 16:14
75 Mark 16:15–16

had been baptized in the Holy Spirit initiating His ministry, His church would experience that same anointing and power in their own lives over the kingdom of darkness. The Holy Spirit would accompany the preaching of the gospel of the kingdom with evident signs and wonders:

> "These signs will accompany those who have believed: in My name they will cast out demons, they will speak with new tongues; they will pick up serpents, and if they drink any deadly poison, it will not hurt them; they will lay hands on the sick, and they will recover."[76]

Very specific signs of the presence of the Holy Spirit were to follow those who believe the church of Jesus Christ. They would have power over every attack of the enemy who desired to hurt them, they would possess power in their hands to heal, but the most obvious sign would be what they were about to experience at Pentecost. They would speak in new tongues.[77] This sign was not to be reserved for a chosen few but all who followed. It was one of the last promises Jesus gave his followers, and they carried it with them into Pentecost.

Go to Jerusalem and Wait

The followers of Jesus, who were much more at home among the small fishing villages around the Sea of Galilee and had fled from Jerusalem at the death of Jesus, returned to the crowded dangerous confines of the city. The resurrected Lord Jesus directed them back into the heart of the ancient city. With obedient excitement, they faithfully gathered, prayed, and waited for ten days to be baptized with the Spirit.[78]

---

76 Mark 16:17–18
77 Mark 16:17
78 Acts 1:4: There is controversy concerning the exact location of the outpouring of the Holy Spirit on Pentecost. Was this the same upper room in which the disciples observed Passover with Jesus the night before his death, or was the room located somewhere in the temple

When they had entered the city, they went up to the upper room where they were staying; that is, Peter and John and James and Andrew, Philip and Thomas, Bartholomew and Matthew, James the son of Alphaeus, and Simon the Zealot, and Judas the son of James. These all with one mind were continually devoting themselves to prayer, along with the women, and Mary the mother of Jesus, and with His brothers.[79]

The exact details of what they would encounter as the Holy Spirit came remained a mystery, but one thing was certain: following the resurrection/ascension of Jesus, these faithful ones were anticipating something thoroughly supernatural. Throughout His earthly ministry, Jesus tenaciously moved toward Pentecost, obviously aware of the messianic destiny encapsulated in His life. Again and again, He urged His disciples that specific events *must* take place.[80] He was committed to accomplishing the full salvific will of His Father. The Lord never considered the climax of His ministry to be the cross or even the resurrection, but His ascension back to the Father to receive His kingdom and baptize His church with the Holy Spirit.[81]

The prophet Daniel saw Jesus, the Son of Man, ascending to the Father to receive His kingdom.[82] From that ascended, highly exalted position, seated upon the throne of His father David in heaven, ruling as King of kings, Jesus reached the apex of His

precincts? How could the large crowd have gathered in the streets surrounding the upper room within the city? Were the followers of Jesus baptized with the Holy Spirit in the upper room and then move to the streets still speaking in tongues? Did Peter speak from the balcony of the upper room or from the porch of the Temple? Based on Acts 2:2, Luke favors the upper room in a private home. John 16:7, "It is to your advantage that I go away; for if I do not go away, the Paraclete shall not come to you."

79 Acts 1:13–14

80 Thirty times in the Gospels Jesus is quoted as stating some event must take place.

81 John 16:7, "It is to your advantage that I go away; for if I do not go away, the Paraclete shall not come to you."

82 Daniel 7:12

messianic ministry.[83] He received both His kingdom and exercised His right to pour the Holy Spirit upon His church.

Pentecost

When the day of Pentecost arrived, they were all together in one place. And suddenly there came from heaven a noise like a violent rushing wind, and it filled the whole house where they were sitting. And there appeared to them tongues as of fire distributing themselves, and they rested on each one of them. And they were all filled with the Holy Spirit and began to speak with other tongues, as the Spirit was giving them utterance.[84]

With the outpouring of the Holy Spirit at Pentecost, the Lord Jesus brought His church into the divine family and poured the life of God into each believer. The disciples had entered the room as old covenant men and women, but inside the room they were born again, baptized with the Holy Spirit, and became true sons and daughters of God, joint heirs with the Lord Jesus. This was the fulfillment of the promise Jesus made concerning the Holy Spirit. Only those who received Him as Lord and Savior would experience the indwelling presence of the Spirit, and that indwelling would occur at the moment of their salvation, not later. Jesus promised, "He who believes in Me ... from his innermost being will flow rivers of living water."[85] The Apostle John explained that the Lord Jesus was speaking of the Holy Spirit, "whom those who believed in Him were to receive"[86] once Jesus was glorified. The promise was fulfilled at Pentecost and then throughout the history of the Church of Jesus Christ.

The baptism of the followers of Jesus with the Holy Spirit at Pentecost mirrored in ways the baptism of Jesus with the Spirit.

---

83 Acts 2:31
84 Acts 2:1–4
85 John 7:37
86 John 7:38

At the baptism of Jesus with the Spirit, heaven opened; with His church, a noise came from heaven. At the baptism of Jesus with the Spirit, the Holy Spirit descended like a dove; with the baptism of the Church, tongues of fire descended. At the baptism of Jesus with the Spirit, the voice of God spoke; with the baptism of the Church, the followers of Jesus all spoke in the heavenly voices of tongues.

The entrance of the Holy Spirit was filled with thoroughly supernatural events that were critically important, for with them the Lord Jesus opened the new covenant. First, one hundred twenty men and women were gathered in a single room inside Jerusalem. Included in this group were the disciples of Jesus who returned to Jerusalem from Galilee immediately following the post-resurrection appearances of the Lord, plus the inner core of the other men and women committed to Jesus. The Holy Spirit did not fall on the entire globe or humanity as a whole. Jesus baptized His church with the Spirit. The doors would be inclusively open to whosoever will, but His church was uniquely and solely the children of God. From that point forward, the activity of the risen King Jesus upon the earth, and therefore the activity of heaven itself, would be exclusively through His church.

Second, this series of supernatural events must be taken as a whole and be understood as occurring simultaneously. The manifestations of the Holy Spirit began with a violent heavenly wind that swept in and filled the room. This wind was the *pneuma*, the breath of God, the Holy Spirit. Throughout the Scripture, wind is an analogy for divine presence.[87] Probably the disciples understood the wind at Pentecost as the same wind experienced by the Prophet Ezekiel when the Lord instructed him to breathe on the dry bones. The Lord directed Ezekiel, "Prophesy to the breath, prophesy, son of man, and say to the breath, "Thus says the Lord GOD, 'Come from the four winds, O breath, and breathe on these slain, that

---

87 Genesis 8:1; Exodus 15:10; Psalm 58:9; Isaiah 66:15

they come to life.'" So I prophesied as He commanded me, and the breath came into them, and they came to life.'"[88]

The bones the prophet saw represented those who would become the church but were then dead, lost without the salvation of Jesus. The breath was the Holy Spirit whose first task was to bring life to those dead ones so they could rise to be a great army, the army of the Lord, the church of Jesus Christ. Ezekiel's prophesied outpouring of the Holy Spirit began on Pentecost and inaugurated the process of salvation by resurrecting individuals to new life. It would continue bringing the life of God to all who come to Jesus as Savior and Lord.

Third, the Holy Spirit entered the room and appeared as "tongues as of fire."[89] Exactly how this manifested is not known, but it seems to be flames of fires rising above the head of each individual present and is most likely tied to the promise of a baptism of the Spirit and fire.[90] As was true with the wind, the analogy of fire as the presence of God is replete in Scripture, but Pentecost stands alone in a manifestation as tongues of fire. [91] Whatever the exact details, it is obvious that the Holy Spirit rested upon each of them in an unexpected, unpredicted, and highly visible manifestation.[92]

Fourth, each of the one hundred twenty in the upper room was filled with the Spirit. As much as the cloven tongues of fire were the outer visible manifestation, the baptism of the Spirit was the inner experience of the disciples. The Holy Spirit brought the life of God into their dead spirits, and each person in the upper room was immediately born again, filled with the Holy

---

88 Ezekiel 37:9–10
89 The King James reads, "cloven tongues of fire." Indicating it is not one flame, but a divided flame over each person.
90 Luke 3:16
91 Exodus 3:2; 13:1; Numbers 14:14; Judges 6:21; 1Kings 18:38; Isaiah 6:6; Ezekiel 1:13; Daniel 7:9
92 There are reports of tongues of fire manifesting in Pentecostal and charismatic meetings throughout the history of the church, including today.

Spirit, and entered the new covenant and the church. Up until that moment, the disciples of Jesus were old covenant people, but then at Pentecost, they were born again, they experienced Christian salvation, became sons and daughters of God, and entered the new covenant.

Spoke in Tongues

Finally, each of the followers of Jesus in the upper room individually and simultaneously spoke in tongues. The Lukan Greek text is very clear:

καὶ ἤρξαντο λαλεῖν ἑτέραις γλώσσαις καθὼς τὸ πνεῦμα ἐδίδου ἀποφθέγγεσθαι αὐτοῖς

That is, "they began to speak in other tongues as the Spirit gave them to speak out." As they were born again, they were baptized by the Holy Spirit, sealed with the Spirit, and began praising the Lord Jesus by the Spirit through their spirits, and it was in tongues. It is critically important to remember who was in the upper room: the eleven disciples and 109 other followers, including Mary, the mother of Jesus, Mary Magdalene, and other women. Each one of these, including the Virgin Mary, spoke in tongues. The experience marked the beginning of that Holy Spirit phenomenon that would continue throughout the life of the church of the Lord Jesus Christ.[93] From that moment forward, the Spirit

93 Some within the church deny the use of tongues continued after the age of the apostles, and therefore believe the present use of tongues is misguided, if not heretical, or even demonic. The arguments against the experience of tongues are extremely varied: tongues have eased; tongues were only for the Jews; tongues causes spiritual pride; there is very limited mention of tongues in the NT; there is no mention of tongues after the Apostles; tongues can cause a Christian to become demon possessed. For these arguments see, Unger, *NT Teaching on Tongues*, 1971; Stollee, *Speaking in Tongues*, 1963; Campbell, *Do Not Speak In Tongues*, 1969; Burdick, *Tongues*, 1969; Coppes, *What Happen To Biblical Tongues*, 1977; Dillon, *Speaking in Tongues*, 1975; Baxter, *Charismatic Gift of Tongues*, 1985; Smith,

would place His mark upon the followers of Jesus. They would speak, sing, pray, rejoice, war by the Spirit in tongues.

The Prophet Isaiah predicted that dimension of the new covenant: "He will speak to this people through stammering lips and a foreign tongue."[94]

It was the mark of the presence of the Holy Spirit and fulfilled this prophesy of Isaiah. However, the most authenticating aspect of tongue speech at Pentecost was that it occurred in response to the promise of Jesus: "You shall be baptized with the Holy Spirit not many days from now."[95]

The experience of the followers of Jesus in the upper room on the day of Pentecost was the fulfillment of the promise of Jesus.

From Pentecost forward and throughout the decades of the church, the active presence of the Holy Spirit baptizing, filling, and gifting the church has been common Christianity. The New Testament is replete with those who entered into a relationship with Jesus by faith, were born again, supernaturally baptized by the Holy Spirit into Christ Jesus, and spoke in tongues. At those salvation moments, the gifts of the Spirit were universally visible and audible. Anything less was not Christianity! Entering into a relationship with Jesus as Lord and Savior was never stale or formal; rather, the gifts of the Spirit, including speaking in tongues, were always present. Christian salvation was always supernatural, and the supernatural was always demonstrated.

The Crowd Gathered

There was no crowd of thousands expectantly waiting outside the upper room for the coming of the Holy Spirit. Indeed, what

---

Tongues, 1972; McArthur, *Speaking in Tongues*, 1988; and many others. It is interesting that some of the arguments used against the present use of speaking in tongues are the same arguments used by those who oppose the authenticity of the New Testament.
94 Isaiah 28:11
95 Acts 1:5

happened in the upper room did not take place for the benefit of a crowd, but for the new birth and empowering of the church of the Lord Jesus Christ. It was only after the events of the upper room that a crowd gathered.

"When this sound occurred, the crowd came together."[96] What sound occurred? Some contend it was the sound of the rushing wind that caused the crowd to come together, but the rushing wind is confined to *the whole house where they were sitting.*[97] The supernatural sound that had in its quality the ability to attract the crowd was the sound of the Spirit, the sound of the one hundred twenty men and women corporately praying, singing, and praising God in tongues. That being the case, it is obvious that the followers of Jesus were speaking in tongues in the upper room for an extended period of time.

The timeline is significant. First, the events in the upper room took place. After time passed, the crowd gathered, and the disciples were still speaking and praying in tongues. Only then does the crowd overhear what was taking place *inside* the upper room. Obviously, then, as the Apostle Paul would later demand, public speaking in tongues was a sign to the lost.[98]

> Now there were Jews living in Jerusalem, devout men from every nation under heaven. And when this sound occurred, the crowd came together, and were bewildered because each one of them was hearing them speak in his own language. They were amazed and astonished, saying, "Why, are not all these who are speaking Galileans? And how is it that we each hear them in our own language to which we were born?"[99]

---

96 Acts 2:6
97 Acts 2:2
98 I Corinthians 14:22
99 Acts 2:5–8. Luke lists those present as: "Parthians and Medes and Elamites, and residents of Mesopotamia, Judea and Cappadocia, Pontus and Asia, Phrygia and Pamphylia, Egypt and the districts of Libya around Cyrene, and visitors from Rome, both Jews and proselytes, Cretans and Arabs–we hear them in our own tongues speak-

Many in the crowd were positively amazed, while others were openly skeptical. "Are these people drunk?" some shouted. Immediately, the disciples understood what was happening and its significance. Based upon what Jesus told them following his resurrection, they did not respond to this powerful moment as though something strange or frightening had taken place; rather, they instantly believed this phenomenon was the work and will of heaven.

Pentecost and the New Covenant

The Apostle Peter quickly decided to address the crowd. In doing so, he preached the first Christian sermon declaring the Messiahship of Jesus and demanding that the outpouring of the Holy Spirit initiated the new covenant. "Men of Judea and all you who live in Jerusalem, let this be known to you and give heed to my words. For these men are not drunk, as you suppose, for it is only the third hour of the day; but this is what was spoken of through the prophet Joel."[100]

Pentecost was not an anomaly; it was not strange; it was not to be avoided, and it was not simply for the moment. Rather, "this is what was spoken through the prophet Joel."[101] Pentecost fulfilled the prophetic promises of Joel and forever established that the age of the messianic kingdom of God's great Son would be the age of the Spirit.

> "And it shall be in the last days," God says, "that I will pour forth of My Spirit on all mankind; and your sons

---

ing the might deeds of God (Acts 2:9–11)."
100 Acts 2:14–16
101 There are some who attempt to deny the clear words of both Joel and Peter. Stanley D Toussaint, "Acts," *The Bible Knowledge Commentary*, ed. Walvoord and Zuck, (Wheaton, IL: Victor Books, 1983) p. 350. "The prophecy of Joel quoted in Acts 2:19–20 was not fulfilled." This is typical Dispensational thought attempting to deny the fulfillment of the Messianic mission of Jesus in the life of His Church.

and your daughters shall prophesy, and your young men shall see visions, and your old men shall dream dreams; even on My bondslaves, both men and women, I will in those days pour forth of My Spirit and they shall prophesy."[102]

The Prophet Joel did not forecast the end of the world or the second coming of Christ; rather, he prophesied that *in the last days* of the old covenant, the Lord Jesus would baptize His church with the Holy Spirit. [103] That was precisely what took place. The day of Pentecost was simultaneously the last day of the old covenant and the first day of the new.

> "I will grant wonders in the sky above and signs on the earth below, blood, and fire, and vapor of smoke. The sun will be turned into darkness and the moon into blood, before the great and glorious day of the Lord shall come."[104]

The Apostle Peter reached back to Joel and interpreted his poetic prophetic language to describe the dual activities of King Jesus throughout the new covenant. From the throne of heaven, ruling as King of kings, the anointed Messiah, King Jesus would baptize His church with the Holy Spirit and pour judgment out on His enemies. The initial baptism of His church occurred at Pentecost. The initial outpouring of His judgment took place with His

---

102 Acts 2:17–18.
103 Acts 2:17. See my book, The End of the Age (Cambridge, MA: Phos Books, 2009)
104 Acts 2:19–20. David Chilton, *The Days of Vengeance*, (Tyler, TX: Dominion Press, 1987), p. 502. Chilton writes of this dual Messianic activity in terms of the ascension of Jesus. "We are not speaking of a single act of ascending into the Cloud, but the direct and immediate consequence of that act; the outpouring of the Spirit on the Church in AD 30 … and the outpouring of wrath upon Jerusalem and the Temple in AD 70."

destruction of Jerusalem in AD 70 at the hands of the Roman prince Titus.

This was the authentic eternal launch of the church of Jesus Christ, which meant that throughout the life of the church, Pentecost, with its attendant charismatic aspects, could not be ignored or pushed aside. Pentecost was the remarkably radical and singularly unique event that gave birth to a very specific Christianity, and as a result, "Everyone who calls on the name of the Lord will be saved."[105]

At its birth, the church was global. Though it would take time for the church to fully understand, because of the outpouring of the Holy Spirit, the gospel of the kingdom was immediately open to everyone with no restrictions. "The Pentecostal phenomena gave an impetus to a community of believers who were destined to break through social, racial, and religious barriers with a message of light and life for all mankind."[106]

Peter continued focusing on the supernatural ministry of the Lord Jesus that came as the result of his baptism of the Holy Spirit.

> "Men of Israel, listen to these words: Jesus the Nazarene, a man attested to you by God with miracles and wonders and signs which God performed through Him in your midst, just as you yourselves know."[107]

The entire earthly ministry of Jesus was one of miracles, signs, and wonders by the power of the Holy Spirit. Peter insisted these miracles did not come from the divinity of Jesus as the Son of God but through his humanity. They were signs that "God performed through Him." Obviously, Peter was referring back to the man Jesus being baptized in the Holy Spirit. One aspect of that

---

105 Acts 2:21
106 T.C. Smith, "Acts," *Broadman Commentary*, Clifton J. Allen, ed. (Nashville: Broadman, 1970), p. 25
107 Acts 2:22

baptism was supernatural power. It was true for Jesus; it would be true for His church. The apostle assigned this power to the anointing of God and that meant the Holy Spirit. Later, Peter clarified this thought at Cornelius's house. "You know of Jesus of Nazareth, how God anointed Him with the Holy Spirit and with power, and how He went about doing good and healing all who were oppressed by the devil, for God was with Him."[108]

Peter declared that this supernatural power and authority was the direct result of His victory over death.

> This Man, delivered over by the predetermined plan and foreknowledge of God, you nailed to a cross by the hands of godless men and put Him to death. But God raised Him up again, putting an end to the agony of death, since it was impossible for Him to be held in its power.[109]

This Man, the Son of God restricted to the form of the man Jesus, could not be held by the power of death! The Apostle Peter stood on the balcony of the upper room and took his audience through the prophecy of Joel and then to the promises to David of the enthronement of His greater Son, the Lord Jesus Christ.

> "Brethren, I may confidently say to you regarding the patriarch David that he both died and was buried, and his tomb is with us to this day. And so, because he was a prophet and knew that God had sworn to him with an oath to seat one of his descendants on his throne, he looked ahead and spoke of the resurrection of the Christ, that He was neither abandoned to hades, nor did His flesh suffer decay."[110]

---

108 Acts 10:38
109 Acts 2:23–24
110 Acts 2:29–31

The apostle declared in the clearest possible terms that the power of sin and death had been defeated by the awesome reality of His resurrection. Jesus had won. As a result of His great victory, all of the promises God made to David concerning the kingdom of David's greater son who was God's Son were fulfilled at the resurrection. David prophetically "looked ahead and spoke of the resurrection of the Christ," not the second coming. The prophetic promise given to David had not been postponed. Jesus had ascended back to His Father and was seated upon the throne of His father David in heaven, ruling as the messianic king.

Peter's Pentecost sermon ended with two climatic declarations: "Therefore having been exalted to the right hand of God, and having received from the Father the promise of the Holy Spirit, He has poured forth this which you both see and hear."[111]

That outpouring on the celebration of the Feast of Pentecost was the beginning, the inauguration of a new age, the age of the Spirit. [112] What Jesus experienced at His baptism with the Holy Spirit would be the model; therefore, Pentecost was not a revival or postponement of the old—it was a birth. It was the culmination of all that had gone before. Only at Pentecost "by the gift of the Holy Spirit were the benefits and blessings won by Jesus in His death, resurrection and ascension applied to His Church."[113] It was the moment at which King Jesus, the Messiah, the resurrected man, the Son of God demonstrated that His church would forever be a supernatural people operating in the power, gifts, and the anointing of the Holy Spirit.

"Therefore let all the house of Israel know for certain that God has made Him both Lord and Christ—this Jesus whom you crucified."[114]

---

111 Acts 2:33
112 Pentecost means fiftieth, from the Greek word. The celebration of the feast of Pentecost took place fifty days after Passover. The feast of Pentecost is first found in Tobit 2:1 and 2 Maccabees 12:23.
113 Dunn, *Baptism in the Holy Spirit*, ibid, p. 44
114 Acts 2:36

What the followers of Jesus had experienced in the upper room and what the crowd overheard was the enthroned Jesus acting upon His kingly prerogative to pour out the Holy Spirit upon His people. This outpouring was the heavenly declaration to the earth with outward, visible, audible demonstrations that Jesus was both Lord and Christ!

The crowd was pierced to the heart with conviction and cried out to Peter, "What shall we do!"[115] Peter responded with what became the essential steps of Christian initiation:

> "Repent, and each of you be baptized in the name of Jesus Christ for the forgiveness of your sins; and you will receive the gift of the Holy Spirit. For the promise is for you and your children and for all who are far off, as many as the Lord our God will call to Himself."[116]

The pattern of initiation was forever established. *Repent.* Christian repentance was not a mere cataloging of sins, but a purposeful turning from sin to receive Jesus as Lord and Savior. *Be baptized.* Christian initiation was a baptism with water and the Spirit. "Baptism is thus a re-presentation of Christ's own baptism, and it necessarily carries with it the gift of the Spirit for those who repent and acknowledge Him as Messiah."[117] Understood correctly, Christian baptism is the baptism of the Holy Spirit. *And you will receive the Holy Spirit.* There was no hesitation for Peter. His assurance was based upon what he knew was the essential expectation: as a part of their salvation initiation, each new Christian would be baptized with the Holy Spirit.

The Apostle Peter assured those who responded to his message that "they could experience what the apostle experienced,"

---

115 Acts 2:37
116 Acts 2:38–39
117 G.W.H. Lampe, "The Holy Spirit in the Writings of St. Luke" in *Studies in the Gospels*, ed. D.E. Nineham (Oxford: Blackwell, 1955), p. 197–198

which was what the Father had promised.[118] [119] Therefore, from Pentecost forward, each individual who comes to Jesus will come through the baptism of the Holy Spirit, and that baptism was to always include the open demonstration of the gifts of the Spirit, which most definitely included speaking in tongues. Since the Lord Jesus chose to initiate His church in this way, no one has the permission or authority to change the pattern.

118 Kilian McDonnell and George T. Montague, *Christian Initiation and Baptism in the Holy Spirit*, (Collegeville, MN: Liturgical Press, 1991), p. 29
119 Acts 1:4

3

The Initiation Continued

The outpouring of the Holy Spirit did not end with the initial Spirit baptism of those followers of Jesus in the upper room on Pentecost. Instead, the baptism of the Holy Spirit became the immediate and essential sign of Christianity, the hallmark of those belonging to the church of Jesus Christ. The Holy Spirit marked each man and woman who genuinely repented and fully committed his or her life to Jesus Christ as Lord and Savior as the Spirit produced forgiveness and salvation. The presence of the Holy Spirit in an individual's life was the guarantee of his or her salvation and relationship with God.[120] For the early church, the baptism of the Holy Spirit was indispensable. If a person had not received the Holy Spirit, he or she had not experienced the salvation of Jesus and was not part of His church.[121]

The Dilemma at Samaria

After recording the initial outpouring of the Holy Spirit on the

---

120 1 John 4:13
121 John 14:17; Galatians 4:6; 1John 3:24

church by Jesus at Pentecost, Luke turned his efforts to documenting the continued outpourings of the Holy Spirit as the gospel of the kingdom was preached by the church. He began this process with a group of believers in Samaria and, in doing so, established the essential role of the Holy Spirit with his historic presentation of the Deacon Philip's ministry.

Philip entered Samaria, probably the cosmopolitan city of Sebaste, and preached the gospel of the kingdom, declaring Jesus to be the Christ, the Messiah. This was a bold and courageous mission for the deacon-evangelist. Sebaste was unlike any city in Israel.

In 31 BC, the Roman commander Octavian gave Samaria to the new king of Judea, Herod the Great, and it quickly became one of his favorite residences. To honor his benefactor, when Octavian changed his name to Augustus, Herod changed Samaria's name to Sebaste, the Greek form of Augustus.[122] As was his method, Herod embellished and enlarged the city, making it even more Greek. On the site of the former temple of Baal, he built and dedicated a large temple to Augustus.[123]

The Samaritans were like ordinary Jews in some ways, but totally unique in others. They were strict monotheists and worshiped Yahweh, as did the Jews, but their religion was not mainstream Judaism. Samaritans were a racially mixed society consisting of both Jewish and pagan ancestry who differed from the Jews on the location of the temple, the line of priests, and the exact books and content of the Torah. [124] In some respects, they were

---

122 Sebaste, in Greek, was equivalent to the Latin, Augustus.
123 The extraordinary staircase is still visible.
124 John 4:20 The Samaritans insisted the temple should not be on Mount Zion in Jerusalem, but on Mount Gerizim near ancient Shichem. They demanded that their line of priests was the legitimate one, as opposed to the line of priests in Jerusalem. They accept only the Law of Moses (Genesis, Exodus, Leviticus, Numbers and Deuteronomy) as authoritative, and have a slightly different text of these books. They did not recognize the prophets and the writings as divinely inspired.

more legalistic than Jews regarding the Mosaic Law, especially the Sabbath regulations, but they did not share the Jewish restriction against pronouncing the divine name Yahweh in their oaths.

Because of their unorthodox adherence to Judaism and their mixed ancestry, the Samaritans were despised by the Jews. Rather than be contaminated by passing through Samaritan territory, Jews superstitiously journeying from Judea to Galilee or vice versa would cross over the river Jordan, bypass Samaria, and cross over the river again as they neared their destination. The Samaritans also harbored a deep-seated antipathy toward the Jews.[125]

There were religious tensions between the Samaritans and the orthodox Jews, economic differences between the urban and peasant economies, and radical distinctions between the cosmopolitan cities of the Samaritans. Samaritans served in the army of Herod, which meant they were sometimes used against the Jews of Judea or Galilee. This did little to increase sympathy between the two peoples.[126] So the sight of a Christian deacon-evangelist from Jerusalem into Sebaste would not have been well received. But that did not deter Philip.

When the deacon demonstrated the veracity of his message by the power of the Holy Spirit with signs, healings, and authority over unclean spirits, the people of the city quickly responded with great rejoicing.[127] As a result of their response to the gospel, Philip did as he was taught to do: he baptized them. "But when they believed Philip preaching the good news about the kingdom of God and the name of Jesus Christ, they were being baptized, men and women alike."[128]

But there was a major problem. Those who were baptized did not receive the Holy Spirit. Something was seriously wrong. How could these Samaritans have believed and been baptized

125 Luke 9:52–53
126 During the Jewish Wars in AD 65–66, the city of Sebaste was razed to the ground by the Jews as they fought the Roman army.
127 Acts 8:5–8
128 Acts 8:12

and yet show no manifestation of the Holy Spirit? Philip quickly sent word to the church in Jerusalem and requested that the church send apostolic help.[129] The Apostles Peter and John were dispatched from Jerusalem to join Philip in Samaria:

> Now when the apostles in Jerusalem heard that Samaria had received the word of God, they sent them Peter and John, who came down and prayed for them that they might receive the Holy Spirit. For He had not yet fallen upon any of them; they had simply been baptized in the name of the Lord Jesus. Then they began laying their hands on them, and they were receiving the Holy Spirit.[130]

At first glance, this account seems thoroughly at odds with the demands of the New Testament and has caused great theological debate.[131] How could individuals have believed, been baptized in the name of the Lord Jesus, and not have received the Holy Spirit? Can a person experience Christian salvation and not receive the Holy Spirit? The Apostle Paul, Luke's mentor, would later answer, absolutely not! "If anyone does not have the Spirit of Christ, he does not belong to him."[132] If Paul were correct, how do these events in Samaria fit into the teaching of the apostle and the other material presented by Luke in the Acts of the Apostles?

It seems obvious that Luke was insistent that his readers rec-

---

129 F. F. Bruce, *The Acts of the Apostles*, (Grand Rapids: Eerdmans, 1960), p. 180. Bruce's contention that the Jerusalem apostles "regarded it as their duty to exercise general supervision over the progress of the gospel" and therefore, Peter and John were simply sent to "inspect this work" seems wholly inadequate. Since Philip was a deacon in the church at Jerusalem, he naturally reached out his community for apostolic assistance in a confusing matter.
130 Act 8:14–17
131 See, Dunn, *Baptism of the Holy Spirit*, ibid, p 55–72
132 Romans 8:9. Many Pentecostals adhere to the baptism of the Holy Spirit as a blessing subsequent to salvation.

ognize something was dramatically wrong with the response of the Samaritans to the gospel of the kingdom, for they obviously had not received Jesus and his salvation. There are several possible causes for this defective response on the part of the Samaritans, but whatever the cause, Luke understood that these baptized Samaritans had not been saved because they had not received the Spirit. [133] Philip knew something was wrong because nothing happened; the apostolic norm was not present. His experience up to that point was that each person who came to the Lord spoke in tongues. For Luke, the most important salvific indicator was the presence or the absence of the Spirit.

The Apostolic Remedy

Once Peter and John arrived to assist Philip, they quickly remedied the situation. Obviously, the brief Lukan description omitted critical details. As the Apostle Paul would be forced to do later at Ephesus, Peter and John probably re-presented the gospel, making sure that the Samaritans understood their surrender to the authentic Jesus as Lord and Savior. Once the apostles were satisfied, and only then, "Peter and John ... prayed for them that they might receive the Holy Spirit ... Then they began laying their hands on them, and they were receiving the Holy Spirit."[134]

When the Samaritans received the Holy Spirit, something

---

133 Dunn, ibid, p. 63–68. Dunn presents many possible reasons for the defective belief of the Samaritans: false Messianic expectation, superstition, mere mental assent, etc. Lamp, The Seal of the Spirit, 1956, p. 70, argues the Spirit was withheld until the Samaritan church comes into relationship with the "mother" church in Jerusalem. Green, I Believe in the Holy Spirit, 1975, p. 136–39, believes the Spirit is only given when the mother church expresses solidarity with the Samaritans. Dillon, New Biblical Commentary, 1990, p. 743, insists the Spirit only operates when there is communion with the apostles. Deere, Surprised by the Spirit, 1993, p. 237, contends the Samaritans refusal to submit to authority caused the Spirit to be withheld until God could "once and for all correct this problem." Calvin, Commentary on Acts, 1844, p. 1:329–48, demands the Samaritans were saved, but needed charismatic endowment.
134 Acts 8:14–17

supernatural and verifying happened. The Spirit entered and brought His gifts. The evidence indicates that, based on the other outpourings of the Holy Spirit in the Acts of the Apostles, each of the Samaritans spoke in tongues. [135] [136] Without a doubt, something very obvious and clearly demonstrative instantly occurred. Before, there were no visible gifts of the Spirit; then Peter and John laid hands on them, and the gifts were present, which meant the Spirit was present. As Dunn accurately declares, "No gifts meant no Spirit."[137] When the gifts were poured out upon these new Samaritan Christians, there was no longer any doubt that they had each entered into the salvation of King Jesus and been born again.

Whatever took place was so impressive that Simon Magus wanted to buy the power to make it happen: "Now when Simon saw that the Spirit was bestowed through the laying on of the apostles' hands, he offered them money, saying, 'Give this authority to me as well, so that everyone on whom I lay my hands may receive the Holy Spirit.'"[138]

Peter was furious, openly rebuked Simon, and declared, "May your silver perish with you, because you thought you could obtain the gift of God with money! You have no part or portion in this matter, for your heart is not right before God."[139] Answering Simon, Peter solved the Samaritan dilemma. Even though the Samaritans had been baptized in water, the Spirit had not been given to them because their *hearts were not right before God.*

Jesus experienced the same frustrating ordeal as Philip, Peter, and John. At the beginning of Jesus' ministry, He was in Jerusalem and many great miracles were taking place. When the crowds

---

135 Acts 2, 10, 19
136 See, Augustine, "Sermons on New Testament Lessons," Nicene and Post-Nicene Fathers, vol. 6, (Peabody MA: Hendrickson, 1999), p. 419
137 Dunn, *Baptism in the Holy Spirit*, ibid, p. 56
138 Acts 8:18–19
139 Acts 8:20–21

saw His miracles, they believed in His name, but Jesus refused to accept them because He Himself knew what was in them.[140] Jesus knew their hearts were not right. The Lord did not desire mental or emotional assent to His power, but a decision from the heart that would lead to a commitment to His as the Christ, the Messiah. Peter and John were with Jesus that day. When they arrived at Samaria to aid Philip, they knew exactly what was needed. They preached, prayed, and laid their hands on these now new believers. And it worked!

Once their defective beliefs were remedied, the Holy Spirit gladly came to accomplish His great salvific work of redemption and empowered the Samaritans without cost. And when the Spirit was poured out, the supernatural manifestation of His presence was obvious to all, for they spoke in tongues. The Samaritans moved out of their sins, beyond the natural, and into the supernatural salvation of Jesus, the reigning King.

The Initiation of Gentiles

The experience of the Roman centurion Cornelius in the city of Caesarea was a series of radical supernatural manifestations that climaxed with each person present being born again, baptized with the Spirit, and speaking in tongues. [141] As a centurion and commander of a Roman cohort, Cornelius was a ranking officer in the Roman Army, commanding nearly five hundred men. His rank allowed him to have his family with him in garrison. What set Cornelius apart were not simply his military courage and ability, but the great love and devotion he and his household shared for God. They prayed continually and helped many of the Jewish people over whom he held political and military control. One day, probably while praying, he had a vision of an angel of God who came to him and said:

---

140 John 2:23–25
141 Acts 10:46

"Cornelius!" And fixing his gaze on him and being much alarmed, he said, "What is it, Lord?" And he said to him, "Your prayers and alms have ascended as a memorial before God. Now dispatch some men to Joppa and send for a man named Simon, who is also called Peter; he is staying with a tanner named Simon, whose house is by the sea."[142]

Cornelius obeyed immediately and ordered three of his soldiers, one of whom was also devoted to God, to go to Joppa and find Peter. The apostle was in prayer awaiting the evening meal when he fell into a trance, and God opened to him His desire to reach the Gentiles.

And he saw the sky opened up, and an object like a great sheet coming down, lowered by four corners to the ground, and there were in it all kinds of four-footed animals and crawling creatures of the earth and birds of the air. A voice came to him, "Get up, Peter, kill and eat!" But Peter said, "By no means, Lord, for I have never eaten anything unholy and unclean." Again a voice came to him a second time, "What God has cleansed, no longer consider unholy." This happened three times, and immediately the object was taken up into the sky.[143]

These orders overwhelmed Peter's Jewish mind and lifelong action. It took a direct order from the Holy Spirit to override Peter's religious heritage and allow him to be used as the instrument of the work of the Spirit. The Holy Spirit spoke to Peter saying, "Behold, three men are looking for you. Get up, go down-

---

142 Acts 10:3–6
143 Acts 10:11–16

stairs and accompany them without misgivings, for I have sent them Myself."[144]

Like Cornelius, the Apostle Peter obeyed. His obedience was a great miracle. As Peter would share with Cornelius, for a Jew to enter the world of a Gentile without being forced was unthinkable.[145] But Peter had received direction from the Holy Spirit Himself. So he went downstairs and presented himself to Cornelius' soldiers.

> "I am the one you are looking for; what is the reason for which you have come?" They said, "Cornelius, a centurion, a righteous and God-fearing man well spoken of by the entire nation of the Jews, was divinely directed by a holy angel to send for you to come to his house and hear a message from you."[146]

After hosting these Gentile soldiers in his home for the night, they departed Joppa the next morning for the trip up the coast of the Mediterranean to Caesarea. Arriving at Caesarea, they went directly to the house of Cornelius. The centurion, his family, and many of his friends who shared his deep desire to know God were anxiously awaiting Peter. "When Peter entered, Cornelius met him, and fell at his feet and worshiped him. But Peter raised him up, saying, 'Stand up; I too am just a man.'"[147]

Peter had walked into a hotbed of spiritual anticipation. There was great excitement among those who had gathered at Cornelius's house. Their hearts were hungry; their expectation was great. After Peter got Cornelius up from his knees and they shared the common visions they had experienced, Peter was thoroughly convinced this mission to Caesarea was a divine appointment. Peter promptly turned the topic to Jesus, His power over

---

144 Acts 10: 19–20
145 Acts 10:28
146 Acts 10:21–22
147 Acts 10:24–26

evil, His awesome ability to heal and forgive sins, and most importantly, Jesus' great victory over death at the cross.

> "You know of Jesus of Nazareth, how God anointed Him with the Holy Spirit and with power, and how He went about doing good and healing all who were oppressed by the devil, for God was with Him. We are witnesses of all the things He did both in the land of the Jews and in Jerusalem They also put Him to death by hanging Him on a cross. God raised Him up on the third day and granted that He become visible, not to all the people, but to witnesses who were chosen beforehand by God, that is, to us who ate and drank with Him after He arose from the dead. And He ordered us to preach to the people, and solemnly to testify that this is the One who has been appointed by God as Judge of the living and the dead. Of Him all the prophets bear witness that through His name everyone who believes in Him receives forgiveness of sins."[148]

Fighting off the reservations of some of those who had come with him, the Apostle Peter faithfully preached the necessary content of the gospel of the kingdom. As Peter did what he could do, the Holy Spirit did what only He could do. "While Peter was still speaking these words, the Holy Spirit fell upon all those who were listening to the message."[149]

This supernatural move of the Holy Spirit absolutely shocked and amazed Peter and the company of Jewish Christians who accompanied him. In their minds, Gentiles coming into the salvation of the Jewish Messiah would never occur. Yet Gentiles were being baptized in the Spirit! The question must be asked: how did Peter and those with him know the Holy Spirit had baptized them? The answer is simple: something supernatural and

---

148 Acts 10:38–43
149 Acts 10:44

conspicuous manifested, and they all heard it. Like Pentecost, like the time with the Samaritans, it was recognizable to all those who were present.

> All the circumcised believers who came with Peter were amazed, because the gift of the Holy Spirit had been poured out on the Gentiles also ... for they were hearing them speaking with tongues and exalting God. [150]

Each individual in Cornelius's house simultaneously spoke with tongues! This was the visible, audible sign, the mark of the Holy Spirit placed upon the Gentile believers. Instantly, the Apostle Peter and the Jewish Christians understood the ramifications. Gentiles had entered the kingdom and were brothers and sisters in the church of Jesus Christ.

That night in Caesarea, Christian initiation was turned on its head. Before the Gentiles were baptized in water, before Peter finished preaching, before the apostle had laid his hand upon them, before they prayed the sinner's prayer, they were born again. It was as though the Holy Spirit was reminding all of those with Peter, and subsequently Christians throughout the church age, that salvation was His prerogative. Peter spoke through his shock and declared, "Surely no one can refuse the water for these to be baptized who have received the Holy Spirit just as we did, can he?"[151]

The silent, resounding answer was, "No!" No one could refuse, no argument could be raised because the Holy Spirit had fallen, and each of these Gentiles had been baptized with the Holy Spirit, just as the church had experienced at Pentecost. This was not a private prayer moment standing in the back of the room. Each one of the new Christians at Cornelius's house simultaneously spoke in tongues! Peter ordered them baptized in water.

---

150 Acts 10:45–46
151 Acts 10:47

4

The Initiation of Paul in the Holy Spirit

It is difficult to imagine a more unlikely convert to Christianity than Saul. Born in Tarsus of Cilicia around AD 5 to powerful parents who had obtained Roman citizenship by their wealth, Saul was an educated radical Jewish zealot who described himself as a descendent of Abraham of the tribe of Benjamin, a Hebrew of Hebrews, [152] a Pharisee and a son of Pharisees who lived according to the strictest sect of Judaism, and one who was blameless according to the Law. [153] This young Jewish extremist, educated under Gamaliel strictly according to the Law of the fathers, was so deeply opposed to Christianity that he saw as his life work the persecution and destruction of what he believed to be a false messianic sect. [154] [155] On his own initiative, Saul sought and received

152 Meaning Paul was from those speaking Aramaic-Hebrew. Since he was reared in Tarsus, he also spoke Greek.
153 See Acts 23:6; 26:5; Romans 11:1; Philippians 3:5–6
154 Acts 22:3
155 Galatians 1:13. The Apostle Paul admitted to the motivation of his work in "his former manner of life in Judaism."

authority from the high priest to arrest Christians and bring them to Jerusalem for punishment. Despite Roman rule, the Sanhedrin claimed the same authority over Jews throughout the diaspora that they exercised at Jerusalem.[156]

> Now Saul, still breathing threats and murder against the disciples of the Lord, went to the high priest, and asked for letters from him to the synagogues at Damascus, so that if he found any belonging to the Way, both men and women, he might bring them bound to Jerusalem.
> [157] [158]

Saul terrorized the church, and they feared his rampage against them.[159] While on the road to Damascus to continue his campaign against the followers of Jesus, something supernatural occurred. Jesus confronted Saul. The Lord would not tolerate this zealot's destruction of his young church. The Lord's confrontation carried with it the ultimate possibility, but not the certainty, of Saul's conversion and fully allowed the exercise of Saul's will.

Questions surround Saul's conversion, especially concerning the process: Was Saul instantly saved on the road to Damascus, or did his salvation take place at the end of a three-day period? The answer lies in the timeline of the actions of Jesus, a Christian named Ananias, and Saul.

First, as Saul continued to Damascus, around noon, "suddenly a light from heaven flashed around him; and he fell to the ground and heard a voice saying to him, 'Saul, Saul, why are you perse-

---

156 "If this is concerning your laws … you see to it …
157 W. J. Conybeare and J. S. Howson, *The Life and Epistles of St. Paul*, (Grand Rapids: Eerdmans, 2004), p. 67. "The Jews in Damascus were very numerous; and there were peculiar circumstances in the political condition of Damascus which may have given facilities to conspiracies or deeds of violence conducted by the Jews."
158 Acts 9:1–2
159 Acts 9:13, 21

cuting Me?'"[160] The entire scene quickly became one of complete bewilderment. The Jewish companions of Saul were speechless and fell to the ground as dead.[161] Each heard the voice but saw nothing. Stunned, dazed, disoriented, bewildered, and probably lying flat on his back, Saul cried out in his confusion, "Who are You, Lord?"[162]

Saul's use of the word *Lord* has led some to see this exclamation as declaration of faith and a moment of salvation. However, the Greek word *Lord* (κύριε) is in the vocative mood, which would carry with it the meaning *sir*. It was a cry of terrorized respect that fell far short of a confession of salvation or even understanding.

Secondly, Jesus did not receive Saul's cry as salvific, for He answered, "I am Jesus whom you are persecuting." This was not Jesus the compassionate Savior or Jesus attempting to convince Saul, for He does not say, "I am the Son of God, the Messiah." Rather, this was Jesus, the head of His church, dealing with its chief antagonist and putting an end to his brutal treachery and murder.[163] Saul was persecuting Jesus and His church, and one way or the other, by conversion or death, Saul would be stopped and His church saved. To test Saul's choice, Jesus added, "Get up and enter the city, and it will be told you what you must do."[164]

The men with Saul quickly moved to help him up from the ground. When he stood, he was blind, so they took him by the hand and led him into Damascus. Saul's entrance into the city was not at all as he had planned. He was not the triumphant Jewish crusader coming to imprison followers of Jesus. Rather, he entered Damascus blind, stumbling, dazed, and escorted through the gate and under the colonnades of Straight Street.[165] Saul

---

160 Acts 9:3–4
161 Acts 26:14
162 Acts 9:5
163 Acts 8:1, Saul participated in the death of the deacon, Stephen.
164 Acts 9:6
165 Conybeare and Howson, ibid, p. 76, Excavations have unearthed a magnificent street with colonnades stretching from the Eastern to

remained in a state of spiritual shock for three days, not eating or drinking.

Third, the Lord spoke to Ananias, a Jewish Christian at Damascus, in a vision and said to him, "Get up and go to the street called Straight, and inquire at the house of Judas for a man from Tarsus named Saul, for he is praying."[166] The dramatic events Saul experienced during the three days between his encounter on the road to Damascus and his baptism were pivotal. This was not an easy conversion. It stretches all credulity to believe that Saul was changed in an instant or to imagine that Saul could immediately embrace a new Lord and religious understanding. This conversion took three days. Saul had literally been stopped in his tracks on the road, physically and spiritually knocked to the ground. The Lord would not allow him to go forward the same.

Throughout the three days of fasting and prayer, Saul was coming to grips with who Jesus was and the content and demands of His gospel of the kingdom. How would Saul respond, what would he believe, what would this mean for his life, would he pay the price the Lord was placing before him? Saul was in the throws of conviction and had been told by Jesus that a man named Ananias would "come in and lay his hands on him, so that he might regain his sight."[167]

Naturally, Ananias was hesitant because of Saul's reputation as a hater and destroyer of the church, but the Lord assured him, "Go, for he is a chosen instrument of Mine, to bear My name before the Gentiles and kings and the sons of Israel."[168] If Saul chose, he would receive both his salvation and commission at the hands of Ananias.

Fourth, Ananias obeyed, knowing that specific steps must be accomplished in Saul's life to complete his commitment to Jesus and assure his salvation. When Ananias entered the house where

the Western gates.
166 Acts 9:11
167 Acts 9:12
168 Acts 9:15

Saul was staying, Saul was blind, gaunt from lack of nourishment, and remained in a state of confusion. Ananias graciously ministered to Saul. "Brother Saul, the Lord Jesus, who appeared to you on the road by which you were coming, has sent me so that you may regain your sight and be filled with the Holy Spirit."[169]

Once again, as Luke does with the Samaritans, he abbreviated the actual contents of the meeting in his writing. Most likely, Ananias was overly precise, desiring to clearly present the gospel of the kingdom to Saul and assure his understanding. Then Ananias laid hands on his head. This was a powerful prayer of healing over Saul to end the blindness. When Ananias prayed, the Holy Spirit moved supernaturally to answer Saul's prayers. He was immediately born again, baptized with the Spirit, and healed from his blindness: "Immediately there fell from his eyes something like scales, and he regained his sight, and he got up and was baptized."[170]

Based on the Lukan text, Saul's conversion must be viewed as one experience lasting from the encounter with Jesus on the road to Damascus and through the ministry of Ananias.[171] To assume his salvation occurred in a single moment on the Damascus road and that his baptism with the Spirit took place later at the hands of Ananias forces his salvation away from the work of the Holy Spirit. But, as is true for Pentecost, Samaria, Cornelius, and the conversion of Saul, the baptism of the Spirit was the moment of salvation.

There is not a specific reference that Saul spoke in tongues at his conversion. What is undeniable is the depth of the experience of Saul. He was radically changed. This event was so dramatic and indelible to Saul that he would carry it throughout his ministry as the Apostle Paul and insist upon its duplication by all who would come into the salvation of Jesus. We know from his own

169 Acts 9:17
170 Acts 9:18
171 See Dunn, ibid, p. 77

testimony that speaking, praying, and singing in tongues were all very important to him, and that being the case, more than likely, speaking in tongues was part of the experience as he was born again, baptized with the Spirit. [172] One thing is for certain: that day in the house of Judas the tanner, at the hands of the powerful man of God, Ananias, something dramatically supernatural happened to Saul. "Paul's conversion was only completed when he called on Jesus as Lord, was filled with the Spirit and had his sins washed away; then and only then, can he be called a Christian."[173]

> Immediately he began to proclaim Jesus in the synagogues, saying, "He is the Son of God." All those hearing him continued to be amazed, and were saying, "Is this not he who in Jerusalem destroyed those who called on this name, and who had come here for the purpose of bringing them bound before the chief priests?"[174]

The young radical Jewish zealot Saul, who vowed to destroy the church, emerged from his time in Damascus as the Apostle Paul to be used of the Lord Jesus to take the message of His kingdom and salvation to the Gentile world. "Saul kept increasing in strength and confounding the Jews who lived at Damascus by proving that this Jesus is the Christ."[175]

With his conversion, the church of Jesus Christ was at peace: "So the Church throughout all Judea and Galilee and Samaria enjoyed peace, being built up; and, going on the fear of the Lord and in the comfort of the Holy Spirit, it continued to increase."[176]

---

172 Acts 19; 1 Corinthians 14:18
173 Dunn, ibid, p. 78
174 Acts 9:20–21
175 Acts 9:22
176 Acts 9:31

The Initiation at Ephesus

Two roads exited southern Galatia in Paul's day that led to Rome. One was the regular lower trade route through the Lycus and Maeander Valleys. The other was the less traveled but more direct route across Asian Phrygia. Desiring to reach Rome as quickly as possible, the Apostle Paul chose to leave his churches in Galatia by the upper route. Ironically, had he journeyed along the regular lower trade route, Paul would have missed Ephesus and his great work there, but instead he arrived in Ephesus from the north side of Mount Messogis. Ephesus was a cosmopolitan seaport city of two hundred thousand located on the Aegean Sea between Mount Pion and Mount Koressos that developed from its early days as a Greek outpost to become the most important city in Asia Minor. [177] Because of its strategic location and great roads to interior markets, the city was constantly visited by ships from all parts of the Mediterranean and served as the common meeting place for traders.

When Paul arrived at Ephesus, he was greeted by a dozen men, presumably Jewish, who—it seems to his surprise—were disciples of John the Baptist but possessed at least some knowledge of Christianity. [178] In the Lukan account, the Apostle Paul immediately began an inquiry to ascertain their relationship to the Lord Jesus. The apostle's targeted question indicated the essentiality of the Holy Spirit in the experience of Christian salvation. Paul did not ask if they knew Jesus, if they had been saved, if they had prayed the sinner's prayer, if they had repented of their sins, if they had been baptized, or even if they understood the gospel. The emphasis was not on a specific prayer, but on experi-

---

177 For geographical details of Ephesus at the time of Paul, see W. J. Conybeare and J. S. Howson, *ibid*, p. 368; and John McRay, *Archaeology and the New Testament* (Grand Rapids: Baker, 1991) pp 250–261
178 Much controversy has come from Luke's use of the word disciple (maqhtaV). The argument is that this word was used as a synonym for Christian, but in this context it is obviously speaking of disciples of John the Baptist.

ence, not on a second work of grace, but on the new birth, not on a third baptism, but the baptism of the Spirit. [179] All of those items would become clear with a single question regarding the Holy Spirit. The apostle asked, "Did you receive the Holy Spirit when you believed?"[180]

This was the salvific question, the normal inquiry that came from Paul's own salvation experience. Certainly Paul would not have asked an abnormal question in an attempt to find truth. Their response clearly indicated their spiritual condition: "No, we have not even heard whether there is a Holy Spirit."[181]

Paul immediately questioned the validity of their baptism. As far as Paul was concerned, if they had not receive the Holy Spirit, their water baptism was illegitimate and their salvation was non-existent! He responded, "'Into what then were you baptized?'" And they said, 'Into John's baptism.'"[182] They had been baptized with John's baptism, not necessarily by John, and had only heard of Jesus within the context of that community.

Recognizing where they were in their faith, the apostle took them methodically, step by step through the claims of Christ and the requirements of salvation within the gospel of the kingdom. Paul taught, "John baptized with the baptism of repentance, telling the people to believe in Him who was coming after him, that is, in Jesus."[183] Once they heard the gospel of the kingdom with its claims of Jesus, these twelve seekers eagerly believed, and Paul had them baptized in water in the name of the Lord Jesus. As each individual came up from the waters of baptism, the Apostle

---

179 Some argue for three baptisms: the baptism by the Spirit as a new Christian is baptized into Christ, then the water baptism, and finally the baptism of the Holy Spirit. In fact, these baptisms are aspects of the one salvific event, not separate events.
180 Acts 19:2
181 Acts 19:2
182 Acts 19:3
183 Acts 19:4

Paul, "laid his hands upon them, the Holy Spirit came on them, and they began speaking with tongues and prophesying."[184]

Something happened! Twenty years following Pentecost, in a demonstrable event, each of these new Christians was baptized with the Holy Spirit with the result that each new Christian spoke in tongues and prophesied.[185] That was the pattern. With the coming of the Spirit at Ephesus, Luke's chronology of the outpouring of the Holy Spirit in the Acts of the Apostles was complete. He had historically established the requirements and expectations of the church age regarding the baptism of the Holy Spirit, "the original pattern."[186]

From that point forward, it was to be expected that each individual who came to Jesus as Lord and Savior was to be baptized with the Holy Spirit, a baptism that could only be understood correctly as the new birth. At that baptism by the Holy Spirit, something supernatural, demonstrative, and immediate would be manifested. For those at Pentecost, Samaria, Caesarea, Damascus, and Ephesus that personal manifestation was "as in all other churches, the miraculous gifts of Tongues and of Prophecy."[187]

---

184 Acts 19:6
185 Helmut Koester, *History and Literature of the Early Church*, (New York: Walter D. Gruyter, 2000), p. 120
186 Smith Wigglesworth, *The Holy Spirit*, (New Kensington, PA: Whitaker House, 1998). 52
187 Conybeare and Howson, ibid, p. 369

5

Paul and the Tongues of Corinth

Every critic who desires to deny the validity of modern tongue speech must develop a scheme to destroy Paul's teaching.

By the time the Apostle Paul entered the city of Corinth to launch the church around AD 51–52, the demonstration of the supernatural was an accepted and expected aspect of the Christian message, especially speaking, praying, and singing in tongues. [188] Corinth required such a demonstration.

Corinth was considered the "light of all Greece" by Cicero, and for good reason.[189] Because of its strategic location, the site of ancient Corinth was first inhabited in the Neolithic period around BC 4000 and flourished as a major Greek city from the eighth century BC. Its commanding position on the Isthmus of

---

188 1 Corinthians 2:4; 14:15. See, Koester, ibid, p. 120
189 Cicero, *In Defense of Manilian Law*, Retrieved on the World Wide Web on October 7, 2009 at: http://www.uvm.edu/~bsaylor/rome/pompeyoration.html

Corinth, the narrow strip of land that separates the Peloponnesus from the northern mainland Greece, was the primary basis of its existence and importance. It was at the center of commerce between Asia and the West. No other city in the ancient world enjoyed the benefit of two major seaports; Cenchreae lay six miles to the east and Lechaion two miles to the north.[190]

In 146 BC, the Roman Army destroyed Greek Corinth, the same year in which they decimated Carthage. Julius Caesar rebuilt Corinth in 44 BC as a Roman city and populated it with numerous colonists from across the Empire. Roman freedmen dominated the city, followed by a significant group of Greeks, many from other nationalities, and a Jewish colony with its own officials and internal management, probably augmented by Claudius's expulsion of the Jews from Rome in BC 49. [191] [192] In BC 29, Augustus made Corinth the capital city of the province of Achaia and the seat of a Roman proconsul.

Corinth quickly regained its ancient splendor and possessed all of the cultural pleasures of a Roman capital city. Looking down on the city from its acropolis was the incomparable temple of Venus. At the heart of the city stood the temple of Apollo, built in the sixth century BC with its thirty-eight magnificent columns. South of the temple of Apollo was the main forum, which was the center of activity in Corinth. It was a colonnaded

---

190 Raymond E. Brown, *Introduction to the New Testament*, (New York: Doubleday, 1997), p. 512. "In antiquity a paved road, the diolkos, across the isthmus facilitated trade between the two seas: and, in addition to transshipment of merchandise, grooves cut into it allowed light ships to be hauled from one sea to the other, thus saving a dangerous journey of about two hundred miles around the treacherous end of the peninsula. Although Nero began to cut a canal, it was only in 1893 that the two seas were connected by the Corinth Canal."

191 Roman Freedmen were former slaves who did not enjoy all the privilege of citizenship.

192 It is not surprising that a Jewish synagogue existed in a large, multicultural city like Corinth. In 1898, archeologists discovered a limestone block with inscriptions appearing to come from the doorway of a synagogue.

square surrounded by workshops, many small venders, halls of rhetoric, schools of philosophy, and a series of small temples to the older Greek gods. At the center of the forum was the bema, the large podium where the Roman proconsuls set in authority and from where Gallio refused to act on accusations against the Apostle Paul.[193] Apollo's son, Asklepios, the god of healing, had a shrine at Epidaurus, the ancient site of miracle healings, about fifty miles southeast.

When Paul arrived, Corinth boasted a population approaching six hundred thousand and as such "had all the problems of a rough, relatively new boomtown adjacent to two seaports."[194] The city was young, dynamic, not controlled by tradition, with a mix of dislocated individuals without strong ethnic identities determined to rise above their former low social status by achieving material success. The Apostle Paul was at home in this climate of a densely populated, bustling, cosmopolitan capital city in which he would spend almost two years and build his greatest work. Like his hometown of Tarsus, Corinth had no dominant religious or intellectual tradition. Instead, the city was filled with various religious ideas from temple prostitutes to legalistic Jews.

As was his custom in following the direction of Jesus, Paul began his work in Corinth inside the Jewish colony every Sabbath.[195] Ultimately, Silas and Timothy joined him in Corinth, and Paul turned all of his attention to the Jews, but not for long. When the Jews resisted his ministry and blasphemed the Lord Jesus, Paul declared, "Your blood be upon your own head! I am clean. From now on I shall go to the Gentiles."[196] The decision to go to the Gentiles was a critically strategic choice and one that worked. Because of the wide religious diversity among the Gentiles and the literal

---

193 Acts 18:12–17
194 Raymond E. Brown, ibid, p.513
195 Matthew 10:5–6 Jesus directed his disciples that the gospel was to go first to the "lost sheep of the house of Israel" until the destruction of Jerusalem in AD 70.
196 Acts 18:6

boatloads who traveled in and out of Corinth, Paul would not have been rejected as an outsider or even a resident alien. The city was filled with tens of thousands who were not bound to or controlled by any heritage that would have kept them from receiving Jesus if they could be convinced of his claims.

In the synagogue, the Apostle Paul presented the gospel of the kingdom to Jewish men and women. His approach was to take the Old Testament, probably in the form of the Septuagint, and attempt to prove that Jesus fulfilled the messianic prophecies, but when he turned to the Gentiles, Paul's method was forced to change. Gentiles were not impressed by a Jewish messiah. So Paul turned to power! The apostle reminded the Gentile Christians in Corinth, "My message and my preaching were not in persuasive words of wisdom, but in demonstration of the Spirit and power, that your faith should not rest on the wisdom of men, but on the power of God."[197]

This was a dramatic turn of events. The church at Corinth was born on the power of the Spirit; it was thoroughly and radically charismatic. Obviously, Paul preached the gospel of the kingdom, proclaiming that Jesus was the risen, enthroned Son of God, but he did more. He demonstrated the validity and authenticity of his preaching with miracles, healings, exorcisms, and other signs. Additionally, as new believers entered into the salvation of Jesus, they were baptized with the Holy Spirit, and as was the Christian norm, they manifested the gifts of the Spirit. Clearly, as was true elsewhere, they spoke in tongues, prophesied, and praised God.

When Paul turned to the Gentiles, he did not go very far. In fact, he only went to the synagogue next door to the home of one Titus Justus, who was himself a worshipper of God.[198] The great charismatic move of the Spirit demonstrated the validity of the gospel of the kingdom, which when Paul preached drew many people. It is easy to imagine that as Jews were coming to the syna-

197 1 Corinthians 2:4–5
198 Acts 18:7

gogue and being told not to believe Paul, next-door people were being healed, demons were being cast out, and people were being baptized with the Spirit, singing and praying in tongues. As a result, many believed and were baptized, even among the Jews.[199] When Crispus, the leader of the synagogue, believed the gospel, he and his family were baptized. The Lord encouraged Paul in a vision: "Do not be afraid, but go on speaking and do not be silent; for I am with you, and no man will attack you in order to harm you, for I have many people in this city."[200]

It is only with this historic understanding that the apostle's instruction to the church at Corinth becomes clear. There was absolutely, positively no possible way Paul was being negative about speaking in tongues or the supernatural manifestations of the Holy Spirit in Corinthians 14. Rather, those demonstrations were the very method Paul employed to bring Corinth to Christ. The church at Corinth thrived on the things of the Spirit. These were Gentile believers who reveled in the gifts and power of the Holy Spirit, knew them, used them, and evangelized with them. Paul's instructions were not to squelch the people and their freedom in the Spirit, but to direct them and help them to be more powerful and effective.

Apostolic Instruction for Tongue Speech

Paul was the apostolic father of the church at Corinth, and it remained his church. As the apostle over Corinth, he did not write to the church at Corinth hoping to correct the church, save it from the excessive use of tongues, or bring it into some higher, more refined enlightenment away from speaking in tongues and other gifts of the Spirit. He certainly was not preparing the church for the ultimate canonization of the New Testament and the cessation of the gifts. Paul birthed the church at Corinth on

199 Acts 18:8
200 Acts 18:10

the strength of the gifts and power of the Holy Spirit, and he was insistent that those gifts, including speaking, singing, and praying in tongues, were to be an ongoing part of the daily life of the believers at Corinth. [201] In fact, his greatest insights concerning speaking in tongues are found in the fourteenth chapter of his first letter to Corinth.

Having spent time demanding that love must rule in their relationships with one another, Paul moved immediately to insist that their pursuit of love must not be at the expense of the demonstration of the Spirit. [202] Both are critically important, and not to the expense of the other. Yes, pursue love, he wrote, but do not let your seeking to walk in love cause you to compromise on the necessity for spiritual gifts. He demanded, "Yet desire earnestly spiritual gifts."[203] The Greek Paul used is enlightening: ζηλοῦτε δὲ τὰ πνευματικά. The word *desire*, ζηλοῦτε is second person plural, which means it included every Christian. The word is also an active imperative; it is an order. So each believer at Corinth was expected by Paul to seek the gifts of the Spirit with all their hearts. There was no word of caution, no word of warning, but Paul did add a requirement that would bring order to the public life of the church: "Especially that you may prophesy."[204]

The Apostle Paul drew a parallel between prophecy and interpreted public tongues. He raised prophecy to its rightful place in the congregation and quickly explained his rationale. In doing so, Paul defined speaking in tongues: "One who speaks in a tongue does not speak to men but to God; for no one understands, but in his spirit he speaks mysteries."[205]

At times, tongue speech was definite languages, as some of the tongues at Pentecost, and at other times, such as Corinth, the

---

201 1 Corinthians 2:4–5
202 1 Corinthians 13
203 1 Corinthians 14:1
204 1 Corinthians 14:1
205 1 Corinthians 14:2

tongues were ecstatic speech, "not foreign languages."[206] The audience was not the congregation; it was God; it was the language of supernatural prayer. One who prophesied, Paul contended, spoke to men "for edification and exhortation and consolation."[207]

Once again, Paul rushed to explain, "One who speaks in a tongue edifies himself."

What a tremendous promise. Whenever any Christian speaks, prays, or sings in tongues, he or she is edified. The Greek word for edify, οἰκοδομεῖ, speaks of building, literally building, a house. Because of its intimate relationship with God, speaking the language of God, the act of speaking in tongues, builds up a Christian's faith, authority, power, and confidence with God. Paul demanded that with tongue speech, the believers in Corinth touched the supernatural and released the will of God into their individual lives. But he continued to explain, "One who prophesies edifies the church."[208]

Again, the apostle drew a parallel. What the church received corporately with the release of the prophetic, the Christian received individually with the release of tongues. Without any reservations or thought of change, Paul insisted, "Now I wish that you all spoke in tongues."[209]

As Paul wrote 1 Corinthians 14, his goal was not a cessation of tongues or even that a selected few spoke in tongues, but that all would speak in tongues. It is extremely important not to see Paul's demand for an ordered assembly as a refutation or even restriction of tongue speech. What the apostle set forth were the rules for the use of tongues that King Jesus intended for His church throughout the age of the new covenant. Paul's wish was the wish of Jesus: that you all speak in tongues.[210]

---

206 Donald G. Bloesch, The Holy Spirit, (Downers Grove, IL: InterVarsity Press, 2000), p. 193.
207 1 Corinthians 14:3
208 1 Corinthians 14:4
209 1 Corinthians 14
210 Mark 16:17

But in the congregational meeting, "even more that you would prophesy."[211] Once again, this is for the edification of the church congregationally. However, this in no way dampens Paul's commitment to and belief in both private and public tongue speech. He maintains, "greater is one who prophesies than one who speaks in tongues, unless he interprets, so that the church may receive edifying."[212]

Interpreted Tongue Speech

This was a strategic moment that forever established public speaking in tongues as a viable and expected aspect of the public life and worship for the church of Jesus Christ. There was no doubt for the Apostle Paul that prophecy in public was greater than tongues. That is, unless tongues are interpreted. Therefore, the Pauline principle was set: interpreted tongue speech is equal to prophecy.[213] He took his understanding a step further in the ensuing verse. When public tongue speech was interpreted in the church, it could manifest itself as revelation, knowledge, prophecy, or teaching.

"But now, brethren, if I come to you speaking in tongues, what will I profit you unless I speak to you either by way of revelation or of knowledge or of prophecy or of teaching?"[214]

Remember, Paul was making his case for the equality of interpreted tongue speech as he was simultaneously arguing for the primacy of prophecy. He does so over several verses arguing against the misuse of uninterpreted public tongue speech in the

---

211 1 Corinthians 14:5
212 1 Corinthians 14:5
213 John Chrysostom would later echo the Apostle Paul and agree that interpreted tongue speech was equal to prophecy. "Accordingly, (Paul) adds, 'greater is he who prophesies, except he interprets; since if he is able to do this, I mean the interpreting, he becomes equal to the prophet." Chrysostom, "Homilies on First Corinthians," *Nicene and Post-Nicene Fathers*, vol. 12, ed. Philip Schaff, (Peabody, MA: Hendrickson, 1999)p. 209 parenthesis added
214 1 Corinthians 14:6

congregation. He continued his argument, "If then I do not know the meaning of the language, I will be to the one who speaks a barbarian, and the one who speaks will be a barbarian to me. So also you, since you are zealous of spiritual gifts, seek to abound for the edification of the church."[215]

And once again, Paul countered to ensure he was *not* being misunderstood as opposing tongue speech. He added, "Therefore let one who speaks in a tongue pray that he may interpret. For if I pray in a tongue, my spirit prays, but my mind is unfruitful."[216] The great apostle placed a high value on both public and private tongue speech. He believed that when a Christian prays in tongues, the Holy Spirit prays through his or her spirit and not through the mind; his or her mind is unfruitful. This was at the heart of the ministry of the Holy Spirit for Paul. Since he believed tongues as equal to prophecy when interpreted, it was not to be mishandled or confusing. It must be allowed to fulfill its supernatural role in the life of the church and the Christian. But while placing demands upon its use, he remained fully committed to its authenticity and irreplaceable standing in the church. Paul focused his thoughts and declared, "What is the outcome then? I will pray with the spirit and I will pray with the mind also; I will sing with the spirit and I will sing with the mind also."[217]

In what is a climatic point in this chapter, Paul refused to abort tongues in his church at Corinth and any church. In fact, he was diametrically opposed to its negation and thereby established its practice as essential for both the individual Christian and Christianity. He declared with no hesitation, "I will allow the Holy Spirit to pray through my spirit. I will allow the Holy Spirit to sing through my spirit." And anyone who fails to do so would fall short of the Pauline desire. The apostle took an additional step to ensure no one could miss his commitment to

---

215 1 Corinthians 14:11–12
216 1 Corinthians 14:13
217 1 Corinthians 14:15

tongue speech. Paul stated as clearly as possible, "I thank God, I speak in tongues more than you all." [218]

The parallelism of Paul was critical in his writing. So he turned again to his concern for uninterpreted tongues in the congregational meetings: "However, in the church I desire to speak five words with my mind so that I may instruct others also, rather than ten thousand words in a tongue."[219] Then to counterbalance his argument, he returned to the efficacy of speaking in tongues and found in its interpreted use an additional task: "So then tongues are for a sign, not to those who believe but to unbelievers; but prophecy is for a sign, not to unbelievers but to those who believe."[220]

As was, continued, and continues to be true for all supernatural manifestations of the Holy Spirit, ultimately it concerns bringing individual men and women into the salvation of King Jesus. Fortunately, the apostle did not share the fear of many that the operation of the gifts of the Spirit would turn people away from the church and its gospel. The fact that Paul believed the exact opposite was obvious in the churches he established. They were alive by the Spirit.

It is easy to imagine the public assemblies of the church at Corinth. It must have been filled with radical praise and deep personal worship of the Lord Jesus. Throughout the worship, individuals were dancing and shouting out to the Lord. The sound of singing in tongues wove its way repeatedly through those worshipping. Angelic visitations were common. The gifts of the Spirit were powerfully evident and freely flowing. As the sound of worship came to a momentary pause, someone would speak out with a message in tongues, then perhaps another, followed by another with each interpreted. Signs and wonders spontaneously occurred across the congregation. Words of prophecy were

218 1 Corinthians 14:18
219 1 Corinthians 14:19
220 1 Corinthians 14:22

spoken, and the gospel of the kingdom was presented. As a result of the life of the church, many in Corinth attended the meetings and received the salvation of Jesus. Without destroying their freedom in the Spirit, Paul set boundaries to establish corporate order and allow the gifts to freely move: "What is the outcome then, brethren? When you assemble, each one has a psalm, has a teaching, has a revelation, has a tongue, has an interpretation. Let all things be done for edification."[221]

These were not the words of one attempting to thwart the supernatural life of the church or dampen the use of speaking in tongues. Paul demanded, *let all things be done* and specifically, let them speak in tongues in the public meeting as long as there is interpretation. Then the Apostle Paul gave a list of several specific ways in which he wanted the church in Corinth to operate in the Spirit.

- If anyone speaks in a tongue, it should be by two or at the most three, and each in turn, and one must interpret; but if there is no interpreter, he must keep silent in the church; and let him speak to himself and to God (1 Corinthians 14:27–28),
- Let two or three prophets speak, and let the others pass judgment (1 Corinthians 14:29).
- But if a revelation is made to another who is seated, the first one must keep silent (1 Corinthians 14:30).
- For you can all prophesy one by one, so that all may learn and all may be exhorted; and the spirits of prophets are subject to prophets (1 Corinthians 14:31–32).
- For God is not a God of confusion but of peace, as in all the churches of the saints (1 Corinthians 14:33).

The apostle ended the chapter mirroring the challenge he gave in the first verse: "Therefore, my brethren, desire earnestly to prophesy, and do not forbid to speak in tongues" (1 Corinthians 14:39).

---

221 1 Corinthians 14:26

6

Tongues in the Letters of Paul

Critics of speaking, singing, and praying in tongues satisfy themselves with the fact that there was no specific mention of speaking in tongues in the New Testament after Paul's letter to the church at Corinth. How can the Epistles of Paul, John, and Peter be filled with constant references to the work of the Holy Spirit, especially surrounding the gospel of the kingdom and its salvation, and there be no mention of speaking in tongues, or for that matter, any of the gifts of the Spirit? It may well be that the answer can be discovered in the structural order of the books of the New Testament canon.

Strategic Canonical Decisions

Clearly, the various sayings of Jesus held a scripture like status from the earliest days of the church.[222] Therefore, the Gospels of Matthew, Mark, Luke, and John were the first of the early

222 Lee M. McDonald, *The Formation of the Christian Biblical Canon*, (Peabody, MA: Hendrickson, 1995), p. 145. Also see, Hans von Campenhausen, *The Formation of the Christian Bible*, trans. J.A. Baker, (Philadelphia: Fortress, 1972)

Christian writings to be universally recognized by the church and given the same status as the Old Testament. [223] A critical aspect of the four gospels was the two-volume work consisting of the Gospel of Luke and the Acts of the Apostles. At the same time the four gospels were being recognized, the writings of Paul were also being accepted. "If both collections were to be regarded as parts of one larger collection of authoritative books, there must be some link between them."[224] The decision to separate the Gospel of Luke from Acts and the placement of the Acts of the Apostles immediately following the gospels and preceding the Epistles was not accidental. [225] [226] By doing so, the church seems to have established the Acts of the Apostles as the paradigm or schema through which the Epistles and pastorals were to be accepted.[227] The Acts of the Apostles served as a filter for doctrinal questions, as well as a definer of terms. "Against the historical background of Acts, the Pauline letters could be read with greater understanding."[228]

There were very strict grounds for an early Christian writing

---

223 Eusebius, *Ecclesiastical History*, (Grand Rapids: Baker Books, 1966), p. 245, quotes Origen (185–254) attesting, "that he knows of only four gospels (Matthew, Mark, Luke, and John) which are the only undisputed ones in the whole church of God throughout the world."
224 F.F. Bruce, *The Acts of the Apostles*, (London: Tyndale Press, 1951), p. 10
225 See, Brown, ibid, p. 279
226 The earliest lists of the NT books (Muratorian Fragment, Eusebius, Athanasius) place the Acts of the Apostles between the Gospels and the Epistles. It is clear the order of the books was purposeful not chronological. First the Gospels, which recorded the life and ministry of Jesus; then Acts, which gave the history of the ministry of the apostles; then the Epistles, which presented the doctrinal development of the church; and then the Revelation. Also see, Francois Bovon, *"The Canonical Structure of Gospel and Apostles," The Canon Debate*, ed. Lee Martin MacDonald and James A. Sanders, (Peabody, MA: Hendrickson Publishers, 2002), p. 516. Bovon contends the "Canonical structure of Gospel and Apostle" was a willful decision to build a "two-part canon" consisting of the ministry of Jesus and the work of the apostles.
227 Bruce, ibid, p. 10, "Without Acts, there might not have been a unified NT as we know it."
228 Bruce, ibid, p. 10

being admitted into the canon, and over many decades, scores of various gospels, letters, histories, and apocalypses were forced through this canonical schema toward orthodoxy, and most failed and were rejected. [229] Ultimately, as each of the distinct writings passed through the judgment of the canonizers, there emerged a single work, the New Testament. [230] [231] Admittedly, not everyone agreed then or now on its exact content, but the process worked, and what were totally disparate, disjointed gospels and letters became seamless, to be understood as a whole. Regardless of the chronology of the Epistles, they each passed the test of canonization, and that process meant the content passed through the Acts of the Apostles, "the pivotal book of the NT canon."[232] Therefore, the material in the Epistles concerning the work of the Holy Spirit was canonized in light of the accepted definitions, understandings, and experiences of the Acts of the Apostles.

In considering the content of Paul's writings on the work of the Spirit, it helps to do so in the order in which Paul wrote. [233]

The Spirit at Galatia

There are many examples of this phenomenon of canonization throughout the Epistles. One is found in the Apostle Paul's letter to the churches at Galatia written around AD 51. Galatia was not a city; it was a region. The churches to which Paul wrote his

---

229 See, McDonald, *ibid*, 2005
230 There was no single group of canonizers. The process took several decades
231 See, McRay, Paul, p. 263. McRay correctly asserts that "the NT is not a book, but a collection of twenty-seven documents of various kinds written over a period of perhaps fifty years by different authors." While McRay is certain correct, the process of canonization brings the divergent into one and does not allow them to continue disjointed and competing. The NT is not a variety of unrelated religious ideas, but through the acceptance by the church it becomes a single document supporting and giving insight into one another.
232 Bruce, ibid, p. 10
233 There is no way to be certain of the exact chronology of Paul's writings, but there is wide agreement regarding the order of those works containing materials regarding the baptism of the Holy Spirit.

Epistle were most likely those around Ancyra in the ethnic Galatian territory of north-central Asia Minor, which he evangelized in AD 50 and again in AD 54. Paul probably wrote the Epistle to the Galatians at some point between those two visits and rebuked the Galatians for allowing others to destroy their confidence in the gospel of the kingdom.[234] "You foolish Galatians, who has bewitched you, before whose eyes Jesus Christ was publicly portrayed as crucified?"[235]

Judaizers from Jerusalem entered the churches of Galatia after Paul departed and attempted to thwart his work and drag the new Christians of Galatia back under the Law of Moses, especially circumcision, food laws, and the observance of Jewish holy days. [236] [237] Paul would have none of it! His single argument against the heretics and enemies of the gospel of the kingdom was to appeal to the validating work of the Holy Spirit: "This is the *only* thing I want to find out from you: did you receive the Spirit by the works of the Law, or by hearing with faith?"[238]

The Spirit was *the* salvific sign. Without the Spirit, there was no salvation. Paul's inquiry was precise and indicative to his understanding of the role of the Spirit in salvation. Clearly, Paul believed these Galatians had the Spirit, but the question was how did they know they had received the Spirit? That knowledge had to have come from some demonstrable presence of the Spirit. If the Acts of the Apostles were to be the guide *at salvation*, the

---

234 See, Brown, ibid, p. 467. There is continuing debate concerning the exact location of the churches of Galatia. Some contend for southern Galatia around Antioch and Lystra.
235 Galatians 3:1
236 The Church at Jerusalem, led by James, the brother of Jesus, had become the center of Jewish Christianity, and as such championed the contention that Christians were to keep certain aspects of the Law. For instance, James and Peter had given place to Jewish food laws (Galatians 2:11–14).
237 These "preachers" (Galatians 1:7) challenged Paul by insisting upon circumcision (Galatians 2:12) and by observing "days and months and seasons and years (Galatians 4:10)." It is sad that some in the church are still attempting to revive the use of Jewish holy days as though they had any significance for Christians.
238 Galatians 3:1–2, emphasis added

gifts of the Spirit were evident. Something supernatural had taken place! It simply does not make sense that Paul would have expected something from the converts in Corinth and something altogether different in Galatia. Following that line of logic, the new Christians at Galatia spoke in tongues, prophesied, and glorified God, and Paul remembered their experience. He reproved them, "So then, does he who provides you with the Spirit and works miracles among you, do it by the works of the Law, or by hearing with faith?"[239]

The answer was obvious. Because these were Christians, they had experienced the Spirit by faith, and the events of that moment could not be denied. At the moment of their salvation, they were baptized by the Spirit into Christ and branded by the Holy Spirit with validating gifts of the Spirit, which included speaking in tongues.[240]

The Spirit at Thessalonica

The Apostle Paul, writing in late AD 51, continued this line of logic defining the experience of the Christians at Thessalonica in the Holy Spirit with the events in the Acts of the Apostles. Thessalonica was a large seaport city in Macedonia shaped in the form of an amphitheater on the slope of a hill at the northeast end of the Gulf of Salonica. Under Rome, Thessalonica became a city of great importance with the largest population in the district and the residence of the Roman governor. When Paul arrived, Thessalonica was a thriving city of seventy thousand consisting of Greeks, a mixture of Romans, and a large Jewish population housing a major synagogue.[241]

---

239 Galatians 3:5
240 Galatians 3:27. Paul was not speaking of water baptism when he stated, "All of you who were baptized into Christ have clothed yourselves with Christ." Rather, he wrote of the salvific baptism of the Holy Spirit, the moment in which the Spirit baptizes the new Christian into Christ.
241 Acts 17:1

As was his strategy, Paul entered the synagogue and confronted the Jews with the demands of the gospel of the kingdom, reasoning with them from the Old Testament scriptures, *"explaining and giving evidence that the Christ had to suffer and rise again from the dead, and saying, 'This Jesus whom I am proclaiming to you is the Christ.'"*[242]

Some of the Jewish men and women, along with a *"great multitude"* of Greeks believed the gospel of the kingdom that Paul preached and were truly born again, baptized with the Holy Spirit. As the church had previously experienced, salvation was accompanied with the demonstrable presence of the Spirit. This evangelistic success stirred up Jewish persecution against Paul and Silas to the point they were forced to flee the city by night for Corinth. Because of the apostle's great concern for his infant church in Thessalonica, he wrote them to encourage and remind them concerning their salvation and the attendant work of the Holy Spirit. He did so with the experiences of Acts of the Apostles in mind. Paul insisted, *"Our gospel did not come to you in word only, but also in power and in the Holy Spirit and with full conviction."*[243]

Paul demanded that the gospel he preached and the gospel the Thessalonians received was replete with demonstrations of the gifts and power of the Holy Spirit. Though he does not use the exact words, it is obvious in the light of the Acts of the Apostles that he spoke of public miracles, healings, and exorcisms. To the individuals who had believed and were baptized with the Holy Spirit, it clearly meant speaking in tongues and glorifying God. Paul demanded, *"You became imitators of us and of the Lord."*[244] How? Just as in all the churches since Pentecost, the Holy Spirit was poured out upon the Christians at Thessalonica.

---

242 Acts of the Apostles 17:3
243 1 Thessalonians 1:5
244 1 Thessalonians 1:5

Paul declared, "*You ... received the word with much tribulation with the joy of the Holy Spirit.*"[245]

Yes, their salvation resulted in persecution, but it was persecution filled with the joy of the Holy Spirit, which meant, according to the pattern of The Acts of the Apostles, the gifts of the Spirit were in operation, and the gifts of the Spirit that imitated the experience of Paul and the other early Christians most definitely included speaking, praying, and singing in tongues. As was true with the other churches, something supernatural happened, something so profound it would keep them through their persecution and struggle. As Paul would demand throughout his ministry, each new Christian was given the Holy Spirit as the definitive act of their salvation, and the coming of the Holy Spirit gave life to their dead spirits, marking them with the demonstration of the Spirit.[246]

The Spirit at Corinth

The church at Corinth was radically charismatic and rightfully so; it was, after all, the work of the Apostle Paul with his consistent emphasis on the Holy Spirit. It is easy to consider Paul's material to the Corinthian church regarding the work of the Spirit to be limited to a few passages, but, in fact, Paul's first letter to them in early AD 53 was replete with expectation and delight at the ministry of the Spirit in the lives of the Corinthian Christians. In the opening verses of the Epistle, Paul immediately wrote of the overflow of the Spirit that came to individual believers from their salvific relationship with Jesus: "I thank my God always concerning you for the grace of God which was given you in Christ Jesus."[247]

---

245 1 Thessalonians 1:5–6
246 Romans 5:5; 8:9, 16; 2 Corinthians 3:17; Galatians 4:6; Titus 3:6
247 1 Corinthians 1:4

These were salvation words for Paul, who constantly insisted upon the grace of God as the basis of the salvation in Christ Jesus. Χάρις(Grace) is best seen as the clothing with which the Spirit comes, and that whereby he manifests himself in charismata."[248] "In everything you were enriched in him, in all speech and all knowledge, even as the testimony concerning Christ was confirmed in you, so that you are not lacking in any gift."[249]

The apostle was thrilled that the church at Corinth was being enriched in the Lord Jesus with all speech (λόγῳ) and all knowledge (γνώσει). Both of those were supernatural manifestations of the gifts of the Spirit. Speech had to refer to something supernatural, and that probably meant speaking in tongues, while knowledge was understood as gifts of wisdom, words of knowledge, and words of prophecy.

Even though the church at Corinth was young and did suffer with division that required the apostolic supervision of Paul, Timothy, and Titus, Corinth was not, as some critics insist, a church out of order or immature with charismatic gifts. [250] [251] It was a church that did not lack any spiritual gift, a church at ease with the power and anointing of the Holy Spirit, a church that constantly experienced the miraculous, and a church that lived in and by the supernatural. The great Apostle had refused to build the church at Corinth on the strength of the natural and

248 Dunn, *Baptism in the Holy Spirit*, p. 116 Dunn defines the gift of grace as "the effectual call of God by means of the Gospel and the Spirit (Rom. 1:5; 15:15; 1Cor. 3:10; Eph. 3:2, 8: 4:7)."
249 1 Corinthians 1:5–7
250 2 Corinthians 7:14–16. It seems to be the ministry of Titus acting as Paul's apostolic deputy to place the church at Corinth in order and heals divisions.
251 Some of those who desire to deny the present operation of the gifts of Spirit seek to damage the reputation of the Church at Corinth by demanding Paul was rebuking an unruly congregation for its misuse of the gifts of the Spirit. Nothing could be further from the truth. Although he did, perhaps for the first time in church history, seek to establish a charismatic order in the public services. See, 1 Cor. 12 & 14, Paul was in no way condemning or seeking to squelch the life and flow of the gifts of the Holy Spirit. See my Chapter 5.

the authority to the world. Its foundations were laid in the visible, audible demonstration of the Spirit. Paul declared, "Christ did not send me to baptize, but to preach the gospel, not in cleverness of speech, that the cross of Christ should not be made void ... and my message and preaching was not in persuasive words or wisdom, but in demonstration of the Spirit and of power."[252]

Paul was an apostle of the Spirit. He knew that the church of Jesus Christ was uniquely built upon the gifts and anointings of the Spirit. To receive Jesus was to receive the Spirit; to know Jesus was to know the Spirit with all His giftings.

> We have not received the spirit of the world, but the Spirit who is from God, that we might know the things freely given to us by God, which things we speak, not in words taught by human wisdom, but in those taught by the Spirit, combining spiritual thoughts with spiritual deeds (literally: "comparing spirituals with spirituals").[253]

The Apostle Paul maintained that true believers in the Lord Jesus Christ spoke with words taught by the Spirit and thus were able to compare the spiritual gifts and revelations already possessed with new spiritual gifts and revelations and judge between the two.[254] What were the spirituals? Without question, they were all of the supernatural gifts of the Spirit leading the church deeper and deeper into its relationship with Jesus. From what was clear in Paul's Corinthian Epistle, the deeds certainly included speaking, singing, and praying in tongues.

The Apostle taught the Corinthians that their entire relationship with the Lord Jesus Christ, as was true in all the churches, was through the work of the Holy Spirit. He pointedly stated

---

252 1 Corinthians 1:17; 2:4
253 1 Corinthians 2:12–13
254 Walter Bauer, *Greek-English Lexicon*, ed. Fredrick William Danker, (Chicago: University of Chicago Press, 2000) p. 953

that they were washed, sanctified, and justified "in the name of the Lord Jesus Christ, and in the Spirit of God."[255] That washing, sanctification, and justification came at their salvation, when the Holy Spirit baptized them into Christ.[256] These new Christians at Corinth were born again. As a result, old things passed away; they entered into a new dimension of life; they were a new creation, supernatural creatures. As would be expected, that baptism of the Holy Spirit came with supernatural release of all the gifts of the Spirit that continued in the life of each believer in the Corinthian church.

The Apostle was not deterred for even a moment by the acceptance or rejection by the skeptics of the power of the Holy Spirit in the church at Corinth. What had taken place in the lives of these new Christians could not be explained or experienced in the flesh; in fact, it could not even be comprehended by those limited to the natural world: "A natural man does not accept the things of the Spirit of God, for they are foolishness to him; and he cannot understand them, because they are spiritually appraised. But he who is spiritual appraises all things, yet he himself is appraised by no one."[257]

Paul then acknowledged the source of knowledge for the Christian as though it were a well-guarded secret. He insists, "We have the mind of Christ."[258] How could it be possible that a believer in the Lord Jesus could possess the mind of Christ and be able to appraise all things? Obviously, for the Apostle Paul, the answer was tied to the presence of the Holy Spirit in the lives of Christians, constantly gifting the believer and through that gifting revealing the full will of King Jesus. As Christians in Corinth spoke, prayed, and sang in tongues, as they spoke words of wisdom, knowledge, and prophecy by the supernatural work

---

255 1 Corinthians 6:11
256 1 Corinthians 12:13 "By the Spirit we were all baptized into one body ... and were all made to drink of one Spirit."
257 1 Corinthians 2:14–15
258 1 Corinthians 2:16

of the Holy Spirit, the thoughts and intentions of the Lord were made known, and, as a result, great faith was released as a gift of the Holy Spirit. The Spirit-filled minds of the church at Corinth became in sync with the mind of Christ. As Paul revealed, "The one who joins himself to the Lord is in one spirit with Him."[259] This relationship with Jesus through the Spirit was not reserved for a chosen few or the radical charismatic fringe. It was the *universal expectation* of the apostle: "For by one Spirit we were all baptized into one body, whether Jews or Greeks, whether slaves or free, and we were all made to drink of one Spirit."[260]

The Apostle Paul was not envisioning water baptism; he spoke of the Holy Spirit baptizing each Christian into the body of Christ.[261] There was no acceptable alternative conclusion other than recognizing that for Paul the baptism of the Holy Spirit was the exclusive salvific door that brought individuals into the body of Christ.[262] The baptism of the Spirit is the moment at which each new Christian is *made to drink of one Spirit*. There was no water in this drink, no water baptism. It was the supernatural baptism of the Holy Spirit, and since the Acts of the Apostles stood as the model, the drink of the Spirit was always demonstrated by the visible, audible gifts of the Spirit, including speaking, praying, and singing in tongues.

The Spirit and Paul's Second Letter to Corinth

Many scholars believe Paul may have written several letters to the church at Corinth and understand Second Corinthians, written AD 56–57, to be a compilation of those letters.[263] Whether or not that is accurate, there is no denying that once again the Epistle is filled with the strategic role of the Holy Spirit. The

259 1 Corinthians 6:17
260 1 Corinthians 12:13
261 Galatians 3:27
262 See, Dunn, *Baptism in the Holy Spirit*, p. 127–131
263 See, Brown, ibid, p. 541

apostle opened the letter by laying the foundation of the role of the Spirit: "Now he who establishes us with you in Christ and anointed us is God, who also sealed us and gave us the Spirit in our hearts as a pledge."[264]

It was the Holy Spirit who God gave to the Christian as the pledge of assurance of salvation. That being the case, the giving of the Spirit had to have occurred in such a vivid way—both internally by way of personal transformation and externally through the release of the gifts of the Spirit—that the experience itself would overcome any doubt.

Once he established the certainty of their salvation by the manifest work of the Spirit, the apostle moved into one of his clearest teachings on the work of the Spirit and the new covenant salvation of Jesus. This was a critical step both to assure those in Corinth of the relationship with Jesus by the Spirit and to refute the false teachers, who desired to put the church back under the law of the old covenant. Paul insisted that by the Holy Spirit, he was the servant of a new covenant, "not of the letter but of the Spirit; for the letter kills, but the Spirit gives life."[265] Paul could not have been more focused. It was the *Spirit that gave life* in the new covenant. Without the Holy Spirit being actively poured out upon the earth by King Jesus, there could be no new covenant. Without receiving the baptism of the Spirit, no one could experience the new covenant and its attendant salvation.[266] That was the Pauline message at Corinth that birthed the church. New covenant life was in the Spirit. The old covenant was death and condemnation, and those without the Spirit were under that covenant of death and were certainly not Christians.

One of the tactics used by those who opposed Paul and his teaching, both inside and outside the Church, was to glorify the Law as the ultimate expression of God. Paul acknowledged the

264 2 Corinthians 1:21–22
265 2 Corinthians 3:6
266 Dunn, *Baptism in the Holy Spirit*, p. 135

glory of the Law, fading as it was, but totally rejected the idea that Moses and those under the old covenant had experienced the full glory of God that could only be encountered by the work of the Holy Spirit: "If the ministry of death, in letters engraved on stones, came with glory, so that the sons of Israel could not look intently at the face of Moses because of the glory of his face, fading as it was, how will the ministry of the Spirit fail to be even more with glory?"[267]

Without question, the ministry of the Holy Spirit and the attendant new covenant would have far greater glory than the Law. The apostle compared the observable glory on the face of Moses with the demonstrable manifestation of the glory of the new covenant in the Holy Spirit, and by doing so, he declared that new covenant glory in the Spirit would in every overt visible manner surpass the glory of the old covenant.

> For if the ministry of condemnation (the Law) has glory, much more does the ministry of righteousness (salvation in Jesus) abound in glory. For indeed what had glory, in this case has no glory because of the glory that surpasses it. For if that which fades away was with glory, much more that which remains is in glory.[268]

This was not an invisible glory! If the glory of the old covenant was a visible, supernatural manifestation on the face and skin of Moses, then the glory of the new covenant must be a far greater supernatural visible manifestation. [269] Beginning with the outpouring of the Holy Spirit at Pentecost, that visible manifestation has been the gifts of the Spirit, which did and must always include speaking, praying, and singing in tongues.

The Apostle Paul concluded this section of Second Corinthi-

---

267 2 Corinthians 3:7–8
268 2 Corinthians 3:9–11
269 Exodus 34:29–35

ans by reaffirming to the church at Corinth that the presence of the Spirit was the presence of Jesus.

> Now the Lord is the Spirit, and where the Spirit of the Lord is, there is liberty. But we all, with unveiled face, beholding as in a mirror the glory of the Lord, are being transformed into the same image from glory to glory, just as from the Lord, the Spirit.[270]

The Spirit at Rome

The Apostle Paul wrote to the church at Rome in late AD 56 as an outsider.[271] It was not his church. From the account in the Acts of the Apostles, Paul had never visited Rome and was known to the church at Rome only by reputation or, more than likely, by exaggeration at the hand of those who opposed both him and his message.[272] For Paul, there was a consistently driven commitment, an intensely understood destiny that he must get to Rome.[273] Many believe the apostle intended to make Rome his new headquarters city as he moved the emphasis of his work to Western Europe.[274] So his letter to the church at Rome was a critically important introduction of his ministry and theology and an attempt to douse some theological fires before his arrival.

Rome was the center of the world, the capital city of the Roman Empire. If the world was to hear and receive the gospel of the kingdom, Rome had to be reached. In Paul's day, Rome was home to Caesar, the most powerful man on earth, but he was not the first target of the church. The Lord Jesus had commanded that the gospel was first to be taken to the Jews, and Rome was

---

270 2 Corinthians 3:17–18
271 See, Brown, ibid, p. 559–564 for a concise presentation of the founding and composition of the Church at Rome.
272 Romans 15:23
273 Acts 19:21; 23:11
274 Romans 16:1–2

home to tens of thousands of Jews. [275] The city had absorbed a significant Jewish population of merchants, immigrants, and captives from early in the second century BC, which by the end of the first century had grown from forty thousand to fifty thousand, who were entrenched throughout Roman society. [276]

The presence of that number of Jewish men and women made Rome an excellent evangelistic opportunity for the early church, especially those missionaries from Jerusalem. "Christianity coming from Jerusalem was likely to be more conservative about the Jewish heritage and the Law than were the Gentiles converted under Paul."[277] Probably under the apostolic direction of James, the brother of Jesus, the church at Rome was birthed in the capital city in the early forties and grew to be a highly respected church.[278] But they were not necessarily prepared for Paul and his teaching because of the Jewish emphasis that came from the church at Jerusalem. Many Jews and Gentiles had believed the gospel of the kingdom, received the salvation of Jesus, and experienced the baptism of the Holy Spirit, but they were so immersed in the Law of Moses that they were continuing to look to the Law as an aspect of their salvation and blessing.[279]

The entirety of Paul's letter was filled with the expectation of the life and work of the Holy Spirit in contrast to the deadness of the Law. It was the Spirit who was alive, bringing the love of God to the church at Rome, not the Law.

---

275 Brown, ibid, p. 559
276 See, Rodney Stark, *The Rise of Christianity*, (San Francisco: Harper, 1997), p. 57. The exact population numbers are uncertain because "many Jews in the Diaspora had changed their names and were no longer Jews in the ethnic sense and remained only partly so in a religious sense."
277 Brown, ibid, p. 562
278 Romans 1:8
279 Regrettably, today there is a group described as Christian Zionists who are attempting to reintroduce Jewish Law, customs, feasts, seasons, holy days and religious celebration back into the Church.

> The love of God has been poured out within our hearts through the Holy Spirit who has been given to us … so that we serve in newness of the Spirit and not oldness of the letter.[280]

The Law was obsolete. The church of Jesus Christ had entered a new world by the reality of their new birth. This was Paul's message. The presence of the Spirit of life in Christ Jesus, which is the Holy Spirit, was the essence of Christianity. Through the power of the victorious death, resurrection, and ascension of Jesus, the Lord was actively pouring forth the Spirit into the earth to baptize the Lord's church and deliver them from both the frustration and condemnation of the Law and set them free from sin. Paul proclaimed, "Therefore there is now no condemnation for those who are in Christ Jesus. For the law of the Spirit of life in Christ Jesus has set you free from the law of sin and of death."[281]

The Lord Jesus Christ, reigning as absolute King of heaven and earth, had established a new law, the law of the Spirit of life in Christ Jesus, and negated the law of sin and death. This was a revolutionary teaching. Paul insisted this was the salvific truth, which was to be experienced by all those who wished to know God. For Paul, the Law had never and would never produce salvation for it was *through the flesh.*

> For what the Law could not do, weak as it was through the flesh, God did: sending his own Son in the likeness of sinful flesh and as an offering for sin, he condemned sin in the flesh, so that the requirement of the Law might be fulfilled in us, who do not walk according to the flesh but according to the Spirit.[282]

---

280 Romans 5:5; 7:5–6
281 Romans 8:1–2
282 Romans 8:3–4

It was a radical new change of understanding, a new worldview. The age of the Law of Moses had ended. Messiah's day was present, and with His day came a new way to God that went through His Son by the Holy Spirit. The choice was clear: either come to God by the way of the Spirit, which led to life, or refuse and attempt to come to God by the Law, which Paul demanded could only lead to death.

> For the mind set on the flesh is death, but the mind set on the Spirit is life and peace, because the mind set on the flesh is hostile toward God; for it does not subject itself to the law of God, for it is not even able to do so, and those who are in the flesh cannot please God.[283]

These are words of salvation, and they are each tied around the work of the Spirit. There was no separation in the mind of the apostle. Either an individual had the Spirit, or he or she did not have Christ, and therefore he or she was not saved! Paul's declaration was emphatic: Christians left the realm of the flesh, and by the salvation of Jesus through the work of the Holy Spirit, they entered the realm of the Spirit, the supernatural world. They were born again. Paul stated, "You are not in the flesh but in the Spirit."[284]

Think of the staggering significance of the apostle's statement. *You are not in the flesh!* Without question, Paul believed that in some supernatural way at salvation a Christian left the restrictions of a purely flesh existence and entered into the supernatural world of the Spirit, "if indeed the Spirit of God dwells in you."[285] Obviously this understanding came from the experience of the church as it walked out its relationship with the Lord Jesus through the Spirit and lived in the power and gifts of the Spirit.

---

283 Romans 8:5–8
284 Romans 8:9
285 Romans 8:9

For the Apostle Paul, it was nonnegotiable. To be a Christian was to have the Holy Spirit. He stated as strongly as possible, "If anyone does not have the Spirit of Christ, he does not belong to him." [286] [287]

This was the primary work of the Holy Spirit: to bring the life of God into the life of the Christian and transform a formerly dead spirit alive by the presence of the Holy Spirit. When that event took place, it was called salvation, and that salvation occurred with the obvious manifestation of the gifts and power of the Holy Spirit beginning at Pentecost. In line with the accounts in the Acts of the Apostles at Pentecost, Samaria, Cornelius's house, and Ephesus, for the Apostle Paul, the single verifying sign of salvation was the gift and reception of the Holy Spirit. Dunn points out, "He does not say, if you are Christ's you have the Spirit, or, if you are sons of God you have the Spirit, far less, if you have believed the right things and/or have been baptized (and so are a Christian) you have the Spirit." [288] Rather, the emphasis of the Apostle Paul, the teaching of the book of Acts, and the expectation of the early church was that the Holy Spirit was *immediately* present at the moment of salvation to demonstrably mark those who had been born again. Thereby, those who experienced the Spirit of Christ by salvation were sons and daughters of God: "For all who are being led by the Spirit of God, these are sons of God." [289]

There could be no greater salvific declaration or definition. Those who possessed the Spirit were the sons and daughters

---

286 There is no distinction between the Spirit of Christ and the Holy Spirit. See Dunn, ibid, p. 149 "The Holy Spirit becomes so related to Jesus and redemption he effects as to be called 'The Spirit of Christ.' The conclusion which Romans 8:9; 1Cor. 6:17; 12:4–6; 15:45 thrust upon us is unavoidable; that in Paul's experience Christ and the Spirit are one, and that Christ was experienced through the Spirit."
287 Romans 8:9
288 Dunn, ibid, p. 145
289 Romans 8:14

of God. Paul succinctly declared, "You have received a spirit of adoption as sons by which we cry out, 'Abba! Father!'"[290]

This was the ministry of the Holy Spirit, the visible, demonstrable, tangible, manifestation of the presence of the Spirit that produced a conscious awareness of being adopted into the family of God. The Apostle Paul insisted that Christians were to know, not guess, not wonder, and certainly not hope, if they were adopted, and the only way of knowing for certain was the presence of the Holy Spirit. Paul continued, "The Spirit Himself testifies with our spirit that we are children of God, and if children, heirs also, heirs of God and fellow heirs with Christ."[291]

How did Paul expect the Spirit to testify with our spirit? Through the gifts of the Spirit, and that meant to the church at Rome, as it had for the other churches, that the Holy Spirit would pray through their spirits. Paul described it as groanings too deep for words. If that phrase was to be understood in the light of the experience of the Acts of the Apostles, it meant praying in tongues.

> In the same way the Spirit also helps our weakness; for we do not know how to pray as we should, but the Spirit himself intercedes for us with groanings too deep for words; and he who searches the hearts knows what the mind of the Spirit is, because he intercedes for the saints according to the will of God.[292]

Paul envisioned Christians participating with the Holy Spirit by praying the will of God with groanings too deep for regular words. The reality of the Holy Spirit interceding through the spirits of believers with prayers in tongues was in every way supernatural. This was the praying in the tongues that Paul fully experienced

---

290 Romans 8:15
291 Romans 8:16–17
292 Romans 8:26–27

in his own life and fully expected to constantly occur throughout the life of all the churches.

The Spirit at Ephesus

The Apostle Paul wrote the letter to the church at Ephesus while imprisoned at Rome in the early sixties and had it delivered to the church by Tychicus. [293] [294] The apostle obviously had a great affinity for Ephesus, for he remained in the city for three years on his third missionary journey. [295] His time at Ephesus was filled with extraordinary supernatural miracles, so much so that handkerchiefs and aprons were taken from his body and placed upon those who were sick, diseased, or those filled with evil spirits, and they were immediately made well and delivered.[296] Prior to leaving Ephesus, Paul had warned the church to be aware of "savage wolves who would come in among them" and attempt to pull them away from things he had taught. [297]

In his letter to the Ephesians, he wrote as the apostle over the work, warning them again of false teaching but primarily reminding them of who they were *in Christ* and how they had become true sons and daughters of God.[298] The entire emphasis of the letter revolves around the work of the Holy Spirit. Paul began the letter by reminding the church of how the Father has

---

293 Pauline authorship is disputed among some critics. They contend the style and theology differ from Paul, and suggest the letter is pseudonymous (written by a follower of Paul who used Paul's name for authorship). Others regard Ephesians as the apex of Paul's writing. The letter was undisputedly accepted in the early church as a work of Paul. Regardless, there is no overwhelming rationale for rejecting Paul's authorship.
294 Ephesians 6:21–22
295 Ephesus was a city of 200,000 located on the Aegean Sea between Mount Pion and Mount Koressos that developed from its early days as a Greek outpost to become the most important city in Asia Minor.
296 Acts 19:11–12
297 Acts 20:29
298 Ephesians 5:6

"blessed us with every spiritual blessing in the heavenly places in Christ."[299] Then Paul moved into a litany of supernatural blessings of being in Christ Jesus: blessings, blamelessness, adoption as sons, redemption, the riches of grace, the mystery of his will, inheritance, and the hope to the praise of his glory.[300] Paul insisted these blessings were not just ethereal or reserved for eternity; they were meant to be experienced daily by the individual Christian, and it was the work of the Holy Spirit that made the blessings of *in Christ* real. The Apostle Paul wrote:

> In him, you also, after listening to the message of truth, the gospel of your salvation—having also believed, you were sealed in him with the Holy Spirit of promise, who is given as a pledge of our inheritance, with a view to the redemption of God's own possession, to the praise of his glory.[301]

This was one great indivisible nugget of truth concerning the work of the Holy Spirit. Paul cried out to his church at Ephesus, "You heard the truth, the gospel of salvation; you believed; and at that moment, you were sealed with the Spirit who was given as a pledge." This apostolic nugget was not to be pealed off and experienced in layers; it was one truth, the message of truth. For the Apostle Paul, salvation was hearing; salvation was believing; salvation was being baptized by the Holy Spirit, which meant being sealed by the Spirit as a pledge of all the blessings of being *in Christ*.

Obviously, it was an experience they knew and remembered. For the church at Ephesus, salvation was not a private moment with no one looking around. Like Jerusalem, Samaria, Caesarea, Galatia, and Corinth, the Christians at Ephesus understood their

---

299 Ephesians 1:3
300 Ephesians 1:3–12
301 Ephesians 1:13–14

salvation in Christ as being baptized in the Holy Spirit. And at their salvation experience, like all the other churches, they had each spoken in tongues.[302]

The apostle closed his letter with a challenge to the charismatic Christians at Ephesus: "With all prayer and petition, pray at all times in the Spirit," and at least at times that would mean praying in tongues. [303]

---

302 Acts 19:1–7
303 Ephesians 6:18

7

Tongues in the Second Century

*A correct reading of history drives
one to the Spirit and his gifts.*

One critical question regarding speaking in tongues is whether the experience outlived the first century or ceased with the original revelatory apostles. If the use of tongues ceased, that cessation would give credence to the belief that the use of tongues was confined to biblical times and holds no place in the current life of Christianity. "If, however, *glossolalia* (speaking in tongues) continued among those who established the foundations of the church, amid the most adverse circumstances," then it cannot be ignored or relegated to the first century AD. [304] [305] The answer is simple: speaking in tongues did stop but started again and again

---

304 The term glossolalia comes from the combination of two
Greek words, tongue; and to speak, and is translated as, speaking in
tongues.
305 Morton Kelsey, *Tongue Speaking*, (NY: Crossroads, 1981), p. 32

and again throughout the history of the church. "The common religious experience of individuals and groups throughout history demonstrates a shared and similar work of one Spirit."[306]

A more intriguing question is not if tongues ceased, but why did they cease and why did they start again? What would cause a clearly canonical experience to cease at various times only to emerge at a later moment? How has the literal meaning of the biblical accounts been bypassed? In order to understand this sporadic phenomenon, it is essential to examine, at least cursorily, the history of Christian thought and worship as it relates to the gifts of the Holy Spirit. To do so requires looking behind the usual cast of selected church fathers (some of whom not only opposed the free flow of the Spirit, but had a great deal to lose if the gifts continued in operation) and attempting to understand the worship, devotional life, and ministry of the early church.

The Acts of the Apostles closed only months before the death of Paul in Rome and just years prior to the destruction of Jerusalem by the Roman Prince Titus in AD 70. With the destruction of Jerusalem, the original manuscripts that ultimately became the New Testament were completed.[307] There is no debate that at the time of their completion, the church was alive by and operating in the gifts of the Spirit. In the light of the New Testament, it is difficult to imagine that any leading Christian did not speak, pray, and sing in tongues during that time.

Following the death of Peter and Paul at the hands of Nero and

---

306 George H. Williams and Edith Waldvogel, "A History of Speaking in Tongues and Related Gifts," *The Charismatic Movement*, ed. Michael P. Hamilton, (Grand Rapids, MI: Eerdmans, 1975), p. 64
307 There is great debate concerning the dating of the books of the New Testament. I agree with J. A. T. Robinson, *The Redating of the New Testament*, that of the writings of the NT were started before the destruction of Jerusalem by Titus in AD 70. It is difficult to imagine that writings by Jews to Jews could have avoided those events. Raymond Brown, *Introduction to the New Testament*, p. 163, desires later dates, but is forced to admit, "The failure of NT works to make specific and detailed mention of the destruction of Jerusalem and the Temple is very hard to explain."

the destruction of Jerusalem, the church fled Palestine as Jesus had instructed and turned its attention to the Gentile world throughout the remainder of the first century. [308] Its message to the nations was the gospel of the kingdom with its attendant supernatural demonstrations of the Spirit, which most certainly included speaking in tongues. Eusebius demanded that the early Christians who took the gospel to the nations were so empowered "by the Holy Spirit that at first hearing, whole multitudes eagerly embraced their piety toward the Creator of the universe."[309] The entire ministry of the early church was dominated by the open, visible, audible demonstrations of the work of the Spirit. Augustine would later write of this patristic period, "Miracles were necessary before the world believed, in order that it might believe," [310] and the miracles meant the presence of the gifts of the Holy Spirit.

The closing years of the first century and the opening decades of the second were highly productive years for the church, which rapidly grew from the one hundred and twenty in the upper room to become the significant emerging religious force in the Roman Empire.[311] During those transitional years, the church proclaimed the gospel of the kingdom, demonstrated the victory of the Lord Jesus, and "the participation of the Christian in it through the Holy Spirit."[312] The victory was not a temporary messianic conquest of some earthly military power but absolute conquest over the powers of Satan and evil. This power was manifested by the gifts of the Holy Spirit with speaking, singing, and praying in tongues.

---

308 Matthew 24:15–21. The Church fled Jerusalem under orders from Jesus, and went north to Pella avoiding the Roman army and its Jewish bloodbath.

309 Eusebius, *Ecclesiastical History 3.37.3, 1927*

310 Augustine, "The City of God," Bk. XII, Ch. 8, *Nicene and Post-Nicene Fathers*, ed. Philip Schaff, (Peabody, MA.: Henderson, 1999), p. 484

311 See, Rodney Stark, *ibid*, p.3–27. There is continued debate concerning exact numbers in the church by the end of the first century. Stark contends the mission to the Jews prior to AD 70 was "far more successful and long-lasting than the NT and early church fathers claim."

312 E. Glenn Hinson, *The Evangelization of the Roman Empire*, (Macon, GA: Mercer Press, 1981), p. 19

Christian thought and practice during this strategic time was filled with struggle and controversy both inside and outside the church, but the leadership of the church was clearly aware and committed to the strategic place the gifts of the Spirit occupied. "It is significant that among those intellectually sophisticated writers, *glossolalia* (speaking in tongues) was known and accepted as one of the special gifts which are given to Christians."[313]

Christian writings during those decades were mainly focused on controversies facing the church. As a result, they were usually reactive in nature, and most certainly did not reflect the deeply spiritual experiences of average individual Christians. One reason for a lack of material concerning speaking in tongues during this time was its non-controversial status. Following the mandates of the Lord Jesus and the Apostle Paul, it was assumed that all would speak in tongues, that the gifts of the spirit would be manifested, and that prophecy, healings, and exorcism would occur throughout the life and ministry of the church. [314] It simply was not necessary to produce materials supporting the place and acceptance of the gifts of the Holy Spirit, which were universally accepted. As a result, Christian literature of this period included only a dim glimpse into the Spirit-empowered life of the church during a time when Christianity was undergoing extensive debate over the nature of its role and identity following the death of the original disciples of Jesus.

The Early Church Fathers and Tongues

The period immediately following the death of the original disciples through the third century AD has been labeled the Patristic Era.[315] The Patristic fathers did not include every bishop or

---

313 Kelsey, ibid, p. 32 parenthesis added
314 Mark 16:17; 1 Corinthians 14:5
315 John McGuckin, "The Early Church Fathers," *Christian Spirituality*, ed. Gordon Mursell, (Minneapolis: Fortress Press, 2001), p. 32. McGuckin writes of the term patristic as denoting elders or bishops and states, "These were the 'fathers': Abbas in the words of

church leader, but only those who were highly respected through-out the church and to whom the churches appealed for matters of doctrine and polity in the struggle between orthodoxy and heresy. The surviving Christian writings from this time came from the pens of those fathers.[316]

However, it is critically important to remember that although they were held in esteem, the Patristics were not always correct; they did not always win the argument, they did not always rise above their own prejudice and political desires, and they most certainly did not always reflect the deep personal devotion to Jesus and genuine dependence upon the supernatural life of the Spirit that existed within the average believer. Early Christianity was "always far richer and more complex than the limited surviv-ing Patristic writings suggest."[317] Therefore, to trace the gifts of the Holy Spirit beginning with the second-century church, it is necessary to analyze both the Patristics and their critics, be will-ing to listen again to those condemned as heretics, and examine as closely as possible the Spirit life of the people of God.

Clement of Rome and the Shepherd of Hermas

There was a very clear, if at times sporadic, trail of the gifts of the Holy Spirit, including speaking in tongues from the Patristic

---

the early Coptic monks, or Patres in the Latin, which gave the word patristic to the vocabulary."

316 Church Fathers wrote to answer the critics of Christianity and achieve acceptance for the Church from an antagonistic Gentile world. Christianity was being accused of all kinds of bizarre behavior such as eating newborn babies, placing curses which produced crop failures and causing floods. With that openly hostile environment, it should not be surprising that little was written concerning speaking in tongues since attempts to explain its use would probably inten-sified the negative rumors. The task of the fathers was to present Christianity as acceptable and understandable.

317 McGuckin, ibid, p. 33. McGuckin sees this limiting principle in several ways, but especially in the role of women in the early church. "If we follow the writings of the fathers alone, we largely miss out on what Christian women were contributing during this period ... and become blind to women's significant activity in the early church."

fathers to Augustine. The trail began with three writings: *First and Second Clement* and *The Shepherd of Hermas*, which emerged almost simultaneously around the turn of the second century and are considered "jewels of early Christian writings."[318] They were some, if not the first, noncanonical Christian writings. Each of these works gives insight into the true spiritual life of the early church, with the consistent emphasis on the work of the Holy Spirit.

The First Letter to the Corinthians by Clement, bishop of Rome, was written in AD 95 to the church at Corinth during the last years of persecution the church endured under Roman Emperor Domitian. The letter, which was held in high esteem by the early church, was an exhortation on spiritual discipline and a severe rebuke to the church because it had allowed "a few rash and self-confident persons have kindled to such a pitch of frenzy, that your venerable and illustrious name, worthy to be universally loved, has suffered grievous injury." [319] [320] Throughout the letter, there is the underlying awareness of the spiritual nature of the church and constant references to the work of the Spirit in bringing order and power to live in righteousness. Clement reminded Corinth that "a full outpouring of the Holy Spirit is upon you all" and that the ministers of God have spoken by the Spirit. [321] Though speaking in tongues is not specifically mentioned, it cannot be overlooked that the letter was written to the church at Corinth, which, from its birth, was a thoroughly charismatic community.

The Second Letter of Clement to the Corinthians, which some believe to have been written by another author, was one of the first noncanonical Christian sermons.[322] The message was one

318 McGuckin, ibid, p. 34
319 See, Eusebius, *Church History*, iii, 16
320 Clement of Rome, "First Letter to the Corinthians," *Ante-Nicene Fathers*, vol. 1, (Peabody, MA: Hendrickson, 1999), Ch. 1, p. 5
321 Clement of Rome, ibid, Ch. 2, p. 5
322 See McGuckin, ibid, p. 36

of impending judgment. To prepare for that certainty, Christians were commanded to live with an emphasis on fasting, prayer, and almsgiving. Understanding the Charismatic nature of the Church at Corinth, there can be no doubt that the call for prayer would be answered by the continued use of praying in tongues.

The *Shepherd of Hermas* was one of the most popular books produced in the early church, and for a time it was frequently quoted and regarded as inspired. The work was radically charismatic and characterized by strong moral demands. It was primarily a call to repentance and adherence to a life of strict morality addressed to Christians, among whom the memory of persecution was fresh. It is believed to have been written in sections between AD 95 and 100 by a Christian freedman living in Rome.[323] The book is structured as a series of prophetic visions that the author experienced and is divided into three sections: five visions that carry an apocalyptic flavor, twelve mandates or sermons, and ten parables in which each parable is followed by a request for and granting of an interpretation, and finally blessings and curses upon those who either do or do not heed the warning. Though there are many fascinating aspects of *The Shepherd Hermas*, the critical factor is that these writings give a glimpse into the spiritual life of individual Christians at Rome during that period. It was a life filled with the supernatural, alive by the Spirit, and one of great freedom in the release of the gifts of the Holy Spirit.

Ignatius, AD 35–107

One of the most important players in the history of tongue speech was Ignatius. He was born in Syria and died a martyr in Rome. Ignatius rose to become bishop of Antioch, one of the most important Christian cities, in AD 69 at age thirty-four. There is no record in his writings concerning speaking in tongues, nor is there any indication that Ignatius spoke in tongues, though he

---

323 See, McGuckin, p. 37

most likely did since he was a disciple of the apostles. In fact, very little is known of him except his remarkable journey across Asia Minor on his way to stand trial in Rome for being a Christian. Ignatius believed his martyrdom was an act of obedience and would not allow the church at Rome to come to his rescue. He demanded, "Let me be food for the wild beast, through which I can reach God."[324] On his journey from Antioch to Rome, Ignatius wrote to the churches at Ephesus, Magnesia, Tralles, Rome, Philadelphia, and Smyrna, together with a personal letter to Bishop Polycarp at Smyrna.

Even though Ignatius wrote of an ability to understand heavenly things by the same Spirit as the prophets and apostles, his importance in the history of speaking in tongues was not his doctrinal stance or charismatic experience, but the hierarchical structure he helped initiate within the church. He was in agreement with the arguments of Clement of Rome in his First Letter to the Corinthians, insisting upon the charismatic selection of a single bishop in each city who could lead the church in purity of heart and under the inspiration of the Holy Spirit. [325] Ignatius's writings, along with those of Clement, were instrumental in establishing the principle of one city, one bishop, one altar, and around that altar one heart and mind constituting the church.[326]

For Ignatius, a sole bishop was to govern the work of the church in a city, assisted by priests and deacons. As the bishop emerged into prominence, the worship life of the church became structured around the liturgy, and the free flow of the gifts of the Spirit in individual lives was placed on hold. Tragically, the bishop became the chief celebrant of the Eucharistic worship of all Christians gathered in one church. The bishop became the high priest of the community, the charismatically appointed leader, the chosen of Christ at the heart of the body, which forced

---

324 Ignatius of Antioch, "Letter to the Romans," *Ante-Nicene Fathers*, vol. 1, (Peabody, MA: Hendrickson, 1999) Ch. 4, p. 75
325 Clement of Rome, ibid, Ch. 44, p. 17
326 McGuckin, ibid, p. 40

the church to find its unity with God through the bishop and less and less through the life and ministry of the Holy Spirit. Repeatedly, Ignatius asserted that the supremacy of the bishop was a divine choice that belonged to the apostolic foundation of the church. He went so far as to insist that the bishop stood in the place of Christ himself. "When you are obedient to the bishop as to Jesus Christ," he writes to the Trallians, "it is evident to me that you are living not after men, but after Jesus Christ … be obedient also to the presbytery as to the Apostles of Jesus Christ."[327] The church was to gather around the bishop not only for its organizational structure, but also for its spiritual life. Ignatius demanded, "Let no man do anything connected with the church without the bishop."[328]

It is difficult to believe that Ignatius purposefully attempted to curtail the work of the Holy Spirit or the manifestation of the gifts of the Spirit among the people, but what he set in place with his writings, the role of the monarchial bishop and hierarchical structure he envisioned, would ultimately rise to discount and even reject the gifts of the Spirit in the individual lives of the believers, especially speaking in tongues and prophecy. The rejection of tongues and other gifts of the Spirit did not take place immediately but through a prolonged process of both cultural and ecclesiastical suppression; speaking, praying, and singing in tongues was relegated to the past. Ultimately, it was bishops, not the New Testament canon that expelled prophecy and tongues from the church.[329]

Polycarp, AD 69–155

Polycarp of Smyrna was a deeply spiritual man who believed the Christian life could only be kept alive by prayer. In an early let-

327 Ignatius, "Letter to the Trallians," ibid, Ch. 2, p. 66
328 Ignatius, "Letter to Smyrna," Ch. 8, p. 86
329 See James L. Ash Jr., "The Decline of Ecstatic Prophecy" in the *Early Church, Theological Studies* 37 (1976), p. 228

ter, Polycarp testified to the important role women played in the church. He referred to one group of women as "our widows."[330] He saw them as powerful charismatic intercessory warriors for the church and encouraged them in what he described as their ministry of spiritual sacrifice. He wrote, "The widows must think soberly about the faith of the Lord and pray without ceasing for everyone."[331]

Given the relationship of Polycarp with the teaching of the apostles, he would have seen the prayers of the widows as including speaking and praying in tongues.

The Rise of Gentile Writers

Until the midpoint of the second century, Christian literature had been profoundly Jewish in character, but then it began to change as more and more Gentiles entered Christianity. New Gentile Christian authors who were more educated and skilled in writing began to produce works that utilized these authors' knowledge of Greek rhetoric to defend the church against its detractors. They are referred to as the apologists.[332] One of these men was Justin.

Justin Martyr, AD 110–165

Justin was born of pagan parents from Flavia Neapolis, a city in Samaria. A highly educated, refined man, Justin became a disciple of Socrates and Plato after much searching. Ultimately, he became intrigued by the fearlessness by which Christians faced death, and through a chance meeting with a man while walk-

330 See McGuckin, ibid, McGuckin displays a picture of a woman in prayer from the tomb stele of Theodora, a fifty-century Coptic burial stone found in Egypt. The woman is praying with her hands raised much like the modern Charismatics who worship and pray with raised hands.
331 Polycarp, "Letter to the Philippians," ibid, Ch. 4, p. 31
332 From the Greek word, apologia, it means a considered legal and intellectual defense of an opinion. These men wrote during the second century AD attempting to prove the validity of the Christian message to those outside the church.

ing on the beach, he encountered the gospel of the kingdom and was radically born again. The conversion of Justin marked a new era in Christianity as this brilliant, deeply spiritual man rose to become the founder of theological literature.

Justin was demonstrably charismatic and held the gifts of the Spirit in high regard. He started the first school of theology at Rome, where he wrote his *Dialogue to Trypho the Jew*, in which he stated, "The prophetical gifts remain among us, even to the present time ... Now it is possible to see amongst us women and men who possess gifts of the Spirit of God."[333] Only the greatest skeptic would contend that speaking in tongues was not one of the gifts Justin experienced and expected. Justin revealed that the gifts of the Spirit were not only in the church in his day, but he connected the outpouring of the gifts with the ascension of Christ. He wrote to Trypho:

"Daily some are becoming disciples in the name of Christ, and are also receiving gifts (of the Spirit), each as he is worthy, illumined through the name of this Christ. For one receives the spirit of understanding, another of counsel, another of strength, another of healing, another of foreknowledge, another of teaching, and another of the fear of God." To this Trypho said to me, "I wish you knew that you are beside yourself, talking these sentiments." And I said to him, "Listen, O friend, for I am not mad or beside myself; but it was prophesied that, after the ascent of Christ to heaven, he would deliver us from error and give us gifts. The words are these: 'He ascended up on high; He led captivity captive; He gave gifts to men.'"[334]

---

333 Justin Martyr, "Dialogue With Trypho," *Ante-Nicene Fathers,* eds. Alexander Roberts and James Donaldson, (Peabody, MA: Hendrickson, 1999) Ch. 39, p. 243
334 Justin, "Dialogue with Trypho," *Ante-Nicene Fathers*, vol. 1, ibid, Ch. 82, p. 215

Justin Martyr's testimony to the ongoing presence of the super-natural work of the Holy Spirit took place nearly a century fol-lowing the death of Paul and his Epistle to the Corinthians. Yet, without question, the gifts of the Spirit, which would have most definitely included tongues, had not ceased or been placed in abeyance.

Irenaeus, AD 130–200

As a young man, Irenaeus heard the legendary Polycarp, AD 69–155, who was reputed to be a disciple of the Apostle John. That expe-rience set the course for his life of commitment to Jesus and his church. During the persecution of Marcus Aurelius, who reigned as Caesar from AD 161–180, Irenaeus was a priest of the church of Lyons.[335] In AD 177, the clergy of Lyons, many of whom were suf-fering imprisonment for their relationship with Jesus, sent him to Rome with a letter to Pope Eleutherius concerning Montanism. The pope was extremely impressed with Irenaeus and following his return to Lyons, elevated him to the office of bishop to replace the martyred bishop of Lyons, Pothinus, AD 87–177.

The rise of Irenaeus was a major watershed moment for the church and its literature. During the last decades of the second century, he produced the first systematic exposition of the church's belief in his now famous *Against Heresies*. There was no doubt as to Irenaeus' belief in and commitment to the gifts of the Holy Spirit. Irenaeus, like Justin Martyr, connected the ascension of Christ with Jesus imparting the gifts of the Spirit to the church. He insisted that the gifts were an aspect of the present reign of King Jesus won by the great victory over evil at the cross and resurrection when He "ascended into the lofty place, led captivity captive, gave gifts to men" and conferred on those who believed

---

335 See, Eusebius, *Church History*

in Him the power "to tread upon serpents and scorpions, and on all the power of the enemy." [336] [337] [338]

Irenaeus never backed away from the gifts of the Spirit, especially tongues. He clearly knew the power and place of speaking, singing, and praying in tongues and took the significance of tongues to a lofty place. "We do hear many brethren in the Church, who possess prophetic gifts, and who through the Spirit speak all kinds of languages."[339]

In what would prove to be a very important decision, Irenaeus purposefully inserted the word *prophecy* for the term *glossolalia* in his work *Against Heresies*. As he described the events of the Apostle Peter's visit to the household of Cornelius in Caesarea, Irenaeus wrote, "Neither for a like reason, would he have given them baptism so rapidly, had he not heard them *prophesying* as the Holy Ghost rested upon them."[340]

Irenaeus changed terms. There is no record of those at Cornelius's house *prophesying*, but there is a clear statement that they *spoke in tongues*. The exact quote in the Acts of the Apostles is, "they were hearing them speaking in tongues," yet Irenaeus substituted the word *prophesy* for the phrase *speaking in tongues*.[341] Why would Irenaeus, who most definitely knew the passage, make such a change? He may have joined the Apostle Paul in believing that interpreted tongue speech was equal to prophecy.[342] If that were the case, it could certainly account for the lack of writings concerning speaking in tongues. At one point, Irenaeus reached back to Paul and maintained that those who were born again had received the Holy Spirit and been made perfect. That

336 Ephesians 4:8
337 Luke 10:19; Mark 16:17–18
338 Irenaeus, "Against Heresies", Ante-Nicene Fathers, ibid, Bk. 2, Ch. 20, sec. 3, p. 388
339 Irenaeus, ibid, Bk. 5, Ch. 4, p. 531
340 Irenaeus, ibid, Bk. iii, Ch. 12, p. 436 Emphasis added
341 Acts 10:46
342 1 Corinthians 14:5

perfection was demonstrated by the manifestation of the gifts of the Spirit.

> For this reason the Apostle Paul declared, *"We speak wisdom among them that are perfect,"* terming those persons "perfect" who have received the Holy Spirit and do speak in all languages, as he used himself to speak. In like manner we do also hear many brethren in the Church, who possess prophet gifts, and who through the Spirit speak all kinds of languages, and bring to light for the general benefit the hidden things of men, and declare the mysteries of God."[343] [344]

Perfection was the result of salvation. They were new creatures, sons and daughters of God, who were alive by the presence of the Holy Spirit. That presence was made obvious by the gifts of the Spirit, and in this case, Irenaeus demanded that the prophetic gift was speaking in tongues that were interpreted and brought benefit to the church. But he does not stop with tongue speech; rather, he insists that all the gifts, including the raising of the dead, were alive and received in his day.

> For some do certainly and truly drive out devils, so that those who have thus been cleansed frequently both believe in Christ, and join themselves to the Church. Others have foreknowledge of things to come: they see visions, and utter prophetic expressions. Others still, heal the sick by laying hands upon them, and they are made whole. Yea, moreover, as I have said, the dead even have been raised up, and remained among us for many years.[345]

---

343 1 Corinthians 2:6
344 Irenaeus, ibid, Bk. 5, Ch. 4, p. 531
345 Irenaeus, ibid, Bk. 2, Ch. 32, p. 409

There are many powerful and exciting teachings from the writings of Irenaeus, but two are clearly apparent in his work concerning the gifts of the Spirit. First, the gifts of the Spirit, which most certainly included tongues, were still in operation in his church at Lyons and therefore in other Catholic churches during his time. He wrote, "It is not possible to name the number of gifts which the Church, scattered throughout the whole world, has received from God, in the name of Jesus Christ."[346] His life and church was one filled with supernatural demonstration, and he believed wholeheartedly that, "The name of our Lord Jesus Christ even now confers benefits upon men, and cures thoroughly and effectively all who anywhere believe on Him."[347] Second, Irenaeus believed that speaking in tongues and all the other gifts of the Spirit would continue until the resurrection took place.[348] He taught that individuals could not fully receive the ultimate promises of God without the gifts of Spirit. "Man is rendered spiritual and perfect because of the outpouring of the Spirit ... It will render us like unto Him, and accomplish the will of the Father; for it shall make man after the image and likeness of God." [349] Therefore, the gifts of the Spirit must continue.

Obviously, Irenaeus lived and believed that one hundred and fifty years after the Apostle Paul wrote his letter to the Church at Corinth, all the supernatural gifts of the Spirit were very much in operation.

Montanus, Priscilla, and Maximilla, AD 170

At some point in the middle of the second century AD, an outbreak of prophecy and speaking in tongues took place within the emerging Catholic Church that was either a genuine move of the Holy Spirit or an emotional overreach by a group of religious

346 Irenaeus, ibid, Bk. 2, Ch. 32, sec. 4, p. 409
347 Irenaeus, ibid, Bk. 2, Ch. 32, sec. 4, p. 409
348 Irenaeus, ibid, Bk. 5, Ch. 8, sec. 1, p. 533
349 Irenaeus, ibid, Bk. 5, Ch. 6, sec. 1, p. 532

zealots. [350] [351] Either way, it was most certainly "a reaction to the structural hardening of main-line (early Roman Catholic) Christianity."[352] It was a renewal movement with an emphasis on the gifts of the Spirit during a time of great anxiety. The significance of this outbreak of prophecy and speaking in tongues has been the subject of intense debate since the moment it occurred.

As the bishop-led church grew more and more hierarchical, liturgical, and male dominated in its leadership, it slowly moved away from the free-flow life of the Spirit that birthed the church of Jesus Christ.[353] And while spiritual stiffness was being formalized, individual believers began seeking a deeper and more supernatural relationship with the Lord Jesus through the life and gifts of the Holy Spirit. "The issue came to a head in the latter half of the second century AD when Montanus began to reassert the importance of spiritual gifts in the church, particularly the gift of prophecy."[354] Thus was born a movement called "The New Prophecy."[355]

The leaders of this movement were Montanus, a second-century prophet from Phrygia, and two female prophets, Prisca/Priscilla and Maximilla.[356] One of the chief characteristics of the New Prophecy was the equality with which women were received and heard as prophets. Together with Montanus, these two women

---

350 The exact date for the rise of what would become Montanism cannot be determined.
351 See Hyatt, *2000 Years of Charismatic Christianity*, (Lake Mary, FL: Charisma, 2002), p. 29. Hyatt insists Montanism represents one of many charismatic awakenings throughout the history of the church. He believes "Montanism was the first Charismatic Renewal within the Church."
352 Michael P. Hamilton, *The Charismatic Movement*, (Grand Rapids: Eerdmans, 1975), p. 64
353 See Ash, ibid, p. 227
354 Hyatt, ibid, p. 26
355 See, Christine Trevett, "Montanism," *The Early Christian World*, Vol. 2, ed. Philip F. Esler, (New York: Routledge, 2000), p. 929–948
356 They were two women who, according to their critics, left their husbands to become disciples of Montanus and were given the rank of virgins. Along with Montanus, they were considered the greatest prophets in the movement.

initiated a prophetic movement within Christianity that spread rapidly and immediately came into conflict with the developing Catholic authority. It is critically important to remember that most of the history of the movement and its leaders was written by adversaries who had much to lose in the success of this outpouring.[357]

The critics were brutal.[358] Catholics deplored the unbridled manner of their prophesying that included speaking in tongues, the prophets' state of ecstasy, and asserted that the New Prophecy leaders violated Christian tradition by their teachings and practices. On the other hand, some of the concerns from the Catholics were much more mundane than theological. For instance, in the New Prophecy, for the first time in church history, there were salaried officials. The priesthood had been reserved for men of high social standing and education. Salaries would have severely undercut the preeminence of the social elite, as well as diverting monies away from the ministries of mainstream churches. Women and individuals from lower classes were empowered through the changes of the New Prophecy, and both were perceived threats by the Catholics. In addition, the new prophets were circulating their own teachings and prophecies that were received as

---

357 See Eusebius, "Church History," *Nicene and Post Nicene Fathers*, ed. Philip Schaff and Henry Wace, (Peabody, MA: Hendrickson, 1999), p. 235–238

358 If the critics of Montanus are to be believed, and that remains very questionable, he was an egomaniac who believed he was the Paraclete, possessed an unquenchable desire for leadership and led his followers into frenzied states of ecstasy where they raved and babbled strange things in contradiction to the traditions of the church. Montanus was accused of being a deranged fanatic who brought foreign practices from his former pagan life into the church, castrated himself, defiled infants, made bloody Eucharistic offerings, and exhibited signs of demons possession. The critics insisted that Montanus and his followers called for renunciation of ordinary relationships including marriage, advocated severe fasting and encouraged celibacy. He elevated martyrdom as the supreme Christian witness and encouraged his disciples to volunteer to be martyred. Montanus and his followers were thrust out of many of the churches very early in the movement.

authoritative by their followers, including the writings of women. It seems the business and the structure of the emerging Catholic Church were threatened by Montanus. Little wonder that he was excommunicated. "The Church never really recovered its balance after it rejected Montanism."[359]

There are many positive and negative aspects of the New Prophecy movement, but most importantly, Montanus, Priscilla, and Maximilla opened a new era in the church, one filled with an emphasis on the gifts and ministry of the Holy Spirit, including speaking in tongues, that spread throughout the church and lasted well into the fifth century.

Tertullian, AD 160–225

Tertullian, Quintus Septimius Florens Tertullianus, was born, lived, and died in Carthage, in what is today Tunisia in North Africa. Tertullian was trained as a lawyer and devoted his life as a Christian apologist. As such, he was the first great writer of Latin Christianity and thus known as the "father of the Latin church." He introduced the term *trinity*, *Trinitas*, the formula: "three persons, one substance," and the designations Old Testament: *vetus testamentum* and New Testament: *novum testamentum*. In his work, *Apologeticus*, he was the first Latin author to qualify Christianity as the true religion and relegated the religions of Rome and other accepted classical cults as mere superstitions.

He denounced Christian doctrines he considered heretical, and in AD 190, desiring a more strict and spiritual relationship with the Lord Jesus, Tertullian left the emerging Catholic Church and joined the Montanists. He became the most renowned follower of Montanus and a staunch defender of validity and essentiality of the gifts and ministry of the Holy Spirit.

Around AD 200, Tertullian wrote his anti-Gnostic work,

---

359 Kilian McDonnell, *The Baptism of the Holy Spirit*, (Notre Dame, IN: Charismatic Renewal Services, 1972), p. 44

Against Marcion. Interestingly, in that writing, he joined with the Apostle Paul and Irenaeus, demanding that when the Lord Jesus ascended back to His Father and received His kingdom, He "gave gifts to the sons of men."[360] Tertullian then listed the gifts of the Spirit and insisted:

> The Spirit's specific graces, as they are described by the apostle, and promised by the prophet Isaiah ... to another, the gifts of healing, and to another the working of miracles ... to another prophecy, and another discerning of spirits, to another divers kinds of tongues, to another interpretation of tongues. [361] [362]

Denouncing Marcion, Tertullian demanded:

> Let him produce a psalm, a vision, a prayer—only let it be by the Spirit, in an ecstasy, that is, in a rapture, whenever an interpretation of tongues has occurred to him; let him show to me also, that any woman of boastful tongue in his community has ever prophesied from among the special holy sisters of his. Now all these signs (spiritual gifts) are forthcoming from my side without any difficulty.[363] [364]

---

360 Tertullian, "Against Marcion," *Ante-Nicene Fathers*, ed. Alexander Roberts and James Donaldson, (Peabody, MA: Hendrickson, 1999), Bk. 5, Ch. 8, p.446. Tertullian quotes Ephesians 4:8
361 Tertullian compares 1 Corinthians 12:8–11 and Isaiah 11:1–3
362 Tertullian, ibid, Bk. 5, Ch. 8, p. 446
363 Marcion, b. 110 AD, responding to the problem of evil, taught a stringent Docetism that insisted the Old and New Testaments were in contradiction to the extent that they presented two distinct Gods: the God of the Old which who the creator, and the God of the New who was the true God of love. Therefore, he totally rejected the Old Testament, and developed his own canon limited to the Gospel of Luke and the writings of Paul, excluding any Old Testament quotes. See Burgess, The Holy Spirit: Ancient Christian Traditions, p. 45: "For Marcion, the incarnation was not only unnecessary, the very concept of a divine Redeemer participating in materiality was disgusting."
364 Tertullian, ibid, vol. 3, Bk. V, Ch. 8, p. 447 Parenthesis included

For Tertullian, in AD 200, the validating proof of the Christian message was the demonstration of the gifts of the Holy Spirit, which he believed came with the laying on of hands, and that demonstration, without question, included speaking, praying, and singing in tongues.[365]

Eusebius, AD 260–339

Eusebius of Caesarea was the undisputed father of Christian church history. His ten books of church history are "a treasure trove of data on the fledgling faith, whose survival and purity were sorely tested by persecution without and heresy within."[366] Writing in the fourth century, he documented Irenaeus's writings:

> He shows that manifestations of divine and miraculous power continued to his time. In another place the same author (Irenaeus) writes: "As also we hear that many brethren in the Church possess prophetic gifts, and speak, through the Spirit, with all kinds of tongues, and bring to light the secret things of men for their good, and declare the mysteries of God."[367]

Eusebius accepted the witness of Irenaeus concerning the presence of the gifts of the Spirit and agreed that "in regard to the fact that various gifts remained among those who were worthy even until that time" it could not be denied. Eusebius seemed to have held the same position, for he made no attempt to assert that the gifts of the Spirit were inoperable in his day.

---

365 E.C. Whitaker, *Documents of the Baptismal Liturgy*, (London: SPCK, 1970), p. 7–10
366 Paul L. Maier, "Eusebius," *Church History*, (Grand Rapids: Kregel, 1999), p. 9
367 Eusebius, "Church History," ibid, Bk. 5, Ch. 7, p. 222 Emphasis added

Origen, AD 185–254

Origen was a theologian, philosopher, teacher, writer, and zealous Christian from Alexandria, Egypt, a thriving city founded by Alexander the Great in the fourth century BC. The city was a center of commerce and culture, the birthplace of Neoplatonism and the home of Philo, the great Jewish philosopher. Origen was the eldest of seven children, whose father was Leonides, a Roman citizen of high standing and probably a teacher of Greek literature. Leonides personally educated his brilliant son in both Hellenistic and biblical studies. According to Eusebius, Origen famously castrated himself so he could tutor women without suspicion and risked his life countless times encouraging martyrs. He was a prolific writer with more than six thousand titles, the most important of which is *On First Principles*.

In his work *Against Celsus*, Origen wrote of miracles taking place in his day through the name of Jesus, and it seems he was involved in many of the miracles himself.

> Some give evidence of their having through this faith a marvelous power by the cures which they perform, invoking no other name over those who need their help than that of the God of all things, and of Jesus ... For by these means we too have seen many persons freed from grievous calamities, and from distractions of mind, and madness, and countless other ills, which could not be cured neither by men nor devils.[368]

Origen's controversial views on the preexistence of souls, the ultimate salvation of all beings, and other topics eventually caused him to be labeled a heretic; yet his teachings were highly influential, and today he is regarded as one of the most important early

---

368 Origen, "Against Celsus," *The Ante-Nicene Christian Library*, ed. Alexander Roberts and James Donaldson (Peabody, MA: Hendrickson, 1999) p. 473

church fathers. In sharp contrast to Latin theologians such as Tertullian, Alexandrian Christians viewed Greek philosophy as a useful means for interpreting and sharing their faith.

The last twenty years of his life were spent in Caesarea. While there, Origen added daily preaching to his regular duties of teaching and writing. This put him in contact with ordinary church members as well as the scholarly elite, and there is corresponding evidence of pastoral concerns in his writings over this part of his career. Almost three hundred homilies preached by Origen have survived, and there are certainly hundreds more that have not. During this period, he was obviously open to the ministry and gifts of the Spirit. He stated:

> Moreover, the Holy Spirit gave signs of his presence at the beginning of Christ's ministry, and after his ascension he gave still more; but since that time these signs have diminished, although there are still traces of his presence in a few who have had their souls purified by the Gospel, and their actions regulated by its influence.[369]

Origen acknowledged the decline of the gifts of the Spirit, but gave no indication of their cessation. In fact, he raised the value of the gifts in his time.

Novatian, AD 210–280

Novatian, a theologian and presbyter of the church at Rome, was known for his great compassion and personal holiness. Novatian opposed Cornelius, the bishop of Rome, because of his leniency with Christians who denied their faith under persecution. Novatian's most important surviving works is his treatise, *The Trinity*. He wrote of the Holy Spirit:

---

369 Origen, ibid, Bk. 7, Ch. 8, p. 614

This is He who places prophets in the Church, instructs teachers, directs tongues, gives powers and healings, does wonderful works, often discrimination of spirits, affords powers of government, suggests counsels, and orders and arranges whatever other gifts there are of charismata; and thus makes the Lord's Church everywhere, and in all, perfected and completed.[370]

As the church approached the third century, Novatian clearly believed healings, miracles, and speaking in tongues were an accepted and expected aspect in the life of the church.

Hilary, AD 300–367

Hilary was born at Poitiers, France, to wealthy pagan parents 190 years after the last of the original apostles died. He was a brilliant original thinker who received a good education. In his drive to find truth, he ultimately turned to the Scriptures and developed a deep-seated conviction that Christianity was the truth. As a result, he abandoned Neoplatonism for Christianity and was baptized with his wife and daughter.

Although he became bishop of Poitiers and was considered one of the greatest doctors of the church, his writings never enjoyed renown for several reasons, the most likely of which was the "difficulty of the thoughts he wished to convey."[371]

Hilary entered Christianity at a time in which the church was satisfied with the traditions that had developed around it. But he was never satisfied; rather, he was driven to find truth. Once he accepted the salvation of Jesus, he became a disciple of Origen and as such, developed both a remarkable sense for the dignity

370 Novatian, "Treatise Concerning the Trinity," *Ante-Nicene Fathers,* eds. Alexander Roberts and James Donaldson, (Peabody, MA: Hendrickson, 1999), Ch. 29, p. 641
371 William Sanday, *Essays on Biblical Criticism and Exegesis*, Craig A. Evans and Stanley Porter eds., with the assistance of Scott N. Dolff, (Sheffield, England, Sheffield Academic Press, 2001)

and freewill of mankind, along with a rudimental doctrine concerning the Holy Spirit.[372] The only Christian writer in his Latin tongue at that time was Tertullian, whom he knew well. His relationship with Tertullian and Origen may explain his openness toward the work and gifts of the Holy Spirit.

In his work *On the Trinity*, he wrote of speaking in tongues and interpretation being an expected aspect of the life of the church: "For God hath set same in the Church, first apostles ... secondly prophets ... thirdly teachers ... next mighty works, among which are the healing of diseases ... and gifts of either speaking or interpreting divers kinds of tongues."

Hilary then forcefully stated, "Clearly these are the Church's agents of ministry and work of whom the body of Christ consists; and God has ordained them."[373]

Hilary was fully committed to both the legitimacy and efficacy of speaking in tongues and believed that the gift of the Spirit, including tongues, was still being poured out upon the church in his day.

> For the gift of the Spirit is manifest ... by kinds of tongues, that the speaking in tongues may be bestowed as a sign of the Holy Spirit; or by the interpretation of tongues, that the faith of those that hear my not be imperiled through ignorance, since the interpreter of a tongue explains the tongue.[374]

There are many who insist that speaking in tongues was a momentary experience that ceased with the canon of the New Testament, the successful spread of the gospel, or the conclusion

---

372 Sanday, ibid, p. vii
373 Hilary of Poitiers, "On the Trinity," Nicene and Post-Nicene Fathers, ed. Philip Schaff, (Peabody, MA: Hendrickson, 1999), Bk. 8, Ch. 33, p. 147
374 Hilary, ibid, p. 146

of Paul's work with the Gentiles.[375] But none of these beliefs can stand the light of history. Clearly, from Pentecost to Constantine, speaking in tongues continued, and its continuation brought life and power to individual Christians and the emerging church.

---

375 See Howard M. Ervin, Spirit Baptism, (Peabody, MA: Hendrickson, 1987), 174–176. Also see, McRay, Paul, ibid, p. 435

8

The Agents of Change:
Constantine and Augustine

Although some assert tongues ceased with the original apostles, proof of individual Christians and congregations singing, speaking, and praying in tongues between the fourth and seventh centuries AD is abundant. These were challenging centuries for the church as it negotiated its way into political power and through the Dark Ages, but it was also a very vibrant time of spiritual activity. It was the period that witnessed the emergence of Constantine and Augustine, the spread of Monasticism, the reach of Christianity into the Anglo-Saxons, the elevation of the church at Rome, and the division of the Empire and the rise of the East.

As the church entered the fourth century, it experienced a new civil freedom and acceptance it had never known that thrust it into the mainstream of the Roman Empire; as a result, thousands of new converts came into the church. The influence of the miraculous on these new believers was dramatic. While Christian writers focused on matters of doctrinal orthodoxy and heresy, their works were also filled with pastoral and apostolic commentary and insight concerning the ongoing daily life and worship of the church, which was highly expressive and filled with expectation of the supernatural.

Unfortunately, during this period, speaking, singing, and praying in tongues took a definitional turn. Augustine defined speaking in tongues as either prophecy or the ability to speak in an unlearned foreign language and insisted that this ability was reserved for the evangelization of the nations during the apostolic age of the church. [376] Because of his enormous influence, subsequent leaders yielded to Augustine's definition of tongues while embracing his acceptance and experience of the supernatural.

Despite this new Augustinian definition of tongues as definite foreign languages, Christian tongue speech continued through these important centuries but under a new name, and proof of its acceptance from Constantine to Gregory the Great can easily be uncovered. To do so, it is necessary to look behind the writings or definitions of the leaders and analyze the worship, praise, and prayer life of the Church.

Constantine, AD 272–337

The foundational character entering fourth-century Christianity was Flavius Valerius Aurelius Constantinus, Constantine I, the first Christian emperor. He entered the world stage in AD 306 as co-emperor of the Roman Empire and rose to be the undisputed ruler from AD 324 to his death. The importance of his embrace of Christianity cannot be overstated. Constantine reversed the persecutions of his predecessor, Diocletian, and proclaimed religious toleration throughout the Roman world, which brought the church out of the catacombs and fully into the life of the empire.

---

376 Augustine, "Homilies on First Epistle of John," *Nicene and Post-Nicene Fathers*, Ch. 6, sec. 10, ed. Philip Schaff, (Peabody, MA: Hendrickson, 1999), p. 498

This amazing turn of events began on the eve of his greatest battle when Constantine had a vision in which he "saw the first two letters—the *chi* and *rho*—Christ's name in Greek superimposed and heard the words, *by this sign you will conquer*."[377]
The following morning, he instructed his army to place the sign on their helmets and shields. They did so and defeated Maxentius's troops near the Milvian Bridge over the Tiber River on October 28, 312.

Constantine immediately took significant steps toward Christianity to show his deep gratitude. In early AD 313, he changed the world by issuing the Edict of Milan in which he extended his protection over Christianity, ended persecution against the church, and ultimately paved the way for Christianity to be established as the religion of the state.[378]

Constantine became the embodiment of the righteous king. While it is true that Christianity offered him an "amazing position of having a theology of government that he could use to consolidate his own secular power," his action was a great boost for the church.[379] Constantine became an active patron and benefactor deeply involved in the life and success of the church, providing funding, granting authority to the hierarchy of the church, and sponsoring councils to settle differences and establish orthodoxy.

Constantine's Imperial Christianity

The full extent of the conversion of Constantine to Christianity continues to be debated, but the positive impact of his life and

---

377 Paul L. Maier, *Eusebius*, (Grand Rapids, MI: Kregel, 1999), p. 340, Emphasis added. See also, Eusebius, The Life of Constantine, *Nicene and Post-Nicene Fathers*, vol. 1, eds. Philip Schaff and Henry Wace, (Peabody, MA: Hendrickson, 1999), p. 490
378 It was not until Theodosius, the last Emperor of both the eastern and western provinces of the Empire, that Christianity was declared the official religion of the Empire in 380 AD.
379 Shaye I.D. Cohen, "Legitimization Under Constantine," *Frontline*, Retrieved December 15, 2008, on the World Wide Web @ http://www.pbs.org/wgbh/pages/frontline/shows/religion/why/legitimization.html

decisions on the church is unquestioned. Taken as a whole, Constantine's actions made his commitment to Christianity perfectly clear.[380] He removed clergy from civic duties and taxation, gave the Christian congregation a place in the law by allowing slaves to be manumitted by declarations in the presence of a bishop, gave church courts official status, declared the Christian day of worship a day of rest, removed old Augustan penalties against celibacy and childlessness, and gave privileges to Christians over Jews. [381 382 383 384 385 386 387] Most significantly, Constantine's patronage of the church was seen by his lavish construction of vast new monumental buildings for public worship. This was especially true of his mother, Helena.[388]

Although there is no indication that Constantine ever spoke in tongues, he was at least an unwitting player in the history of tongue speech through several actions he took to empower the church and free it to develop a highly expressive worship. The one action that affected Christianity most was his decision to build a new capital city for the empire in the east. "It was a decision as important as the dethronement of the gods of old Rome."[389] Upon his defeat of Licinius on September 18, 324, Constantine became the sole ruler of the Empire. Two months later, on Sun-

---

380 See, Bill Leadbetter, "Constantine," *The Early Christian World*, ed. Philip F. Esler, (New York: Routledge, 2000), vol. 2, p. 1069
381 Theodosian Code 16.2.1,2
382 Theodosian Code 16.2.10
383 Theodosian Code 4.7.1; 2.8.1
384 Code of Justinian 1.27.1
385 Code of Justinian 3:12.2
386 Theodosian Code 8.16.1
387 Theodosian Code 16.8.1; Code of Justinian 1.9.3; Sirmondian Constitutions 4
388 It is common knowledge that Helena, the mother of Emperor Constantine, journeyed to various sites connected to the life of Jesus and directed to be built more than eighty church buildings—at Bethlehem where Jesus was born, on the Mount of Olives where the Lord ascended to heaven, and at Gethsemane where Jesus prayed before enduring the cross.
389 W.H.C. Frend, *The Rise of Christianity*, (Philadelphia: Fortress Press, 1984), p. 501

day, November 8, 324, he consecrated Byzantium as his new residence, Constantinoupolis, the city of Constantine, and committed to build Constantinople as the Empire's Christian capital.[390]

Temporarily, Rome remained the capital of the empire where Constantine built many new monuments: his famous arch, the churches of Saint Peter and Saint Paul, and his mausoleum (now called Santa Costanza). It was in Rome that Constantine celebrated his *Vicennalia*, his twenty-year jubilee of his reign. To his great frustration, there were some riots during the festival, and at about the same time, there was a political crisis that led to the downfall of Constantine's second wife, Fausta. Motivated by those events, the emperor decided to leave Rome behind, and on Monday, November 4, 328, new rituals were performed to dedicate Constantinople as the capital of the empire.

A year and a half later, on Monday, May 11, 330, when the festival of Saint Mocius was celebrated, the city was finally dedicated, and in AD 336, the new Christian capital of the empire was completed. Constantine the Great celebrated his *Tricennalia*, his thirty-year jubilee, in his new capital. One year later, he was baptized and died.

Following Constantine, the church was free and would never again face the tyranny of persecution. Its influence flourished, and its freedom of worship and expression blossomed, spurred on by its robust commitment to and demonstration of the gifts of the Holy Spirit.

Enter the Barbarians

The fifth century AD began a series of Germanic and later Islamic invasions across Europe that lasted for six hundred years and deeply disrupted the life of the church. In AD 407, Alaric, the king of the Visigoths, entered Italy, surrounded Rome, and prepared to attack. Rome's bishop, Innocent I, entered negotiations with Alaric,

---

390 Constantinople is present-day Istanbul.

agreeing to pay him four thousand pounds of gold to leave the city. But the payment only postponed the inevitable, for later Alaric returned and again laid siege to the city. Finally, the Roman Senate agreed to pay a substantial tribute of five thousand pounds of gold, thirty thousand pounds of silver, four thousand silken tunics, three thousand hides dyed scarlet, and three thousand pounds of pepper.[391] Alaric's forces moved back up Italy's boot, continuing his conquests, but once again his attention turned to Rome. In doing so, he demanded the Emperor Honorius make him a Roman general and commander of the army. Honorius refused, and a year later, Alaric returned to Rome and sacked the city on August 24, AD 410, and became the first Germanic leader to conquer the city of Rome. Because Alaric was a Christian, the churches remained untouched throughout the Gothic sack. Romans found safety inside the churches; outside, the carnage took thousands of lives. After sacking the city, Alaric took his army down Italy's boot, hoping to conquer Sicily, but died before achieving his goal.

Rome was in a battle for survival. As the civil government disintegrated under the barbarian invasions, the Roman church developed as the only viable organization of civilized life and was forced to take upon many of the functions of secular authority. As a result, the church in the West was driven in two distinct directions. It intentionally incorporated a practical concern for everyday life, since the people were reaching out to the bishops for support and answers with the deterioration of Roman civil authority, and simultaneously moved toward an even greater, powerful, deeply spiritual, and highly expressive worship filled with the miraculous and the gifts of the Spirit.

---

391 John Julius Norwich, *Byzantium: The Early Centuries*, (New York: Knopf, 1989), p. 134

Augustine, AD 354–430 and the Embrace of Jubilation

At the center of the leaders at this critical juncture in the church was Augustine, bishop of Hippo in North Africa. By the time Augustine rose to prominence, two significant events were taking place. Rome was under attack, and it seemed as though the gifts of the Holy Spirit had come to a temporary halt. Augustine wrote around AD 400 and expressed the sad charismatic state of the church in the West. "For who expects in these days that those on whom hands are laid that they may receive the Holy Spirit should forthwith begin to speak with tongues?"[392] Speaking in tongues had ceased.[393]

Coming into the church at the moment he did initially convinced Augustine that the age of the miraculous had passed; the supernatural was no longer required for the current role of the church. Perhaps in an overreaction to Montanus and his followers, the Catholic hierarchy had taken a stand against speaking in tongues and prophecy. It is easy to observe the negative reaction to Montanism during this time by the attention it received from Catholic writers and the overt, intense opposition of Pope Innocent I, AD 410–417, and the laws set in place by the Emperor Honorius I against Montanism in AD 407.[394]

But something happened. It may have been a personal awakening on the part of Augustine or some outside influence, but Augustine changed. At one point, he embraced what appears to be a form of praying and singing in tongues that he labeled

---

392 Augustine, "On Baptism Against the Donatists," *Nicene and Post Nicene Fathers*, vol. 4, ed. Philip Schaff, (Peabody, MA: Hendrickson, 1999), p. 443

393 Augustine, "The Epistle of Saint John," *Nicene and Post-Nicene Fathers*, vol. 12, p.497–98 Some have taken this to mean that the gifts of the Spirit, especially speaking in tongues, ceased and were not to be part of the life of the Church which is a gross misreading of the New Testament and the history of the church.

394 For a succinct understanding of the church's official reaction to Montanism, see The New Catholic Encyclopedia, vol. 9, p. 1079

jubilation. Augustine explained that jubilation occurred when the mouth could not express the words the heart was singing and the individual continued to make sounds, but the words were inarticulate. Augustine insisted, "Your heart may rejoice without words, and your unbounded joy may not be confined by the limits of syllables."[395]

Jubilation was a way of praying and singing without understandable words in any language. The word jubilation comes from the Latin *jubilatio*, meaning *loud shouting, whooping, rejoicing,* or *gladness.* At several points in his work *On the Psalms*, Augustine mentions jubilation as an aspect of his commentary.[396] It is critical to understand that Augustine is not referring to mere excitement or enthusiasm. Jubilation was an experience of the Holy Spirit: "To manifest his joy, the man does not use words that can be pronounced or understood, but bursts forth into sounds of exaltation without words." Augustine continued, "What is jubilation? Joy that cannot be expressed in words; yet the voice expresses what is conceived within and cannot be explained verbally; this is jubilation."[397]

The church fathers of the late Roman Empire and Dark Ages were clearly acquainted with a variety of wordless expressions and regarded wordless prayer and singing as an important aspect in the life of the church. Augustine wrote, "Do not look for words, as if you could put into words things that please God. Sing in jubilation: singing well to God means, in fact, just this: singing in jubilation."[398]

Augustine clearly participated in jubilation and encouraged people to jubilate, but what was the relationship between jubila-

---

395 Augustine, Expositions on the Book of Psalms, vol. 1, (Oxford: John Henry Parker, 1847), p. 317. Also see Francis Sullivan, ibid, p.147
396 See Paul Hinnebusch, *Praise: A Way of Life*, (Ann Arbor, MI: Word of Life Publishers, 1976)
397 Augustine, "On the Psalms," *Nicene and Post-Nicene Fathers*, ed. Philip Schaff, (Peabody, MA: Hendrickson, 1999), p. 488
398 Augustine, "On the Psalms," ibid, vol. 8, p. 488

tion and singing in tongues? Once again, the answer can be found in what Augustine and others did, not simply what they wrote, or even their understanding at that moment. Augustine considered singing in tongues and jubilation to be two different experiences since he explicitly stated that in his time the gift of tongues was no longer present while jubilation was in the present.

It appears that Augustine and other church fathers restricted their meaning of the gift of tongues to the ability to speak in unlearned human languages for the purpose of spreading of the gospel, and they believed it was no longer needed. As a result, they would not define jubilation as tongue speech. Instead Augustine related jubilation to other scriptures, such as the expressions of joy in the Psalms. Yet it seems clear that what Augustine and others were experiencing as jubilation was in fact singing and praying in tongues, as defined by the Apostle Paul in First Corinthians.

Almost all the major fathers—Augustine, Jerome, John Cassian, Ambrose, Peter Chrysologus, John Chrysostom, Gregory the Great, Isidore of Seville, and Cassiodorus—wrote of jubilation. Obviously, most of the fathers of the late Roman Empire and Dark Ages believed jubilation was the continuation of a biblical and apostolic tradition. To the fathers, the relationship Christians enjoyed with God was at its best a mystery. For them, praying and singing without understandable words was a way of entering into that mystery, a way of experiencing God that was too great for ordinary words. It was a means of entering into the mystery, of being led into the mystery with body and soul. And it worked. It seems to have been the use of jubilation that kept Augustine open to the supernatural. Later in his life, Augustine, writing his famous work, *The City of God*, acknowledged his great joy at the miraculous move of the Holy Spirit in his church at Hippo: "Even now, miracles are wrought in the name of Christ, whether by sacraments or by prayer or by the relics of his saints."[399]

---

399 Augustine, "The City of God," *Nicene and Post-Nicene Fathers*, ed. Philip Schaff, vol. 2, (Peabody, MA: Hendrickson, 1999), p. 485

Augustine described a miracle that occurred in a woman with breast cancer. Having been told by her doctor that the cancer was incurable, she was instructed by the Holy Spirit in a dream to wait for the first woman who came out of baptistery after being baptized on Easter. "She did so, and was immediately cured."[400] Powerful supernatural manifestations of the miraculous were overwhelming to Augustine. When Augustine was at Milan, "a blind man was restored to sight."[401] "An old comedian of Curubis was cured at baptism not only of paralysis, but also of hernia."[402] Augustine recorded the exorcism of demons from a neighbor named Herperius, who asked one of the presbyters "to go with him and banish the spirits by his prayer."[403] He documented a "young countryman who was paralytic...yet went away on his own feet perfectly cured."[404]

Obviously, the miracles in his bishopric at Hippo were staggering. Augustine attempted to document them, but rejoiced. "I cannot record all the miracles I know."[405]

The people of Augustine's church showed every indication of a fully charismatic congregation. "They shouted comments, sighed, and laughed, like children at a cinema."[406] One Easter Sunday, a young brother and sister were miraculously healed:

> Everyone burst into a prayer of thanksgiving to God. The entire Church rang with the clamor of rejoicing... Such wonder rose up from men and women together that the exclamations and tears seemed as if they would never

400 Augustine, "The City of God," ibid, p. 486
401 Augustine, "The City of God," ibid, p. 485
402 Augustine, "The City of God," ibid, p. 487
403 Augustine, "The City of God," ibid, p. 487
404 Augustine, "The City of God," ibid, p. 487
405 Augustine, "The City of God," ibid, p. 484–492, Augustine records many amazing miracles which he witnessed in his bishopric. He saw first-hand people being healed, exorcised, raised from the dead, etc.
406 Fredrick Van Der Meer, *Augustine the Bishop*, (New York: Sheed and Ward, 1961), p. 339

end ... They shouted God's praise without words, but with such a noise that our ears could scarcely stand it.[407]

Obviously, in Augustine's church during the fifth century, the congregation was shouting praises to God, and they did so in tongues. Without question, speaking, praying, and singing in tongues, known as jubilation, had not ceased, not before Augustine, and not after.

Jubilation, which unquestionably was speaking, praying, and singing in tongues, played a major role in the worship of the church for several centuries. The worship of the church during these years was alive, vibrant, even rowdy; the miraculous demonstrations of the Holy Spirit were powerful and convicting. Congregations reacted with laughter, tears, sighs, and shouting phrases such as "Glory to God." Singing was accompanied by clapping of hands and dancing. These powerful believers would have been shocked to learn that what they were experiencing with jubilation was supposed to have ceased!

---

407 Augustine, "The City of God," ibid, p. 491 Emphasis added

9

Tongues and the Early Monastics

As the gifts of the Holy Spirit were waning among some of the emerging hierarchy of the Roman church, they continued to be manifested with a devout group of Christians who were choosing to isolate themselves and live as hermits in order to experience an intensely personal move of the presence of the Holy Spirit. These were the forerunners of the Monastics.[408] Immediately following the rise of Constantine and the civil freedom he granted to the church with his edict of Milan in AD 313, men gathered in isolated self-sufficient monastic settings to devote themselves to the worship of the Lord Jesus, to prayer, and the presence of the Holy Spirit. During this period, "most supernatural phenomena

---

408 The word monastic is derived from the Greek, meaning 'to live alone.' Those who participated in a monastic lifestyle were called monks, and their dwellings were monasteries. The earliest extant use of the word is found in the work of the Jewish philosopher Philo, *On Contemplative Life*.

were either recorded by monastics or by those who venerated the monastic lifestyle." [409]

Throughout the fourth and fifth centuries, the monastic movement became so popular and powerful in the church that its leaders slowly overtook the role of the bishops, and by the fifth century, more and more important bishops rose among the leading monks. The monastic communities ultimately developed into monasteries that grew to serve as centers of learning, prayer, and meditation throughout the Middle Ages.

Some of the leading monks developed highly respected ministries of miraculous power. The fact that people embraced the ministries of monasteries indicates a widely held belief in and expectation of the supernatural among Christians, so much so that thousands flocked to the monasteries for healing and deliverance from demonic oppression at the hands of these miracle-working monks.

Antony, AD 251–356

Antony, considered the founder of monasticism, was known for the great power he possessed in prayer. He was reared in an affluent Christian home in Egypt. Following the death of his parents at age eighteen, he sold his family's three-hundred-acre estate, retired to a cave, and entered a life of absolute devotion to the Lord Jesus. He continued to move further and further into solitude, and as he did so, his notoriety for holiness and power in prayer eventually spread throughout the Roman Empire. Disciples soon gathered around Antony seeking a solitary life. As a result, the monastic movement quickly developed in two distinct branches. On one hand were individuals who lived in complete seclusion. At times these men sought for spiritual advice, but basically they committed themselves to a life of extreme simplicity and constant prayer. On the other hand were groups of monks

409 Hyatt, ibid, p. 38

who gathered in communities around a single teacher. The older and most honored teachers who headed the various communities became known as abbots and rose to an equivalent authority of the bishops.

According to Athanasius in his work *Life of Antony*, Antony's life was filled with great miracles including healing the sick and casting out demons.[410] For nearly twenty years, he continued in stark solitude, seldom seen by anyone, but ultimately emerged from the cave "filled with the Spirit."[411] In keeping with the experiences in the New Testament and those of other monastics, the evidence of his relationship with the Holy Spirit included speaking and praying in tongues. On one particular occasion, many gathered at the entrance of Antony's cave, pleading to receive his prayers. After some time, Antony appeared and "through him the Lord healed the bodily ailments of many present, and cleansed others from evil spirits."[412]

Pachomius, AD 292–346

Pachomius organized the first monastery around AD 320 at Tabennisi on the Nile. He was a monk anointed with great power for miracles.[413] It was reported that on several occasions, after hours of prayer, he spoke in languages of angels and with tongues he had never learned. [414] [415] This certainly indicates that speaking, praying, and singing in tongues were very common in the life of the monasteries.

---

410 See, Athanasius, "Life of Antony," *Nicene and Post-Nicene Fathers* vol. 4, ed. Archibald Robertson, (Peabody, MA: 1999) p. 188–221. The work is filled with the accounts of miracles at the hand of Antony.
411 Athanasius, "Life of Antony," ibid, p. 200
412 Athanasius, "Life of Antony," ibid, p. 200
413 Jerome and Gennadius, "Illustrious Men of the Church," *Nicene and Post-Nicene Fathers*, vol. 3, p. 387
414 Alban Butler, *The Lives of the Saints*, (Baltimore: Murphy & Co., 1889), p. 218
415 Schaff, ibid, iii, p. 197

Athanasius, AD 295–373

Bishop Athanasius of Alexandria, Egypt, was known as the father of orthodoxy, most notably for his demand that Christ was coequal, coeternal, and consubstantial with God the Father. Based upon his writings concerning the life of Antony and the validity he placed upon the miracles he performed, Athanasius appeared very committed to the supernatural ministry and gifts of the Holy Spirit. He never indicated that he believed the gifts of the Spirit had ceased.

Ambrose, AD 340–397

Ambrose abandoned a successful political career to follow the demands of the Lord Jesus. As such, he was one of the significant fathers who ministered under the protection of Constantine as bishop of Milan. He rose to be one of the most eminent bishops of the fourth century and, together with Augustine of Hippo, Jerome, and Gregory I, was considered one of the four doctors of the church. In his work *Of the Holy Spirit*, he wrote of his belief in the unity of the trinity, demanding that what is true of the Father and the Son is likewise true of the Holy Spirit. Ambrose also revealed his belief in and commitment to the supernatural manifestations of the Spirit and in doing so endorsed the tongues as a continuing aspect in the life of the church.

> As the Father gives the gift of healings, so too does the Son give; as the Father gives the gift of tongues, so too has the Son also granted it. In like manner we have heard also concerning the Holy Spirit that He too grants the same kinds of graces.[416]

---

416 Ambrose, "Of the Spirit," in *Nicene and Post-Nicene Fathers*, ed. Philip Schaff and Henry Wace, (Peabody, MA: Hendrickson, 1999), p. 134

Ambrose demanded, "This is the inheritance of apostolic faith and devotion."[417] He wrote of the gift of tongues in the present, not the past tense.

Jerome, AD 340–420

Jerome was born at Stridon in what is today Croatia. At around age twenty, he traveled to Rome and became deeply interested in matters of the church. Following his theological studies, he journeyed to the east and first settled in Antioch, where he heard Apollinaris of Laodicea, one of the first exegetes. In his early thirties, Jerome entered the desert of Chalcis, southwest of Antioch, and began the life of an asceticism and study with only a brief return to Rome. In AD 386, he reached Bethlehem and settled there in a monastery near a convent founded by two Roman women, Paula and Eustachian, who followed him to Palestine. It was at Palestine that he completed his greatest work, *The Vulgate*, the Latin translation of the Scriptures.

Jerome fully believed in the supernatural ministry and gifts of the Holy Spirit. In his work *The Life of Saint Hilarion*, Jerome records many of Hilarion's miracles, the greatest being that of Hilarion calming what seems to be a raging tsunami caused by a large earthquake around the time of the death of Julian. According to Jerome, Hilarion encountered a "mountain-high" wave dashing on shore. After making the sign of the cross three times on the sand, Hilarion "faced the sea, stretched out his hands, and no one would believe to what height the swelling sea stood like a wall before him. It roared for a long time as if indignant at the barrier, then little by little sank to its level."[418] Jerome explained that even the most dramatic miracle could "be literally fulfilled if one has such faith as the Lord commanded the apostles to

417 Ambrose, ibid, p. 135
418 Jerome, "Life of Saint Hilarion," *Nicene and Post-Nicene Fathers*, ibid, avol. 6. p. 313

have."[419] Clearly, Jerome firmly believed in the manifestation of the supernatural power of the Holy Spirit.

Jerome, being deeply committed to prayer and worship, was one of the first to recognize the importance of jubilation. In describing jubilation, Jerome gave the clear indication that the experience he was having in the early fifth century was the same praying in tongues the disciples enjoyed. "By the term jubilus we understand that which neither in words nor syllables nor letters nor speech is it possible to express or comprehend how much man ought to praise God."[420]

Benedict, AD 480–547

Benedict was the son of a Roman noble of Nursia, Italy, and a twin to his sister Scholastica. As a young man, he was sent to Rome for his education. While in the capital city, he was drawn to and influenced by a group of ascetic Christians. He was so troubled by what he saw and experienced in Rome, he departed the city as a totally corrupt place, abandoned his studies, and renounced the wealth of his father to dwell in the village of Enfide and pursue a solitary monastic life living in a cave. In that setting, Benedict became a great miracle worker. At Enfide, he founded the monastery of Monte Cassino. It was there he worked his first miracle by restoring to perfect condition an earthenware wheat sifter that his old servant had accidentally broken. Benedict cured the sick, raised the dead, possessed a power gift of prophecy, and was a fearless exorcist of demons.[421] Though there is no specific record of Benedict speaking in tongues, it is difficult to imagine that he did not do so since he enjoyed a powerful, fervent prayer life and died in his prayer chapel with his hands raised in prayer.[422]

---

419 Jerome, "Life of Saint Hilarion," ibid, p. 313
420 Jerome, "The Psalms," as found in Ensley, ibid, p. 8
421 Michael Walsh, ed., *Butler's Lives of the Saints*, (San Francisco: Harper, 1991), p. 212
422 Walsh, ibid, p. 212 The Monte Cassino Monastery was destroyed by bombing during World War II, but has been completely rebuilt

The monastic movement consisted of many other highly committed and deeply devout men and women who held to the supernatural manifestations of the Holy Spirit, though many in the church were drifting away. By AD 600, the life of the Spirit, including speaking, praying, and singing in tongues, centered in the monasteries and was associated almost exclusively to the monastic lifestyle.

Cassiodorus, AD 490–583

Cassiodorus, Flavius Magnus Aurelius Cassiodorus Senator, was a Roman writer, statesman, and monk. Although of Syrian ancestry, his family was one of the most important in southern Italy. He lived at a time when Roman society was in collapse and constantly under the attack of barbarian tribes.

Cassiodorus wrote a massive work, *Explanation of the Psalms*, in which he repeatedly refers to jubilation as "excessive joy, but not the sort that can be expressed in words."[423] He continued, "What the speech of a confused voice cannot explain, the devout bursting forth of the rejoicing believer declares."[424]

Isidore of Seville, d. AD 636

Isidore was the last of the great Latin fathers. He was undoubtedly the most learned man of his age and exercised a far-reaching and immeasurable influence on the educational life of the Middle Ages. His contemporary and friend, Braulio, bishop of Saragossa, regarded him as a man raised up by God to save the Spanish people from the tidal wave of barbarism that threatened to inundate the ancient civilization of Spain.

---

to it former glory. At the entrance of the monastery stands a large bronze grouping depicting the death of Benedict with both hands raised in praise.

423 Cassiodorus, *Explanation of the Psalms*, 61:1, Ensley p. 18
424 Cassiodorus, *Explanation of the Psalms*, 97:5, Ensley p. 21

"Language cannot explain … words cannot explain … it is an effusion of the soul … when the joy of exultation erupts by means of the voice, this is known as jubilation."[425]

---

425 Isidore, Ensley p. 22

10

Tongues in Eastern Christianity

The Church in the Eastern Roman Empire developed in contradistinction to the West. Unlike Rome, Constantinople was secure. That governmental security enabled a multifaceted civilization to develop that never passed into the Dark Ages. Though Constantinople experienced several sieges throughout its history, the city remained free from pagan control until AD 1453. Thus the Church in the East was never forced to assume the secular functions that were forced upon the Western Church.

The Greek Church remained far more mystical and continued the Greek propensity for introspection and individuality. Greek monasticism, even though it came to play an important part in Byzantine politics, was never as organized or controlled as that which emerged in the West. The overarching spiritual climate of the Christian East emerged as an inward-looking mystical character.[426] There was a strain of wild enthusiasm and individual liberty in the Greek tradition. In this tradition, the gifts of the Spirit flourished, and speaking in tongues was never rejected. It is clear

---

426 See McGuckin, *Christian Spirituality*, Ch. 4

that speaking in tongues simply continued within the tradition of Greek monasticism without attracting much fanfare.

Cyril of Jerusalem, AD 315–386

Little is known of Cyril of Jerusalem except his *Catechetical Lectures*. They are among the most precious remains of Christian antiquity. The lectures are divided into eighteen divisions, including one on the work of the Holy Spirit. He obviously held great love for the Holy Spirit and wrote that the Spirit was "great indeed, and all-powerful in gifts ... The gifts of the Father are none other than those of the Son, and those of the Holy Spirit."[427]

Cyril wrote of being baptized in the Holy Spirit at salvation and receiving "gifts of grace of every kind." He taught that the very God who spoke by the Holy Spirit through the prophets and sent the Holy Spirit upon the apostles at Pentecost would also "send him (the Holy Spirit) forth at this time upon you."[428]

Basil of Caesarea, AD 329–379

Basil, the bishop of Caesarea, was a highly respected theologian and a tireless defender against heresy, who focused his writings against those he believed to be heretical. With his friend Gregory of Nazianzus, his brother Gregory of Nyssa, and sister Macrina, made up the Cappadocians. One of his most important works was *On The Holy Spirit*. However, it is in his letter to the clergy of Neocaesarea that he defended his practices in prayer "at night in the house of prayer in continual tears until at last they rise from prayer to sing psalms." Basil emphatically wrote of praying "in the oracles of the Holy Spirit,"[429] or the language of the Spirit. In doing so, he demanded he was following the expected custom of

---

427 Cyril of Jerusalem, "Catechetical Letters," NICENE AND POST-NICENE FATHERS, vol. 7, p. 121
428 Cyril of Jerusalem, ibid, p. 133, parenthesis added
429 Basil, "Letters," *Nicene and Post Nicene Fathers*, vol. 8, p. 247

Gregory in prayer, and was mirroring the demand of the Apostle Paul and Jude, the half brother of Jesus, to pray in tongues. [430] These were not rigorous, legalistic prayers, but free, powerful, individual prayers that lasted until dawn.

Evagrius of Pontus, 346–399 AD

Evagrius of Pontus, a disciple of Basil and of Gregory of Nazianzus, was one of the most important monastic writers specializing in the life of prayer. He was a strong advocate of "imageless prayer" and argued that any image the mind entertained in prayer falsified the reality of God. In his work *Chapters on Prayer*, Evagrius contended, "Struggle to make the mind deaf and dumb at the time of prayer, for only then will you be able to pray."[431] The striking similarity with the Apostle Paul's teaching that "if I pray in tongues, my mind is unfruitful"[432] is unavoidable. Obviously, Evagrius prayed in the Spirit.

John Chrysostom, AD 347–407

Chrysostom was born at Antioch, the second city of the eastern Roman Empire. The city was torn by religious factions, including the schism among the Catholic bishops Meletius and Paulinus. In 367, Chrysostom met Bishop Meletius, and his life was radically changed. The earnest, mild, and winning character of the bishop captivated Chrysostom to such a degree that he soon began to withdraw from classical studies and devoted himself to an ascetic and religious life. Three years later, he received baptism and was ordained as a lector.

Chrysostom desired a deeper relationship with the Lord Jesus and entered one of the ascetic communities. Four years later, Chrysostom resolved to live as an anchorite in one of the

---

430 1Corinthians 14:14; Jude 20
431 Evagrius of Pontus, *Chapters on Prayer* 11
432 1Corinthians 14:14

caves near Antioch. He remained there two years, but then, as his health was quite ruined by indiscreet washings and fastings in frost and cold, he prudently returned to Antioch to regain his health and resumed his office as lector in the church.

In 381, Meletius ordained Chrysostom as a deacon, and in 386 he was made a priest. Twelve years later, on February 26, 398, following great tension in the church at Constantinople, he was hurriedly ordained bishop of the most important city in the eastern Roman Empire. His time at Constantinople was filled with great success and devastating political intrigue that ultimately led to his exile and death on September 14, 407.

Chrysostom gained his place in church history not simply as bishop of Constantinople, but chiefly as a doctor of the church. He was a gifted preacher, talented exegete, theologian, and the most prolific writer of all the Greek fathers. His sermons were filled with brilliance and enthusiasm. Often, the audience interrupted his messages with applause. One of his favorite subjects was the power and manifestation of the Holy Spirit. In his *Homilies on First Corinthians*, Chrysostom lamented the lack of the gifts of the Spirit in his day. Rebuking the church for the cessation of the gifts of the Holy Spirit, he reminded them of the commitment of the early church to the work of the Holy Spirit and demanded, "Whoever was baptized he straightway spoke with tongues and not with tongues only, but many also prophesied, and some also performed many other wonderful works."[433]

> As the Apostles themselves had received this sign first, so also the faithful went on receiving it, I mean, the gift of tongues; yet not this only but also many others: inasmuch as many used even to raise the dead and to cast out devils and to perform many other such wonders:

---

433 Chrysostom, "Homily on Corinthians," *Nicene and Post Nicene Fathers*, vol. 12, ed. Philip Schaff, (Peabody, MA: Hendrickson, 1999)p. 209

and they had gifts too, some less, and some more. But more abundant than all was the gift of tongues among them.[434]

Chrysostom was obviously distraught with the condition of the church and the lack of the supernatural manifestations of the Spirit to such as extent he believed the church had fallen from its rightful place and condition. Obviously, Chrysostom believed that had the life of the church been functioning correctly, the gifts would have been present.

What now can be more awful than these things? For in truth the Church was a heaven then, the Spirit governing all things, and moving each one of the rulers and making him inspired. But now we retain only the symbols of those gifts ... they thus used to speak, not of their own wisdom, but moved by the Spirit. But not so now: (I speak of mine own case so far). But the present Church is like a woman who hath fallen from her former prosperous days, and in many respects retains the symbols only of that ancient prosperity; displaying indeed the repositories and caskets of her golden ornaments, but bereft of her wealth: such a one doth the present Church resemble.[435]

This is the first written account of deep disappointment that the gifts of the Spirit were no longer being allowed to manifest in the church.

Diadochus of Photike, AD 400–486

Diadochus was bishop of Epirus in northern Greece. He expanded the teaching of Evagrius and believed the heart was the spiritual center of the individual and the place of meeting God. Diadochus

---

434 Chrysostom, , "Homily" ibid, p. 168–169
435 Chrysostom, "Homily," ibid , p. 219–220

insisted upon the power of the *Jesus Prayer* and taught that the repetition of the phrase, "Lord Jesus Christ, Son of God, have mercy on me" quietly spoken hundreds of times would lead to the heart of prayer. This prayer opened the heart to an entire ecstatic world. Diadochus insisted, "When the whole person has turned toward the Lord, then grace reveals to the heart its presence there with a feeling which words cannot express."[436] Prayer which words cannot express is the very essence of praying in the Spirit. Diadochus continued, "The person who dwells continually within the heart is detached from the attractions of this world, and such a person lives in the Spirit."[437] The radicalism with which Diadochus and other believers lived and experienced the life of the Spirit four hundred years following the original apostles is a clear indication of the ongoing availability of all the gifts of the Spirit, and that would have included speaking and praying in tongues.

Isaac of Nineveh, d. AD 700

Isaac of Nineveh was born in the region of Qatar in the Persian Gulf. As a young man, he entered a monastery and gained considerable renown as a teacher. Isaac was ordained bishop of Nineveh, but after only five months abdicated and went to the wilderness of Mount Matout and lived a life of solitude for many years, eating only three loaves a week with some uncooked vegetables. Eventually, blindness and old age forced him to retire to the monastery of Shabar, where he died and was buried. At the time of his death, he was nearly blind, a fact that some attribute to his devotion to study.

Isaac wrote many spiritual homilies on the inner life, consciously avoiding topics that were disputed or discussed in the contemporary theological debates. Isaac lived in the tradition of the eastern mystical saints and placed great emphasis on the

---

436 Diadochus Of Photike, On Spiritual Knowledge, 85
437 Diadochus Of Photike, On Spiritual Knowledge, 56

work of the Holy Spirit. He believed the gifts of the Spirit were released during times of prayer.[438] In one of his *Ascetical Homilies*, he wrote of the sensation the Holy Spirit produced in the soul as a sign of his gifts and ministry: "The love of God is fiery by nature and when it descends in an extraordinary degree onto a person it throws that soul into ecstasy…This is the spiritual passion which inebriated the apostles and martyrs."[439]

Isaac employed two terms by which he identified his praying in tongues. First, he wrote of the ecstasy of the Spirit and second he identified praying in tongues as being inebriated in the Spirit which the followers of Jesus experienced at Pentecost.[440]

The Hesychast Movement

Hesychasm means *quietness* and comes from the tradition of the desert fathers, such as Diadochus of Photike. Diadochus demanded, "The same stress on the need for inner quietness is there; the central position of the Jesus prayer; the importance of finding an experienced spiritual guide; and the teaching of the heart as the focal point of the encounter with God."[441] The Hesychast were deeply spiritual and committed to the works and gifts of the Holy Spirit.

Symeon the New Theologian, AD 949–1022

Symeon was the last of three men the Orthodox Church gave the title theologian, following the Apostle John and the Cappadocian father, Gregory of Nazianzus, 329–391. Symeon, born at Paphlagonia in Galatia and educated at Constantinople, abandoned his potential political career to enter the monastery under the direc-

438 Stanley Burgess, *The Holy Spirit: Eastern Christian Traditions*, (Peabody, MA: Hendrickson, 1898), p. 104
439 Isaac of Nineveh, *Ascetical Homilies*, 35
440 Acts 2:15, Peter declared, "These men are not drunk as you suppose."
441 McGuckin, ibid, p. 148

tion of Elder Simeon the Pious at Studion at age twenty-seven. Ultimately, he became abbot of the monastery of St. Mammas in Constantinople.[442]

Symeon credited the prayers of the Elder Simeon as the vehicle through which God seized him on the first day of a series of visions of the divine light. This experience had a profound impact on Symeon. So much so, he became a true ecstatic, totally devoted to intense prayer, and insisting that all Christians must experience the life-changing power of the Holy Spirit. "Symeon called on Christians to return to a radical living of the gospel, to the charismatic and prophetic life of the primitive church." [443] That call included a life of praying in tongues.

In his theology of light, Symeon taught that Jesus became transfigured in radiant light to the disciple who truly comes close to Him in prayer.[444] This teaching of Symeon, along with his absolute commitment to the work of the Holy Spirit, merged in succeeding generations with the leading theologians of the late Byzantine period, Gregory of Sinai and Gregory of Palamas, to form the intellectual and spiritual leadership of the Hesychast movement. Thus, the "profound and luminous transfiguration came to be the dominant motif of the entire hesychast school."[445]

Gregory of Sinai, AD 1260s–1346

Gregory was born at Smyrna in Asia Minor. As a young man, he was captured by marauding Muslim pirates, along with his family and other Greek townsmen, and held for ransom. While in detention, he was noted for his ability as a chanter by the Christian

442 For a recent study of the life and impact of Symeon, see Hilarion Alfeyev, *St. Symeon, the New Theologian, and Orthodox Tradition*, Oxford, England: Oxford Press, 2000)
443 Burgess, *Eastern Christian Tradition*, ibid, p. 62
444 John A. McGuckin, "The Eastern Christian Tradition," *The Story of Christian Spirituality*, ed. Gordon Mursell, (Minneapolis: Fortress Press, 2001), p. 146
445 McGuckin, ibid, p. 146

155

worshippers living under Muslim rule. Once ransomed, although still young, he left his family and journeyed to Cyprus and became a rassoforos monk, [446] then to Sinai, where he became a fully professed monk at St. Catherine's Monastery, Mount Sinai, Egypt. Later, in what would be described as a milestone in the Hesychast movement, Gregory journeyed to Crete where he studied the practices of Hesychasm from a monk named Arsenios.[447] In 1310, he moved to Athos in Macedonia, where he remained until 1335. Muslim raids on Athos pushed Gregory and some disciples into Bulgaria, where he found protection under Bulgarian Emperor Ivan Alexander and where he founded a monastery near Paroria.

Gregory constructed cells for his own disciples and, at some distance, a cell for himself. In his cell, he committed himself to prayer, and using the Jesus Prayer, "Lord, Jesus Christ, Son of God, have mercy on me," he began to undergo a powerful transformation as the presence of the Holy Spirit transformed his inner man. Just as had been predicted by the monk Arsenios, his cell was filled with "light, the effulgence of Grace," while Gregory overflowed with joy, weeping tears, filled with divine love. His desire for God was overwhelming, and he, as well as his cell, was filled with light.

Gregory was a Charismatic and wrote of prayer,

> No one on his own account and without the help of the Spirit can mystically invoke the Lord Jesus, for this can be done with purity and in its fullness only with the help of the Holy Spirit (1 Corinthians 12:3). Like children who can still speak only falteringly, we are unable by ourselves to articulate the prayer properly.[448]

---

446 Rassoforos is the first grade of an ascetic monk.
447 David Balfour, *Saint Gregory the Sinaite: Discourse on the Transfiguration*, (Athens: 1982), p. 65
448 *The Philokalia*: Volume IV, ed. and trans. G.E.H. Palmer, Philip Sherrard, and Bishop Kallistos Ware, (London: Faber and Faber, 1995) p. 275

There is not an exact statement that Gregory prayed in tongues, but considering his use of 1 Corinthians 12:3 and his relationship with the teachings of Symeon, who firmly states his use of tongues in his remarkable experiences of prayer, it is logical to believe this was the case for Gregory of Sinai.

Gregory Palamas, AD 1296–1359

Palamas was a native of Constantinople. Having been born in 1296 to a noble family close to the Byzantine Emperor, Andronicus II, he was well educated despite the death of his father when Palamas was only seven. He joined the monasteries on Mount Athos, the Great Lavra of Saint Athanasius, at the age of twenty and began what would be a lifelong monastic journey into the "Theology of Light."[449]

Palamas was a great theological thinker. In one of his most important works known as the *Triad*, he confronted the Greek-Italian philosopher Barlaam the Calabrian in a series of debates concern the ability of man to experience God.[450] In the second *Triad*, Palamas wrote that the passions, when properly focused and directed through prayer, possess the ability to draw up the flesh to a dignity near to that of the spirit and that in this state the Holy Spirit gives the body the experience of divine things.[451]

In his third *Triad*, Palamas reconciled the seeming inconsistency between a belief in the absolute transcendence of God and hesychasm, which taught that God could be known and experienced but that individuals could and should fully participate in God. Palamas argued that God could not be known in His

449 Vladimir Lossky, "The Theology of Light in the Thought of Saint Gregory Palamas," *In the Image and Likeness of God*, (New York: St. Vladimir's Press, 1947) p. 45–69, and, John Meyendorff, trans. Adele Fiske, *Saint Gregory Palamas and Orthodox Spirituality*. (New York: St. Vladimir's Seminary Press, 1974)
450 See, Gregory Palamas: *The Triads*, trans. Nicholas Gendle, ed. John Meyendorff, (Ramsey, NJ: Paulist Press, 1983)
451 Triad11.2.12

essence, but He can be known as He is in His energies which he saw as the person of Jesus and the gift of the Holy Spirit deifying individual Christians.[452]

Palamas believed the ability to know and experience God was lost in the fall of Adam into sin, but since the redemptive work of Jesus, the divine Holy Spirit can be received again, bringing the energies of God back to individual men and women. The released energy of God, Palmas believed, was the result of the work of the Holy Spirit when He encapsulated the Christian in light of God. Christians become the instruments of the Holy Spirit, having received the same energy the Holy Spirit possesses.[453] Palmas insisted Christianity was nothing unless it was the direct and personal experience of the believers, who pray and know the power of God in and through prayer.

Palamas believed in and obviously practiced speaking and praying in tongues. He wrote that gifts such as tongues, interpretation of tongues, the word of instruction, the gift of healing, and the performing of miracles are granted at times of intense mental prayer. He did believe that it was possible that the gifts of instruction and of tongues and their interpretation may operate even without prayer, but the reception of such gifts would require the laying on of hands.[454]

---

452 See endnote 4, *Burgess, Eastern Christian Traditions*, ibid, p. 70. Burgess correctly shows that Palamas was not the first to use the distinction between the essence and energies of God.
453 Burgess, ibid, p. 71
454 Gregory Palamas: *The Triads*, ibid, p. 52–53

11

Tongues Among the Celtics

In the first century AD, Britain had its own set of religious icons: pagan gods of the earth and Roman gods of the sky. Into this superstitious and violent world came Christianity. The exact date Christianity reached into Britain is uncertain, though tradition has held it to be early in the life of the church. One account contends that James, the brother of the Lord Jesus, preached in Britain around AD 41.[455] The Apostle Peter was supposed to have preached in Britain, founded churches, ordained bishops, elders, and deacons.[456] On the other hand, the gospel could have come to Britain as Roman artisans and traders arrived and spread the story of Jesus. There are many possibilities, but even though Christianity was just one religion among many, unlike the cults of Rome, Christianity demanded exclusive allegiance from its followers and quickly began to grow.

---

455 Thomas MacLauchlan, *The Early Scottish Church: The Ecclesiastical History of Scotland, from the First to the Twelfth Century*, (Edinburgh: T & T Clark, 1864), p. 38
456 MacLauchlan, ibid, p. 39

The early entrance of Christianity into Britain is critical to the freedom of the Spirit and the acceptance and manifestation of the gifts of the Holy Spirit, including speaking, praying, and singing in tongues as an accepted aspect of Celtic Christianity. The Celtic church was never under the domination of the Roman Church or its belief in the cessation of the gift of tongues. [457] The Celtic church was born from the life and ministry of those who received the gifts of the Spirit and spoke in tongues. The Celtic church produced leaders who believed and experienced all the gifts of the Spirit.

There was a remarkably close relationship between the churches of Britain and Gaul (France). In many ways, the church of Britain received the church in Gaul as the "Mother Church" and dedicated a number of British churches under Gallican names: St. Martin, St. Germanus, and St. Lupus.

The Christianization of Britain intensified following the legalization granted the church under Constantine and subsequent Christian emperors. In AD 407, Rome withdrew its armies from Britain to defend Italy from Visigothic attack. With the sack of Rome in AD 410, legions of Rome never returned to Britain.

The absence of Roman military and governmental influence and overall decline of Roman imperial political power enabled Britain and the surrounding isles to develop distinctively from the rest of the West. A new culture emerged around the Irish Sea among the Celtic peoples with Celtic Christianity at its core. What resulted was a form of Christianity distinct from Rome in many traditions and practices. From Britain, this Celtic Christianity spread to Ireland, Northern England, Cornwell, Scotland, Wales, and the Isle of Man and established a unique spirituality.

---

457 James a.m. Hanna, *A History of the Celtic Church from its Inception to 1153*, (Ann Arbor, MI: Edward Brothers, 1963) p. 15

Martin of Tours, AD 316–397

Martin was a Roman soldier who became a monk around AD 350, and twenty years later, he rose to the position of bishop of Tours following Hilary, AD 300–367. Hilary was fully committed to both the legitimacy and efficacy of speaking in tongues and believed that the gifts of the Spirit, including tongues, were still being poured out upon the church in his day. As Hilary's disciple, Martin would have been thoroughly immersed in the expectancy of speaking in tongues.

Martin of Tours was a powerful prophetic voice within the Celtic-Anglo Saxon church, challenging those in authority for their corruption and cruelty. He freely operated in the power of the Holy Spirit, performing many miracles of healing, exorcisms, and raising at least two from the dead. One was a young man who died while awaiting baptism. When Martin arrived, the man was dead. He sent the others from the room and:

> Stretches himself at full length on the dead limbs of the departed brother. Having given himself for some time to earnest prayer, and perceiving by means of the Spirit of God that power was present, he then rose up for a little, and gazing on the countenance of the deceased, he waited without misgiving for the result of his prayer and of the mercy of the Lord. And scarcely had the space of two hours elapsed, when he saw the dead man begin to move a little in all his members, and to tremble with his eyes opened for the practice of sight.[458]

Ninian, AD 360–432

Ninian, the son of a Christian prince, was born in southwest

---

458 Sulpitius Severus, "The Life of Saint Martin," *Nicene and Post-Nicene Fathers*, vol. II, eds. Philip Schaff and Henry Wace, (Peabody, MA: Hendrickson, 1999), p. 7

Scotland, in the province of Galloway.[459] Because of his family, as a young man, he was able to travel extensively and study in Rome for ten years, encountering Christian leaders from throughout the empire. Completing his education, he returned to Britain to evangelize his people. On his way home, he stayed with his uncle Martin of Tours. Ninian became a disciple of Martin and, through him, of Hilary, both of whom walked in great anointings of the Holy Spirit and freely operated with the gifts of the Spirit.[460]

Tradition, first mentioned by Bede, states that around AD 397, Ninian set up his base at Whithorn in southwest Scotland, building a stone church there known as the *Candida Casa*, which means the *white house,* and dedicating it to Martin of Tours.[461] From there, he began work among the northern Brythons of the surrounding area. Later, he undertook a journey northward along the east coast in order to spread Christianity among the Picts.[462] Evidence and local tradition suggest that he may have traveled as far as the Shetland Islands. Ultimately, Ninian and his followers founded the Great Monastery, an imitation of Martin's Marmontier. There, he trained many missionaries who in turn taught others and founded scores of churches. Ninian converted the Eastern Picts.[463]

Patrick, AD 390–460

The sole Roman British Christian about whom significant infor-

---

459 George G. Cameron, *Highlights of Our Heritage; Some Landmarks in Our Church's Advance,* (Edinburgh: MacCorquodale & Co., 1953), p. 12
460 See, Hilary, in chapter 7
461 Bede, Ecclesiastical History of the English People, trans. Thomas Stapelton, ed. Philip Hereford, (London: Burns, Oates, Washbourne, 1935)
462 Richard A. Fletcher, *Who's Who in Roman Britain and Anglo-Saxon England,* (Chicago: St. James Press, 1989), p.19
463 William Cumming Skinner, *Candida Casa The Apostolic Center of Scotland,* (Dundee, Scotland: David Winter and Son, 1931), p.18

mation exists is Patrick. Born in Britain, he was the son of the deacon Calpurnius and his wife, Concessa. At age sixteen, he and other young men were kidnapped from his father's villa by pirates to work as a slave in the west of Ireland, but they managed to escape. He spent six years in captivity, praying one hundred times a day and one hundred times a night.[464] His time in captivity had a major impact upon him and his faith, so much so that upon his return to Britain, he became a priest. Though he was freed from Ireland, he felt called to return and bring ministry to the very ones who held him captive. He spent his life as a missionary bishop to the Irish people. Under the care of Patrick, Ireland became a powerful center of Christian culture and monastic spirituality.[465]

Patrick was a man of deep contemplation, and in his *Confessions*, he wrote of a genuine experience of praying in tongues in a vision:

> Another night I saw Him praying in me earnestly with groans. I was in amazement, wondering who it could be who was praying within me; but at the end He told me it was the Spirit: "He who gave His life for you; He it is who speaks within you." At that I woke up full of joy.[466]

Columcille, AD 521–597

Columcille, the abbot of Iona at Garten, County Donegal, Ireland, belonged to the Clan O'Donnell and was of royal descent. His great-great-grandfather was Niall of the Nine Hostages, an Irish king of the fourth century. Columcille lived in the manifestation of presence of all the gifts of the Holy Spirit, which

464 Edward C. Sellner, *Wisdom of the Celtic Saints*, (Notre Dame, IN: Ave Maria Press, 1993), p. 182
465 Dales, ibid, p. 77
466 Patrick, *Confessions of Saint Patrick*, 24, Retrieved on the World Wide Web on December 16, 2008 @ http://www.ccel.org/ccel/patrick/confession.html

included speaking and praying in tongues. He was constantly surrounded by angels, experienced prophetic visions and dreams, and possessed the power to perform great miracles, even raising one young man from the dead. The brothers who ministered with him often saw an immense blaze of heavenly light surrounding him. "One winter's night … Columcille entered the sacred house to pray. Along with him, at the same time, a golden light came down from the highest heavens and filled that part of the church."[467]

Columcille's preaching also provided instruction of new Christians and the motivation for founding numerous churches and monasteries. When not engaged in missionary journeys, he always resided at Iona. Many individuals came to him there to receive spiritual help and physical healing. From Iona, he governed those numerous communities in Ireland and Caledonia, which regarded him as their father and founder.

Samthann, d. AD 739

Samthann of Clonbroney was a deeply devout woman who had profound influence on Celtic Christianity. Like many other women saints, her life of commitment to the things of the Lord Jesus began with her refusal to accept a marriage arranged by her foster father, Cridan, an Irish king. On her wedding night, she persuaded her new husband to delay the consummation until all the residents of the Tuath had retired. During the delay, she gave herself to fervent prayer for deliverance, and God provided an illusory fire that panicked the residents and allowed her to escape. When Cridan eventually found her, she reproached him for binding her to a marriage against her will. The king relented and asked for her choice of husband. Samthann would have none but God, and both the king and her husband agreed and allowed her to enter a convent. Ultimately, she founded Clonbroney Abbey in

---

467 Sellner, ibid, p. 95

County Longford and refused large donations for the house for fear of losing the simplicity of their lives.

Samthann was undoubtedly a charismatic. Her life was replete with the supernatural: words of knowledge, prophecies, healings, and miracles. She often appeared in the dreams of others to offer direction and advice. She possessed a genuine ability to heal. She was regarded as a woman of great power in and commitment to prayer and freely entered into an ecstatic state while praying.[468]

There are scores of other major men and women who were and are extremely important to the life and spiritual history of the Celtic Anlgo-Saxon church. The temptation is to produce a history of each one, but the focus is limited to documenting the use of speaking, praying, and singing in tongues. Following in the charismatic traditions of Martin, Ninian, Patrick, and Columcille, the Celtic church remained open to the gifts and manifestations of the Holy Spirit and never surrendered to the cessationist views of the church of Rome.

468 See, Sellner, ibid, p. 193

12

Tongues in the Early Middle Ages, AD 590–1050

The exact starting dating for the Middle Ages is debated, but most scholars contend it can start no later than the ascendancy of Gregory the Great to the papal throne in AD 590.[469] Because of the significance of the Catholic Church in this critical moment in which the Roman Empire was being overrun, a new epoch does begin with Gregory. Throughout the early Middle Ages, only the Catholic Church came close to uniting all of Europe, and it developed as a geopolitical entity that achieved both spiritual and political power. While the exact extent of the church's political power and influence on the material culture of medieval Europe has been and continues to be debated, there is no denying

---

469 The most common time frame for the Middle Ages is approximately AD 500–1500. Some choose the dates of 476, the date of the fall of the Western Roman Empire to the Germanic warrior Odoacer; and 1453, the fall of the Eastern Roman Empire when the capital city of Constantinople fell to the Turks and Islam. Others prefer the dates of 590, the year Gregory the Great rose to the papal throne, and 1517 the year Martin Luther posted his 95 theses challenging the Catholic Church.

that it had a significant impact on international events and personal lifestyles throughout the era. The rise, establishment, and ultimate fracturing of Catholicism as the single most influential religion in Europe clearly mark the beginning and end points for the Christian Middle Ages.

Gregory the Great, AD 540–604

In AD 325, Constantine called the Council of Nicaea, the first ecumenical council of the Catholic Church. This convocation of bishops from all over the known world was an important step in building the organized church that would have enormous influence over the next twelve hundred years. However, Gregory was key in establishing the medieval papacy as a strong sociopolitical force, without which the Catholic Church would never have achieved the power and influence it wielded throughout the Middle Ages. It was Gregory who gave the papacy the title "servant of the servants of Christ."[470]

Gregory was born to Gordianus, a wealthy patrician who owned large estates in Sicily and a mansion on the Caelian Hill in Rome.[471] His mother, Silva, was also from a powerful Roman family, although little else is known of her life. She was honored as a saint. Gregory was an outstanding student of the law and held the important office of prefect of Rome. His education prepared for the strategic role he would ultimately play in establishing the powerful papacy, equipped to take its major role in the sixth century.

Following the death of his parents, Gregory surrendered his fortune and entered a Benedictine monastery. In AD 574,

470 Douglas Dales, "Celtic and Anglo-Saxon Spirituality," *The Story of Christian Spirituality*, ed. Gordon Mursell, (Minneapolis: Fortress Press, 2001), p. 81
471 The ruins of his family mansion in Rome are believed to be in a good state of preservation still awaiting excavation beneath the Church of St. Andrew and St. Gregory.

he founded seven monasteries and became a monk at one, St. Andrews, in AD 575. While in the monastery, he developed into a gifted leader, and upon the death of Pope Pelagius in AD 590, Gregory succeeded him to the papacy.

Under the direction of Gregory, the Christianization of Anglo-Saxon England began around AD 600, influenced by Celtic Christianity from the northwest and by the Roman Catholic Church from the southeast, and gradually replaced Anglo-Saxon polytheism. Gregory's instructions were clear: no conversion by compulsion and no automatic destruction of pagan shrines; instead they were to be transformed into Christian churches.[472] Gregory installed his trusted Augustine as the first archbishop of Canterbury in AD 597. In AD 601, the new Archbishop Augustine baptised the first Christian Anglo-Saxon king, Ethelbert of Kent. Anglo-Saxon Christians regarded Gregory with great affection and respect as the one who brought them to Christianity.[473]

Gregory was openly charismatic and recorded many miracles in his *Dialogues*, including people being raised from the dead.[474] He fervently believed miracles were at the heart of Christianity and that the miraculous work of the Holy Spirit was to continue throughout the life of the church. Like others before him, Gregory believed jubilation was a work of the Holy Spirit that produced a joy that could not be concealed, yet could not be expressed in words. He stated, "By the term jubilation we mean a joy of the heart that cannot be expressed in speech, yet the person who is rejoicing makes this joy known in certain ways—this joy that cannot be concealed, yet cannot be fully expressed (in words)."[475]

Gregory also wrote of the work of the Holy Spirit in indi-

---

472 Dales, ibid, p. 81
473 Dales, ibid, p. 81
474 See Gregory, Dialogues
475 Gregory the Great, *Morals on Job*, Bk. 8, 88, Retrieved on the World Wide Web on December 30, 2008 @ http://www.lectionary-central.com/GregoryMoralia/Book08.html

vidual Christian lives and rejoiced, "We can see holy men and women who shine with virtues and gleam with miracles."[476]

Cuthbert, AD 634–687

Cuthbert, one of the most beloved saints of England, was a man of angels. Little is known of his early life, but it is believed he was born into a wealthy Anglo-Saxon family. Even so, he was a "Celt by temperament and deeply influenced by Celtic spirituality.[477]

Cuthbert had his first angelic encounter when he was a child and insisted angels had ministered to him through several difficulties, including the healing of his diseased leg. One night as he tended sheep, Cuthbert was keeping watch and praying. As he prayed, "he suddenly saw light streaming from the skies … and choirs of angels coming down to earth. The angelic hosts quickly took a human soul, shining brightly, into their ranks. Then they returned to the home above."[478] Cuthbert dropped to his knees and began to praise the Lord. It was at that moment he made a commitment to give his life to ministry.

In 651, Cuthbert joined the Celtic monastery at Melrose and rose to become the bishop of Lindisfarne. He became famous for miracles and for prayers that healed all kinds of diseases. He delivered some who were demon possessed by laying his hands directly on them, exhorting them, and exorcising them. Others were healed from great distances merely by praying or predicting their healing. Cuthbert encouraged his people to lift their hearts and give thanks to the Lord God more by the yearning of their heart than the sound of their voice. In what was reminiscent of Paul's encouragement to the church at Rome to allow the Holy

---

476 Gregory the Great, *Forty Gospel Homilies*, trans. Dom David Hurst, (Kalamazoo, MI: Cistercian Pub., 1990), p. 246
477 Sellner, ibid, p. 101
478 Sellner, ibid, p. 105

Spirit to pray through their spirits.[479] He motivated his people more by his signs than by his preaching.[480]

Bede, AD 672–735

Bede was highly respected for his thorough scholarship as a writer and the "Father of English history," having authored his *Ecclesiastical History of England.*[481] He described himself as a servant of Christ and a priest of the monastery of the blessed apostles Saint Peter and Saint Paul, which is at Wearmouth and at Jarrow.[482] At the age of seven, his parents placed Bede in the care of Abbot Benedict and afterward to Ceolfrid to be educated. From that time forward, he spent his life within that monastery.

Bede rose through the ranks to ultimately become a priest and committed his life to the study of the Scriptures, its meaning and interpretation, to prayer, and to writing, producing commentaries of the Gospels of Mark and Luke, the Acts of the Apostles, the Revelation of Jesus Christ, Genesis 1–20, Exodus 24:12–30:21, Samuel, Kings, Song of Solomon, Ezra, and Nehemiah, and Tobit. In his ecclesiastical history, he wrote of finding "the Celtic and Anglo-Saxon cultures were abounding in manifestations of tongues and the gifts of the Spirit."[483]

The Spread of Monasticism

Throughout the sixth and seventh centuries, Christianity rapidly spread across Western Europe, especially with the spread of monasticism. The monasteries were centers of prayer and mediation where the gifts of the Spirit were a natural aspect of daily

---

479 Romans 8:26
480 Sellner, ibid, p. 108
481 J.M. Wallace-Hadrill, ed., *Bede's Ecclesiastical History of the English People*, (New York: Oxford University Press, 1993)
482 See Bede, *Ecclesiastical History of the English Nation*, (Rochester, NY: Dutton, 1910)
483 Hamilton, *The Charismatic Movement*, ibid, p. 69

life. It is unthinkable that any individual, male or female, living in that intense spiritual life would not experience the gifts of the Spirit, especially speaking and singing in tongues. The work of individuals such as Samson, AD 450–535, and his ministry in Ireland and Brittany; Gildas, AD 500–570, who was a key to monastic discipline in Ireland and Wales; and Columba, AD 521–597, who was a great healer and prophet often visited by angels, helped to turn Britain, Wales, and Ireland into a dynamic Christian culture and monastic spirituality. Columbanus, AD 543–615, left Ireland and birthed monasteries in France and Italy. Throughout this period, monasticism never lost its vigor and commitment to the supernatural and the gifts of the Holy Spirit.

By the eighth century, the Anglo-Saxon church began sending missionaries to the Low Countries and Germany, who were each deeply committed to the work and ministry of the Holy Spirit. The mission on the continent assisted the Christianization of practically all of the Frankish Empire by AD 800. Each of their missionary ministries was noted for its miracles and exercise of all the gifts of the Spirit. Two of these extraordinary individuals were Willibrord, AD 658–739, the Benedictine bishop of Utrecht and the apostle of the Frisians; the other was Boniface, AD 680–754, an English Benedictine missionary known as the apostle of Germany. In AD 718, he was authorized by Pope Gregory II to preach Christianity to all the tribes of Germany.

The opening years of the Middle Ages were a time of great charismatic ministry with all the gifts of the Spirit in operation. These critical years paved the way for the overt outpouring of the Holy Spirit during the remarkable time know as the Age of Faith.

13

Tongues in the High Middle Ages, AD 1000–1300

"The High Middle Ages in Europe was a richly creative period, with brilliant art, important literature, and great social change—all coming forth as the feudal system gave way to capitalism, cities, and a new middle class."[484] Even limiting its duration to a mere three hundred years, the High Middle Ages saw such significant events as the east-west schism that divided Western Catholicism from Eastern Orthodoxy in 1054; Norman conquests by William the Conqueror in Britain and Sicily in 1066; the submission of Henry IV to Pope Gregory VII in 1077, which established papal rule over European heads of state for over 450 years; the earlier Crusades beginning in 1099; the founding of University of Oxford in 1117; the cornerstone laid for the Notre Dame Cathedral in Paris in 1163; the recapture of Jerusalem by Saladin and the Muslims in 1187; the founding of the University of Cambridge in 1209; and the signing of the Magna Carta in 1215, marking the

---

484 Stanley M. Burgess, *The Holy Spirit: Medieval Roman Catholic and Reformation Traditions*, (Peabody, MA: Hendrickson, 1997), p. 87

first time a medieval ruler was forced to accept limits on power. During this period, there was also an explosion of stone castle building and the construction of some of the most magnificent cathedrals in Europe.

By the end of the eleventh century, Europe was thoroughly Christianized except for much of Spain. The papacy was firmly established as a significant political force in constant struggle with some governments and in alliance with others. In terms of material productivity and glimmers of political freedom, the High Middle Ages rose to new levels. Feudalism[485] was firmly established in Britain and in many parts of Europe; trade in luxury items, as well as staples, flourished; some towns were granted charters of privilege[486] and even new towns were established by feudal lords; and a well-fed population was beginning to burgeon. By the end of the thirteenth century, Europe was at an economic, cultural, and spiritual high.

The Age of Faith

Mystics, Ecstatics, Jubilation, Inebriation

Mystics were few, but they are very significant and served as great spiritual challenges to their contemporaries. For six hundred long years between AD 500 and AD 1100, hordes of barbarians overran Europe. Germanic tribes, followed by the challenge of Islam, plunged the west into the Dark Ages. The darkest years were between AD 900 and AD 1000 as Asiatic tribes and Scandinavian and Saracen pirates pillaged Europe. But throughout this diffi-

485 Feudalism was a political, economic and social system in the Middle Ages in which individuals known as serfs were bound to land received by members of the military elite known as vassals in exchange for military and loyalty to overlords.
486 Charters of privilege were granted towns during the Middle Ages that held a "free status." It drew a distinction between that of freeman and vassals of a feudal lord. The charter affirmed the recipients enjoyed the privileges to own property, the right to trade, and protection within the town.

cult time, the church maintained its love for Jesus and its mission, which prepared the way for the High Middle Ages, three centuries of peace, "an epoch which may be likened to spring after the barbarian winter."[487]

The robust commitment to and demonstration of the gifts of the Spirit, including speaking, praying, and singing in tongues, continued unabated during the Middle Ages. The entire worship experience of the church grew more and more spontaneous with jubilation punctuated by clapping and dancing and an abundance of miracles. This was the worship and prayer lives of both ordinary Christians and mystics.

Those who insist that tongues did not occur during these years run counterfactual with history. In fact, there was such a miraculous outpouring of all the gifts of the Spirit, such a continuation of the practice of jubilation, such radical expressions of faith, and such spiritual freedom and power in the three hundred years from 1000 through 1300 that some identify this time as the Age of Faith.[488]

At various times in this period, there were remarkable groups and individuals both inside and outside the Roman Catholic Church who were deeply committed to walking in a radical faith and freedom of the Holy Spirit with all the signs and gifts of the Spirit in operation. Most remained in the Church, but some chose to leave the confines of the church in order to live out what they considered correct. The best known of the groups which left the Church were the Catharis and the Waldeneses, both of whom were radical Charismatics.

---

487 H. Daniel-Rops, *Cathedrals and Crusades* (New York: Dutton & Co., 1957), p. 2
488 Eddie Ensley, ibid, p. 31

The Cathari, AD 1200–1400

Cathari means *pure*.[489] This title was given to a collection of groups and individuals during the medieval period who left the Catholic Church to pursue what they considered to be *pure* biblical faith. [490] The Cathari held various beliefs, but generally were identified with a deep evangelical faith and an openness and expectation for the miraculous ministry of the Holy Spirit, including speaking in tongues.[491]

The Roman Catholic Church officially considered them heretics, even to the point of accusing them of witchcraft because of the significant number of miracles they experienced. They burned many of them at the stake and branded others on the forehead in an attempt to destroy the movement. Yet there is no doubt that these were significant groups of orthodox, charismatic Christians fully devoted to the Lord Jesus and freely operating in all the gifts of the Spirit. The Cathari represented a growing discontent within the church against the structured hierarchy and a desire for the manifestations of power enjoyed by the early apostolic church.

The Waldeneses

Peter Waldo, AD 1140–1217, a wealthy merchant of Lyons, France, was a loyal Roman Catholic. In AD 1176, he obtained a copy of the New Testament that he could read, and his life was dramatically altered. He was so deeply convicted by the words of Jesus to preach the gospel without concern for material comfort that he gave up his possessions and entered an itinerant preaching

---

489 The term Cathari was first used by Eusebius in the fourth century referring to the Novatians. See Eusebius, *Church History*.
490 Some have seen the Cathari as non-Christians in large part due to the writings of their enemies. Others believe them to be true Christians and forerunners of the Protestant Reformation, see John Foxe, *Foxe's Book of Martyrs*.
491 Neander, ibid, p. 590

ministry, declaring the gospel he found in the Scriptures.[492] His radicalism attracted others, and soon he led a significant group of Catholic laypeople, who were going two by two preaching the gospel, experiencing the release of the gifts of the Spirit, and seeing miracles. In AD 1179, he applied to the church for its blessings on their work and was denied. Pope Innocent III refused to bless their work not because they were heretics, but because he considered them to be ignorant laypeople. Choosing to obey God rather than man, they continued in their work and in AD 1184 were excommunicated.

The Waldeneses, like the Cathari, sought to live out what they perceived as the biblical pattern for their lives and ministries, which opened them to the supernatural ministry of the Holy Spirit and all the attendant gifts, which most definitely included speaking, praying, and singing in tongues. [493]

While the Cathari and Waldeneses departed the Latin church, the vast majority of the leaders and laity who operated in the gifts of the Holy Spirit remained and greatly impacted the Roman church with their commitment to the Lord Jesus and the power of the Spirit that they experienced.

Hildegard of Bingen, AD 1098–1179

Hildegard was considered the most important woman in the church during her day.[494] She was the leader of a Benedictine convent near Bingen on the Rhine and widely recognized for her power in prayer. Hildegard both spoke and sang in tongues. Her colleagues referred to her spiritual songs as "concerts in the Spirit."[495] In AD 1184, Pope Eugenius personally visited her and

---

492 See Matthew 10:5–13
493 J.D. Douglas, ed., *The New International Dictionary of the Christian Church* (Grand Rapids, MI: Zondervan, 1974), p. 1026
494 John S. Oyer, *Lutheran Reformers Against the Anabaptists* (The Hague: Martinus Nijhoff, 1964), p. 231
495 A. J. Gordon, *The Healing Ministry*, (Harrisburg, PA: Christian Pub. 1961) p. 92

after investigating her revelations "recognized the genuineness of her miracles and encouraged her to continue her course."[496]

Francis of Assisi, AD 1181–1226

Francis was born of wealthy parents and early in his life heard a voice calling him to the work of the ministry. Francis possessed a deep devotion to Jesus. "He was always taken up with Jesus: he carried Jesus in his heart."[497] He established the Franciscans as a monastic order committed to studying the Scripture, preaching the gospel, praying, and helping the poor. The order, which elected to renounce all earthly possessions and live in poverty, was endowed with great spiritual power and described as "the most thoroughly Charismatic, in its primitive period, the Church had ever known."[498] They were constantly in prayer, which was usually highly exuberant and expressive. "Francis loved loud praise."[499]

Jubilation was a normal aspect of Franciscan prayer. Francis was once described as breaking out in songs of jubilation. "Intoxicated by love and compassion for Christ … melodies would often well up within him and found expression in French melodies, and the murmurs of God's voice, heard by him alone, would joyfully pour forth in French-like jubilation."[500]

Thomas of Celano described the day of Francis's canonization as a saint by Pope Gregory IX as a day filled with great jubilation by the people. "New songs were sung, and the servants of God jubilated in melody of the Spirit."[501]

---

496 Gordon, ibid, p. 94
497 *Early Franciscan Classics*, trans. Friars of Saint Barbara California, (Paterson, NJ: St. Anthony Press, 1962) p. 119
498 Francis A. Sullivan, *Charisms and Charismatic Renewal*, (Dublin, Scotland: Gill and Macmillan, 1982), p. 42
499 Ensley, ibid, p. 58
500 Ensley, ibid, p. 59
501 Thomas of Celano, *Vita Prima*, p. 718, as quoted by Ensley, ibid, p. 60

Dominic, AD 1174–1221

Dominic, a contemporary of Francis of Assisi, began a preaching order known as Dominicans. His ministry was filled with visions and miracles, including at least one report of raising the dead.[502] Dominic spoke in tongues. At one point, Dominic encountered a group of Germans who offered him their hospitality. He was deeply concerned that he was not able to understand them or talk with them to share the gospel. Dominic challenged his friends, "Pray God to teach us their language for we are not able to announce to them the Lord Jesus."[503] He prayed and was given the supernatural ability to speak and understand German.[504]

Bonaventure, AD 1217–1274

Bonaventure of Bagnoregio, born John of Fidanza, received great veneration even during his lifetime because of his impeccable character and the miracles attributed to him. Bonaventure was undoubtedly one of the great Christian philosophers of the Middles Ages and a radical ecstatic. There is a story of Saint Thomas visiting Bonaventure's monastic cell while the latter was writing the life of Saint Francis and, finding him in an ecstasy, demanded, "Let us leave a saint to work for a saint."[505]

---

502 Francis C. Lehner, *Saint Dominic: Biographical Documents* (Washington D.C.: Thomist Press, 1964) p. 165–166
503 George B. Cutten, *Speaking with Tongues: Historically and Psychologically Considered* (New Haven, CT: Yale University Press, 1927), p. 41. I believe the supernatural ability to speak and understand a foreign language is a unique type of tongue speech. It is a miracle and best understood as a "sign and wonder." Many years ago I was speaking at a youth camp in South Texas to hundreds of Hispanic teenagers. Almost all of them spoke and understood English, so I was not using an interpreter. After I spoke, a young man came up with a friend and asked me how long I had spoken Spanish. To his amazement, I assured him I had never spoken Spanish. Through the English speaking friend he said, "I heard you speaking perfect Spanish." I was shocked and thrilled. This was a great miracle of God.
504 Horsch, *The Faith of the Swiss Brethren*, vol. II, p. 11–16
505 Paschal Robinson, Saint Bonaventure, *The Catholic Encyclopedia*. Vol. 2.(New York: Robert Appleton Company, 1907). Retrieved 12.18.2008 @ *http://www.newadvent.org/cathen/02648c.htm*

He was an unabashed Christian mystic who contended that all the sciences were the handmaids of theology; reason can discover some of the moral truths, but others can only be received and understood by the revelatory power of the Holy Spirit. This revelation requires prayer and meditation that rises to ecstatic union with God. Once again, it was in the action of this intellectual giant, not simply his writing, that his commitment to the gifts and power of the Holy Spirit was seen.

In his *Triple Way*, one of his major works on mysticism, the tradition and practice of jubilation is plainly evident. Bonaventure made clear that first the soul was to be cleansed through genuine sorrow and tears. Then he believed a perfecting of the soul comes through praise, thanksgiving, and jubilation. He taught:

> Perfection through gratitude implies an awareness that rises to a hymn of thanksgiving for the quality of graces that are offered, a joy that rises to jubilation for the value of the gifts we have received, and a delight that culminates in an embrace because of the Giver's bounty.[506]

---

506 Bonaventure, *The Triple Way*, *The Works of Bonaventure*, trans. Jose de Vinck (Paterson, N.J.: St. Anthony Guild Press, 1960), p. 90

14

Tongues in the Late Middle Ages, AD 1300–1600

The three hundred years that composed the Late Middle Ages can best be characterized as a transformation. Through a series of both catastrophic and remarkable events, Europe slowly moved from the medieval world and entered the early modern period. The fourteenth century encountered the Babylonian captivity of the papacy to Avignon, France, in 1309, which was accompanied by a profound compromise of the papacy's spiritual integrity, especially in the alleged subordination of the powers of the church to the ambitions of the Frankish emperor; experienced the start of the Hundred Year War in 1337, in which England and France fought for dominance; endured the ravages of the Black Death in Europe in 1347 for the first of many times with thirty percent of the population perishing in the first year; lived through the Western Schism in 1378 in which three popes were elected simultaneously; rejoiced with the Bible being translated into English

1381; and in 1381, experienced the Peasants' Revolt, which began the end of serfdom and increased the rights of the serf class.

During the fifteenth century, Joan of Arc was executed in 1430; the Strasbourg Cathedral was completed in 1439, making it the tallest building in the world; Leonardo da Vinci was born in 1452; Constantinople fell to the Ottoman Turks in 1453, officially ending the Roman Empire; Johann Gutenberg printed the first Bibles on his new printing press in 1454; Christopher Columbus reached the New World in 1492. The sixteenth century experienced Martin Luther launching the Protestant Reformation in 1517, which is considered the end of the Middle Ages.

Though the possibility of death by famine and disease was always present, the Late Middle Ages saw the horrific results of both in abundance. The Black Death, preceded by famine and overpopulation, wiped out at least a third of Europe and marked the end of the prosperity that had characterized the High Middle Ages. The church, which had enjoyed tremendous acceptance by the general populace, suffered reduced status when some of its priests refused to minister to the dying during the plague and sparked even greater resentment when it enjoyed enormous profits in bequests from plague victims. Throughout this period, more and more towns and cities wrestled control of their own governments from the hands of the clergy or nobility while the monumental reduction in population triggered economic and political changes that would never be reversed. Throughout this period, the Holy Spirit continued to move powerfully among many people, and the gifts and manifestations of the Spirit were clearly present.

Vincent Ferrier, AD 1350–1419

The renowned Dominican preacher Vincent Ferrier received a vision of Jesus during an illness that instructed him to go through the world preaching Christ. When the vision ended, he was completely well. Immediately, he set out preaching throughout Europe from Spain to Greece and discovered many individuals who spoke in tongues.[507] Everywhere he preached, remarkable miracles were reported. In fact, so many miracles occurred that he was forced to set an hour aside daily for the healing of the sick.[508] Vincent spoke in tongues. "Various ethnic groups where he traveled and preached heard him speaking in their own language."[509] Many of his biographers hold that Vincent Ferrier was endowed with the gift of tongues.[510]

Jean Gerson, AD 1363–1429

Gerson, rector of the University of Paris, was one of the top scholars of the Middle Ages and an outstanding preacher. He insisted that Christian jubilation came out of a deep experience of the Lord's joy and was best experienced during ecstasy. He insisted:

> The hilarity of the devout…in a certain wonderful and unexplainable sweetness seizes the mind…so that now it does not contain itself. There happens some sort of spasm, ecstasy or departure…the mind springs forth; it leaps, or dances by means of the gestures of the body, which are comely, and then it jubilates in an inexpressible way…the purity of the heart sings along with the voice.[511]

---

507 Arnold, ibid, p. 262
508 Herbert Thurston and Donald Attwater, eds. *Butler's Lives of the Saints*, vol. 4, (New York: P.J. Kennedy, 1963), p. 32
509 Thurston and Attwater, ibid, p. 33
510 A. Reinhart, "St. Vincent Ferrier." In: *The Catholic Encyclopedia*. (New York: Robert Appleton Company) Retrieved November 19, 2008 from New Advent: http://www.newadvent.org/cathen/15437a. htm
511 Jean Gerson, *Oevres Complete*, vol. V, p. 284 as quoted by Ensley, ibid, p. 55

Colette, AD 1380–1447

Colette, founder of *Colettine Poor Clares*, was born at Corbie in Picardy, France. She successively joined the Bequines, the Benedictines, and the Urbanist Poor Clares. Later, she lived for a while as a recluse and exercised the gift of tongues speaking in both Latin and German.[512]

Francis Xavier, AD 1506–1552

Francis Xavier was a man who possessed an extraordinary love for the Lord Jesus Christ and his gospel. Given the time in which he lived, it is amazing that in the short space of ten years, AD 1542–1552, he could have preached the gospel of the kingdom to so many nations and converted so many individuals. Xavier possessed an incomparable apostolic zeal that motivated him and a remarkable power for miracles that God released through him.

Xavier spoke in tongues. Although he had never learned Japanese, he spoke it on his mission trip to the Far East "as if he had lived there his whole life."[513] Urban VIII spoke of Xavier possessing the gift of tongues at his canonization and said, "He spoke to various tribes with ease in their languages."[514]

Xavier had an unparalleled reputation as a miracle worker. In AD 1546, while in the Moluccas, Xavier lost a crucifix during a storm at sea, and a crab brought it back to him. Several times Xavier's prayers calmed storms at sea, preserved ships from pirate attacks, and steered them safely into port. One story, reported by two eyewitnesses, told how Xavier, while sailing on the Santa Cruz from Malacca to China in 1552, converted seawater into freshwater.[515]

---

512 George Barton Cutten, *ibid*, p. 40
513 Cutten, ibid, p. 45
514 Cutten, ibid, p. 44
515 Cutten, ibid, p. 46

The Women Mystics

The Middle Ages were filled with powerful Christian women who led the church into the manifestations of the Holy Spirit. There were certainly deeply spiritual forerunners: Maragret, Queen of Scotland, 1045–1093; Hildegard of Bingen, 1098–1179; and Christina of Markvate, 1095–1155, all experienced the gifts and power of the Holy Spirit. But the late medieval period produced some women who were prominent in the movements of the time, while others were enclosed in contemplative nunneries and unknown.

Catherine of Siena, AD 1340–1380

Bridget of Sweden, AD 1303–1373, Rita of Cascia, AD 1381–1457, and Julian of Norwich, AD 1342–1417, were all important mystics who spent hours in meditation and prayer. It is highly likely each of these women spoke, prayed, and sang in tongues, but the most notable woman mystic was Catherine of Siena. Being unable to write, she dictated her famous work, the *Dialogue,* and 380 surviving letters. They were filled with her overwhelming love of the Lord Jesus Christ. Her director wrote of her death as "not for any natural cause, or for any other reason that the sheer intensity of her love for God."[516]

Margery Kemp of King's Lynn, AD 1373–1440

Margery Kemp was from a wealthy family, wife of a mayor, mother of fourteen children, and a mystic. When she was in her twenties, she began having visions in which she talked to Jesus, Mary, and the saints. In one vision, Jesus told her to go deeper in her religious practices. Kemp manifested the presence of the Holy Spirit in an unusual state by weeping, screaming, and praying for Christians during religious services. She became so involved that

516 Mary Ann Fatula, *Catherine of Siena's Way,* (London: Darton, Longman, and Todd, 1987) p. 203

she detached her daily life from her husband and children and set out on a long journey, ending up in Jerusalem. In her autobiography, *The Book of Margery Kemp*, she gave real insight into her visions, what she described as her madness and the criticism she received from the clergy. [517] Margery Kemp was a deeply devout and sincere woman who experienced great freedom and power in the Holy Spirit.

The actions, even more than the writings, of these individuals put flight to the false idea that speaking in tongues ceased with the apostles or even with the arrival of the canon. There were, of course, many others who gave their lives to prayer and therefore prayed, spoke, and sang in tongues and jubilation, experienced great miracles, spoke prophetic words, and were used as instruments of the Holy Spirit to change the world during this period. Despite the gaps in the chronology, the same experience of the disciples at Pentecost and the Apostle Paul at Corinth continued throughout the period from the fourth to the sixteenth centuries.

---

517 Fatula's mental illness, which has been used as a way to negate her experiences, is better understood as an indication of manifestations of the Spirit across the range of human conditions.

15

Tongues from Martin Luther to John Wesley

Martin Luther, AD 1483–1546

The Christian world dramatically changed on October 31, 1517, the moment Martin Luther, a Catholic priest and professor of theology at the University of Wittenberg, nailed his ninety-five theses on the doors of the *Schlosskirche*, Castle Church, in Wittenberg, Germany. It was a brazen move. The church's abuse of authority deeply offended Luther, particularly the selling of indulgences as a means by which, in exchange for money, the church completely forgave an individual's sin without regard for repentance. Luther strongly opposed monies from indulgences funding the extravagant life of the church hierarchy. He launched a revolution.

In limited ways, Luther was a charismatic. He certainly believed tongues had ceased, at least to some extent, but had great faith for miracles. [518] Luther prayed for Pastor Fredrich Myco-

---

518 Burgess, *Medieval Roman Catholic and Reformation Traditions*, ibid, p. 151 "Luther has a curious conversation with Karlstadt over

nius, a close friend and colleague, who was dying with tuberculosis. Luther wrote to him, "The Lord will never let me hear that you are dead but permit you to survive me. For this I am praying, this is my will, and may it be done because I seek only to glorify the Name of God."[519] Myconius was healed and outlived Luther by two years.

Andreas Carlstadt, a professor of theology at the University of Basel, and the renowned Greek scholar Erasmus had a lengthy scriptural discussion with Luther. They pleaded with him to restore the pattern of the early church, including all the gifts of the Holy Spirit. Luther accused Carlstadt of misunderstanding the expression "speaking with tongues." Luther did not reject speaking in tongues but demanded that it must be interpreted. "If one should speak in tongues, he ought, in addition, to put what he says into German (the local vernacular), or interpret it in one way or another, so that the congregation may understand it."[520]

Within years, the Roman Catholic monopoly over Christianity in the West was shattered, and a plethora of new radical leaders emerged to lead segments of the church. Some continued the official Roman Catholic policy that tongues had ceased, but many, such as the Anabaptists, French Prophets, Mendicant Friars, Little Prophets of Cevennes, Jansenists, Quakers, Method-

---

tongues. Karlstadt argues that Paul's direction to the Corinthians concerning tongues excluded preaching in Latin. Luther responds that Paul was not forbidding speaking in tongues when it was accompanied by an interpretation. In the absence of an interpreter, no other language other than the vernacular should be used." The fact that Luther's great hymn "A Mighty Fortress is Our God" contains the phrase "The Spirit and gifts are ours" is an obvious indication that he was open to the manifestations and gifts of the Holy Spirit. See Hyatt, *2000 Years*, ibid, p. 74–75

519 Hyatt, *2000 Years*, ibid, p. 75

520 Martin Luther, *Against the Heavenly Prophets*, ed. Conrad Bergendorff, "Works," XL, 142 As quoted by Williams and Waldvogel, "A History of Speaking in Tongues and Related Gifts," *The Charismatic Movement*, ed. Michael P. Hamilton, (Grand Rapids, MI: Eerdmans, 1975), p. 72

ists, and others, embraced the supernatural including speaking, praying, and singing in tongues.

The Anabaptists, AD 1500–1800

There were several distinct groups of Anabaptists, but the largest and most influential were evangelical Anabaptists who attempted to follow what they believed to be a model of the New Testament by creating pacifistic communities. Among this group were the Swiss Brethren, the Hutterites, and the Mennonites.[521]

The Swiss Brethren, AD 1525

Following the lead of Martin Luther, Ulrich Zwingli, 1484–1531, a Swiss Roman Catholic priest, insisting the Bible, not the church, was the ultimate source of Christian truth, instituted a similar series of reforms in the city of Zurich in 1520–1523 that attracted several young radical reformers, including Conrad Grebel, 1498–1526, Felix Manz, 1498–1527, and George Blaurock, 1491–1529. At first, these men and others were ardent followers of Zwingli but ultimately believed the Zwingli's reforms were not proceeding as thoroughly or expeditiously as needed. The breaking point came primarily over the issues of infant baptism and the authority of the state to determine the nature of the Reformation. As a result, Grebel, Manz, and Blaurock broke with Zwingli in 1525, and Anabaptism was born.[522]

---

521 The Hutterites derived their name from the founder of the movement, Jacob Hutter, an early Anabaptist leader. Doctrinally they were closest to the old order Amish, stressing complete separation from the world and the communal ownership of all property. Hutterites were total pacifists.
522 Identifying the origins of Anabaptism is a notoriously complicated matter. Previous disputes have centered around whether Anabaptism began in Zurich with the initiation of believers' baptism in January of 1525, or in 1521 and 1522 with Luther's confrontation of the Wittenberg radicals, whom he labeled Schwärmer (enthusiasts). Recently, the disputed nature of Anabaptism's origins, has led scholars away from an attempt to establish a single moment of origin, and to accept a plurality of possible origins and to engage the

On January 17, 1525, the conflict between Zwingli and Grebel reached its peak. In a public debate on baptism, Grebel, Manz, and Wilhelm Reublin argued their case against infant baptism. Zwingli followed, using arguments he would publish in *Concerning Baptism, Rebaptism, and Infant Baptism*. Zwingli's argument prevailed, and on January 18, the Zurich Council mandated that all infants be baptized within eight days. Three days later, the council would demand that Grebel and Manz desist from arguing about infant baptism. As a result of these rulings, Grebel, Manz, and others gathered in Manz's home on January 25 and witnessed the first adult baptism in Zurich. Grebel baptized George Blaurock, after which Blaurock proceeded to baptize others present.

By the end of the month, Grebel had baptized Wolfgang Ulimann, a former monk, by immersion in the Rhine River. He spent the next several months preaching the need for repentance and baptism with much success in the area of St. Gall, baptizing as many as five hundred adults in St. Gall. In October of 1525, Grebel was arrested and sentenced to life in prison. Friends helped him escape in March of 1526, and he continued his ministry until he died of the plague later that summer. Felix Manz was arrested on January 5, 1527, accused of boasting of special revelation of the writings of the Apostle Paul, and condemned to death. He was drowned in the River Limmat that day.

As the Anabaptist movement spread beyond Zurich and throughout Switzerland, its followers became known as the Swiss Brethren. They were renowned "for their primitivism, or desire to restore a simple, biblical pattern of life; for biblical literalism, or fundamentalism in the interpretation of Scripture; for a disciplined communal life; and for adult baptism and free faith."[523]

Anabaptists as a whole were radically Charismatic, and their

---

complexity of Anabaptism. For well-established and detailed treatments of Anabaptism, see Claus-Peter Clasen, *Anabaptism, a Social History 1525–1618: Switzerland, Austria, Moravia, South and Central Germany* (Ithaca, Cornell University Press, 1972)
523 Burgess, *The Holy Spirit: Medieval Roman Catholic and Reformation Traditions*, ibid, p. 201

churches throughout Europe were filled with those who spoke in tongues and were very zealous to worship God in Spirit and truth.[524] Their worship was highly demonstrative, excited, and enthusiastic. They would shout and dance and always sang hymns with great fervor.[525]

A Swiss Anabaptist document produced between 1532 and 1534 was entitled *Answer of Some Who Are Called Anabaptists Why They Do Not Attend the Churches*. The primary reason was simple: the churches do not permit the members of the congregation to exercise spiritual gifts according to the Christian order as "taught in the gospel or the word of God in 1 Corinthians 14."[526] Of course, that is the chapter in which the Apostle Paul gives rules for the public use of tongues and prophecy.

The Mennonites

Facing persecution in Switzerland, the Anabaptists moved to neighboring countries, and with the move, Anabaptist groups emerged throughout Europe under different names. Some of those groups taught that speaking in tongues was the evidence of being born of the Spirit. One such group was known as the Mennonites, who were led by the Dutch reformer Menno Simons, 1496–1561.

Simons, a very prominent Anabaptist, was evidently very familiar with speaking, praying, and singing in tongues. He insisted speaking in tongues was the expected evidence of receiving the Holy Spirit. In his *Treatise on Christian Baptism*, Simons wrote, "You are plainly taught that Peter commanded that those

---

524 Williams and Waldvogel, *The Charismatic Movement*, ibid, p. 74
525 Crane Brinton, *A History of Civilization*, (Englewood Cliffs, NJ: Prentice Hall, 1976), p. 472–480
526 Paul Peachey and Shem Peachey, trans. "Why They Do Not Attend The Churches," *Mennonite Quarterly Review* 45, no. 1 (1971): 10. as quoted in Hyatt, *2000 Years*, ibid, p. 80

only should be baptized who had received the Holy Ghost, who spoke with tongues and glorified God."[527]

The French Huguenots

The Protestant Reformation began by Martin Luther spread rapidly in France, especially among those having grievances against the established order of government. Seizing the reformation moment, Lefevre, a professor at the University of Paris, prepared the way for the rapid dissemination of Lutheran ideas in France with the publication of his French translation of the New Testament in 1523, followed by the Old Testament in 1528. The two most famous of Lefevre's students, William Farel and John Calvin, were deeply committed to the reformation. Farel became a leader of the Swiss Reformation, establishing a Protestant government in Geneva, and Calvin, with his theological mind, rose to be a global force in the Reformation movement. Sometime between 1550 and 1580, members of the Reformed church in France came to be commonly known as Huguenots.

The newly reformed Christianity practiced by many members of the French nobility and social middle class, based on a belief in salvation through individual faith without the need for the intercession of a church hierarchy and on the belief in an individual's right to interpret Scriptures for themselves, placed these French Protestants in direct theological and ecclesiastical conflict with both the Catholic Church and the king of France in the theocratic system, which prevailed at that time.

The Revocation of the Edict of Nantes by Louis XIV in October 1685 began a new persecution of the Huguenots, and hundreds of thousands of Huguenots fled France to other countries.[528] A group of Huguenots, mostly peasants, who resisted the

527 Menno Simons, *Treatise on Christian Baptism, Collected Works,* trans. and ed. Leonard Verduin, (Scottdale, PA: 1956) p. 276f
528 The Edict of Nantes was signed by Henry IV in April 1598 and ended the War of Religion and allowed the Huguenots religious freedom.

attempts of Louis XIV's government to convert them to Roman Catholicism were imprisoned, tortured, and martyred.[529] Many were cruelly tortured and then executed; others died in prison or of extreme hardship.[530] Simultaneously, there occurred a sudden and mass outbreak of speaking in tongues.[531] Speaking, praying, and singing in tongues became an important aspect of prayer and worship among the Huguenots of France.[532] Observers reported enthusiastic, demonstrative worship, individuals being seized by the Spirit, uneducated peasants speaking in tongues, and young children prophesying in pure, elegant French.[533] The first occurrence of tongues came from the prophetic utterance of a ten-year-old, Isabeau Vincent. Soon adults and "little prophets of Cevennes" were speaking in tongues and prophesying throughout their province for over a decade.[534]

The Jansenists

The charismatic manifestations of the Cevennes had deep repercussions in France. A French Catholic holiness sect known as Jansenists had similar experiences beginning around 1730. Although they were outspoken in their criticism of the Protestant enthusiasts, they revolted against what they saw as a lack of freedom in the spiritual life among the Jesuits.[535] In reaction, the Jansenists sought and found the fullness of the Holy Spirit, including speaking in tongues. The movement existed for nearly eighty years.[536]

---

529 Vessie D. Hargrave, *The Glossolalia Phenomenon*, (Cleveland, TN: Pathways Press, 1966), p. 101
530 It was not until the Edict of Toleration in November, 1787 that the civil and religious rights of Huguenots in France were restored.
531 Kelsey, ibid, p. 52
532 Vinson Synan, *Aspects of Pentecostal-Charismatic Origins*, (Plainfield, NJ: Logos, 1975), p. 126
533 Hamilton, ibid, p. 75
534 Kelsey, ibid, p. 53
535 Hamilton, ibid, p. 76
536 Kelsey, ibid, p. 55

The Moravian Revival

Wednesday, August 13, 1727, was a day of the outpouring of the Holy Spirit in Saxony, Germany, among the Moravian Brethren gathered at the estate of Count Nicholas Zinzendorf, 1700–1760. [537] For centuries, the followers of John Huss, 1373–1415, the martyred Bohemian reformer, had endured persecution and death. Fleeing imprisonment and torture, they found refuge in Germany when Zinzendorf offered asylum on his estates.

No one present could tell exactly what happened at the specially called communion service. They hardly knew if they had been on earth or in heaven.[538] Zinzendorf described the morning as a time "the Savior permitted to come to us a Spirit of whom we had hitherto not had any experience or knowledge. The Holy Spirit himself took full control of everything and everybody."[539] The radical change in the Brethren was immediate. Their emotionally expressive worship was punctuated with fervent prayer and much singing.

It was through their detractors that the presence of speaking in tongues was revealed. They were accused of reviving the activity of the Montanists: speaking in tongues.[540] Although speaking in tongues was not officially endorsed by the Moravian leadership, it did occur at their meetings.[541] One of the most significant dimensions of the Moravian Revival was their commitment to prayer. Twenty-four men covenanted together on August 26, 1727, to continue praying in allocated intervals of one hour each day and night. That astonishing prayer meeting beginning in 1727

537 John Greenfield, *Power From On High*, (London, Marshall & Scott, 1931) p. 12 Greenfield wrote his book honoring the 200 anniversary of the revival. The revival was highly significant resulting in great missions work and the establishment of a prayer commitment that lasted for one hundred years.
538 Greenfield, ibid, p. 14
539 Greenfield, ibid, p. 14
540 John Roche, *The Moravian Heresy*, (Dublin: printed for the author, 1751), p.44
541 Hamilton, ibid, p. 77

went on for one hundred years and spawned scores of ministries and missionaries around the world. It made a strong impact on many, including John and Charles Wesley.[542]

George Fox, 1624–1691, and the Quakers

The life of George Fox was remarkable in every way and worthy of the volumes written concerning him.[543] He was born into a wealthy religious family who considered making him a priest when he was young. His ability to guide his Quakers through the treacherous years and remain alive though repeatedly imprisoned was miraculous. His commitment to avoid politics, live a simple life, yet speak to power remains a compelling, puissant model. His belief in the authenticity of the Bible while remaining open for a direct word from the Holy Spirit made him unique among the reformers. It was through his powerful preaching beginning in 1647 that his Society of Friends was formed.[544] His success with the group was remarkable. Under his leadership, Quakers became the fastest growing movement in the Western world. By 1656, Fox had over fifty associates who were traveling preachers, and by 1660, it is believed the movement had forty thousand to sixty thousand followers.[545]

Both Fox and the Quakers were fervent prayers. The degree to which they spoke and prayed in tongues is not certain, but it is obvious that many were highly charismatic. The record seems to indicate that speaking in tongues was a common occurrence, especially among the early Quakers. Edward Burroughs, a close ally of Fox, wrote of Quaker meetings, waiting for hours in silence for the manifestation of the Holy Spirit. When the Holy Spirit

542 Greenfield, ibid, p.
543 For an in-depth look at Fox and the Quaker movement see, Elton Trueblood, *A People Called Quakers*, (New York: Harper & Row, 1966)
544 John L. Nickalls, ed. *The Journal of George Fox*, (Cambridge: University Press, 1952) p. 18–19. Several editions of Fox's Journal have been published since it was first published in 1694.
545 Hyatt, ibid, p. 93

was released, "We received often the pouring down of the Spirit upon us ... as in the days of old, and our hearts were made glad, and our tongues loosed, and our mouths opened, and we spoke with new tongues, as the Lord gave us utterance, and as his Spirit led us."[546]

John Wesley, 1703–1791, and the Methodist Revival

John Wesley was born into a family of highly educated, deeply committed Christian parents, Samuel and Susannah Wesley. His father was the rector of the Anglican (Church of England) parish in Epworth, England, and his mother was a brilliant woman who knew Hebrew, Greek, and Latin. Wesley graduated from Oxford with its highest degree and was ordained into the Anglican priesthood in 1728 at age twenty-five.

It was at Oxford that John and his brother Charles founded a group, the "Holy Club," whose participants became known as Methodists because of the methodical way in which they sought the presence of God. From six until nine each evening, the group met for prayer and Bible study; they fasted each Wednesday and Friday. However, none of this brought him satisfaction or peace.

On the evening of May 14, 1738, while listening to a reading of Luther's *Preface to Romans* at a meeting on Aldersgate Street in London, Wesley found the spiritual peace he had sought. "I felt my heart strangely warmed. I felt I did trust in Christ, Christ alone for my salvation and an assurance was given me that he had taken away my sin, even mine, and saved me from the law of sin and death."[547]

Wesley believed the gift of tongues was readily available in his day. In fact, he believed it had an authentic existence in other,

---

546 George Fox, *The Works of George Fox*, vol. 3, (New York: AMS Press, 1975), p. 13
547 Curnack, ed. *The Journal of the Rev. John Wesley* A.M, (vol.1, p. 476

if not all, post-apostolic centuries.[548] Many of the early Methodist leaders openly sought for the manifestations of the Holy Spirit, such as John and Mary Fletcher. Mary insisted, "We must look for the baptism of the Holy Ghost. I've tasted, but I want the fullness."[549] Other early Methodist leaders did speak in tongues. One was Thomas Walsh, a close friend and colleague of Wesley. Walsh wrote, "This morning the Lord gave me a language I knew not of, raising my soul to him in a wonderful manner."[550]

Breaking with tradition, Wesley regarded Montanists, who were radically charismatic, as genuine spiritual Christians and Montanus himself as "one of the best men then upon the earth."[551] His openness to the things of the Spirit and his determination to follow Jesus fully enabled John Wesley to bring thousands to receive Jesus as Lord and positively change the world.

---

548 Hamilton, ibid, p. 80
549 Henry Moore, ed., *The Life of Mary Fletcher*, (New York, 1840), p. 270–324
550 William R. Davies, *Spirit Baptism and Spiritual Gifts in Early Methodism*, (Jacksonville, FL: Cross Fire Ministries, 1974), p. 12
551 John Wesley, *Journal, III*, 496; Wesley, *Works*, ed. John Emory (New York, 1856), VI, 556. As quoted in Hamilton, ibid, p. 81

16

Tongues and the Great Awakening 1726–1750

The American colonies entered the eighteenth century facing a growing spiritual skepticism and moral deterioration. Many of the long-established churches, which had been beacons of faith and moral certainty, had degenerated into dying religious institutions diluting the demands of the gospel and denying the supernatural power of the Spirit. Across the frontier a genuine scarcity of churches and pastors had left many small towns and villages without a voice of spiritual life and care. These conditions combined to lead Jonathan Edwards, pastor of the Congregational Church in Northampton, Massachusetts, to decry a "general deadness existed across the land."[552]

Edwards was a brilliant, Yale-educated, third-generation pastor who, responding to the conditions he saw in the colonies, determined to seek God for real spiritual renewal. He wholeheartedly believed in the power of prayer and often spent twenty

552 David S. Lovejoy, *Religious Enthusiasm and the Great Awakening*, (Englewood Cliffs, NJ: Prentice Hall, 1969), p. 5

hours a week praying. In 1726, God answered their prayers with a genuine spiritual awakening that swept along the east coast. Without any manmade plan or evangelistic strategy, hundreds received Jesus as Lord and Savior. Churches filled to capacity with "everyone eager to drink in the words of the minister as they came from his mouth; the assembly from time to time in tears while the word was preached; some weeping with sorrow and distress, others with joy and love, others with piety and concern for the souls of their neighbors."[553]

Edwards did not speak in tongues, but he did embrace some of what would be seen as Charismatic manifestations. He described positively one event he experienced upon his return one day to Northampton which is what Charismatics would call "being slain in the Spirit." "There were some instances of persons lying in a sort of trance, remaining perhaps for a whole twenty-four hours motionless, and with their senses locked up; but in the mean time under strong imaginations, as though they went to heaven and had there visions of glorious and delightful objects."[554] In his *Treatise Concerning Religious Affections*, Edwards attempted to distinguish between what he saw as true manifestations of spirituality and emotionalism. His staunch Calvinism kept him from embracing what he referred to as "the extraordinary gifts of the Holy Ghost,"[555] which included tongues. The strength of Edwards' opposition to the gifts of the Spirit is a clear indicator of the widespread manifestations of the gifts during the Great Awakening. In fact, he openly rebuked those who believed the that gifts of the Holy Spirit were to be expected in the Great Awakening, and insisted they were "deluded."[556]

But many others, including the other hero of the Awakening, George Whitfield, disagreed with Edwards' rejection of the

---

553 Jonathan Edwards, *Jonathan Edwards on Revival*, (Carlisle, PA: Banner of Truth, 1984), p. 14
554 Edwards, ibid, p. 154
555 Edwards, ibid, p. 71
556 Edwards, ibid, p. 71

"extraordinary gifts." Whitfield was born in Gloucester, England, studied at Oxford, and became a colleague of John and Charles Wesley in their "Holy Club." Whitfield rose to become the "Grand Itinerant" and a major leader in the Great Awakening. He was a great preacher who traveled extensively throughout the colonies, preaching the need of personal salvation with fervor and emotion. Unlike Edwards, "Whitfield believed the human will was less guided by intellect than emotions."[557] The crowds that gathered outdoors to hear Whitfield preach were amazing. "At a time when the population of Boston was twenty-five thousand, Whitfield preached to thirty thousand on the Boston Common."[558] When he preached, manifestations of the Holy Spirit were always present. Remembering individuals in a large crowd that had heard him preach, Whitfield wrote of some whose faces "drowned with tears, others struck pale as death … others lying on the ground, and most lifting their eyes to heaven and crying out to God."[559]

As to the question of tongues being present in Whitfield's meetings, Lovejoy quotes one critic who gave real affirmation. "These meetings would continue until 10, 11, or 12 o'clock at night; in the midst of them sometimes 10, 20, 30, and sometimes many more would scream and cry out, or send forth the most lamentable groans, while others made great manifestations of joy by clapping their hands, uttering ecstatic expressions, singing psalms, and inviting and exhorting others."[560]

The Great Awakening had a major impact on the entire society of colonial America. Tens of thousands received Jesus as Lord and Savior, filled existing churches, and helped give life

557 Stephen R. Graham, "The Protestant Tradition in America," in *Christian Spirituality*, ed. Gordon Mursell, (Minneapolis: Fortress Press, 2001), 285
558 Hyatt, ibid, p. 110
559 George Whitfield, George Whitfield's Journal, (London: The Banner of Truth Trust, 1965), p.425
560 Lovejoy, ibid, p. 77

to hundreds of new congregations. The spiritual climate radically changed. Colleges such as Princeton, Columbia, and others were formed to train new leaders for the church. Taken as a whole, despite Edwards' rejection of the gifts of the Spirit, Hyatt believes the Great Awakening must "be embraced as a Charismatic movement."[561]

---

561 Hyatt, ibid, p. 112

17

Tongues from the Irvingites to the Welsh Revival

The United States entered the nineteenth century spiritually reeling. Decades filled with war, the negative influences of the French Revolution, and the rise of deism had passed since the revivals of Jonathan Edwards and the Great Awakening. America was poised to abandon Christianity. The Presbyterian General Assembly, in 1798, circulated a pastoral letter describing the existing condition of the country in these terms:

> Formidable innovations and convulsions in Europe threaten destruction to morals and religion. Scenes of devastation and bloodshed unexampled in the history of modern nations have convulsed the world, and our country is threatened with similar calamities. We perceive with pain and fearful apprehension a general dereliction of religious principles and practice among our fellow citizens, and a visible and prevailing impiety and contempt for the laws and institutions of religion, and an abounding infidelity, which in many instances

tends to atheism itself. The profligacy and corruption of the public morals have advanced with a progress proportionate to our declension in religion. Profaneness, pride, luxury, injustice, intemperance, lewdness, and every species of debauchery and loose indulgence abound.[562]

In this setting, the Church cried out to the Lord Jesus, and He sent revival. The century opened with a sequence of charismatic eruptions around the globe that intensified with each decade and served as a precursor of things to come. Through a succession of remarkable men and women, the Lord Jesus moved to again establish the essentiality of the manifestations and gifts of the Holy Spirit in the life of his church and the church to the life of the nation. The power and range of this Second Great Awakening "deserves to be with the religious upheavals of seventeenth-century England and even with the European Reformation itself."[563]

Revival at Yale and Dartmouth, 1800

College campuses were filled with students claiming to be spiritual skeptics, if not outright atheists. Ironically, it was these campuses that saw revival, and Yale University was first. In 1795, Timothy Dwight, the son-in-law of Jonathan Edwards, had become president of Yale. Before he came to Yale, the college was spiritually dead. The college church was almost extinct.[564] President Dwight preached a series of chapel sermons on infidelity in 1800. The Holy Spirit moved powerfully, and one-third of the student body

562 William W. Sweet, *Religion of the American Frontier*, (New York: Cooper Square, 1964), p. 55
563 Richard Carwardine, "The Second Great Awakening in Comparative Perspective: Revivals and Culture in the United States and Britain," *Modern Christian Revivals*, ed. Edith L. Blumhofer and Randall Balmer, (Chicago: University of Illinois Press, 1993), p. 84
564 Lyman Beecher, *The Autobiography of Lyman Beecher*, (Cambridge, MA: Harvard University Press, 1961)

received Jesus as Lord and Savior.[565] The revival quickly spread to Dartmouth College in New Hampshire, Williams College in Massachusetts, and then throughout cities and towns along the East Coast.

The Revival at the University of Georgia, 1800–1801

A great revival swept the University of Georgia in 1800–1801, and the students "shouted and talked in tongues."[566]

The Kentucky Revival, 1800–1801

Deep in the Allegheny Mountains, James McGready, 1763–1817, a Presbyterian pastor of three small congregations on Gasper, Red, and Muddy Rivers in Logan County, Kentucky, sparked revival. Logan County was called "Rogues' Harbor." Refugees from all parts of the Union fled to the area to escape punishment or justice, and created an extremely violent society. Murderers, horse thieves, highway robbers, and counterfeiters came until they combined and actually formed a majority.[567]

McGready understood the need for revival and led his congregations into a covenant of prayer and fasting. Four years of prayer passed and nothing changed. Then a revival broke out that would change the condition of Logan County and the nation. The first move of the Holy Spirit occurred at the Red River Church. McGready described the moment:

> The power of God seemed to fill the congregation; the boldest, daring sinners in the country covered their faces and wept bitterly. After the congregation was dismissed, a large number of the people stayed about the doors,

---

565 Hyatt, ibid, p. 114
566 Synan, , ibid, p. 25
567 Peter Cartwright, *The Autobiography of Peter Cartwright*, (Nashville: Abington Press, 1956)

unwilling to go away. Some of the ministers proposed to me to collect the people in the meetinghouse again, and to perform prayer with them; accordingly we went in, and joined in prayer and exhortation. The mighty power of God came amongst us like a shower from the everlasting hills—God's people were quickened and comforted; yea, some of them were filled with joy unspeakable and full of glory. Sinners were powerfully alarmed, and some precious souls were brought to feel the pardoning love of Jesus.[568]

The revival at Red River was accompanied by unusual demonstrations of the Holy Spirit in increasingly informal services of worship. The manifestations were remarkable. Hundreds would simultaneously fall to the ground. Shouting, singing, and exhorting interspersed with laughing, jerking, and barking became characteristic of the meetings.[569] Speaking in tongues was not emphasized, but as in all the outbreaks of revival at the opening of the nineteenth century, many spoke, prayed, and sang in tongues.

George Baxter, a prominent Presbyterian minister and president of Washington Academy, went to Kentucky to investigate the effects of the revival. His report was extremely favorable. He said:

On my way to Kentucky I was informed by settlers on the road that the character of Kentucky travelers was entirely, changed; that they were now as remarkable for sobriety as they had formerly been for dissoluteness and immorality. And, indeed, I found Kentucky, to appearances, the most moral place I had ever seen.[570]

568 James Smith, *History of the Christian Church*, (Nashville: Cumberland Presbyterian, 1835), p. 672–673
569 Vessie D. Hargrave, "Reformation to 20th Century," *The Glossolalia Phenomenon*, ed. Wade H. Horton, (Cleveland, TN: Pathway Press, 1966) p. 106
570 George A. Baxter, "The Great Revival in Kentucky," *The Connecticut Evangelical Magazine*, II. 354, (Hartford: March, 1802)

Cane Ridge Revival, 1801

Barton Stone, 1772–1844, pastor of Presbyterian churches in Concord and Cain Ridge in Bourbon County, Kentucky, attended the revival at Red River. Convinced it was a genuine work of the Holy Spirit, Stone followed McGready's principles, and revival broke out in his two congregations. Such supernatural and extraordinary gifts of the Spirit accompanied the revival that it was seen to be a resumption of apostolic faith.[571]

It was estimated by military personnel that twenty to thirty thousand attended from all ages, representing various cultures and economic levels. Hundreds came on foot and on horseback, many bringing wagons with tents and camping provisions. Because of the numbers of people attending and the length of the meeting, Cane Ridge has become the metaphor of the Great Revival. Historic accounts recall the contagious fervor that characterized the meetings that continued day and night. Descriptions abound of individuals, taken by great emotion, falling to the ground, crying aloud in prayer and song, and rising to exhort and assist others in their responses to the moment. Worship continued well into the week following the serving of communion on Sunday. Stimulated by the revival spirit, "people appropriated for their own experiences the full and perfect accomplishment of Joel's prophecy."[572] "Like wonders have not been seen, except the Kentucky Revival last summer, since the Apostle's days. I suppose the exercises of our congregation this last winter, surpassed anything ever seen or heard of."[573] In truth, many experienced the same breakthroughs of the Holy Spirit. Cane Ridge was lived out in England, Massachusetts, North Carolina, Georgia, New York City, Boston, Richmond, and many others.[574]

---

571 Richard McNemar, *The History of the Kentucky Revival*, (New York: reprint by E.O. Jenkins, 1846) p. 32
572 McNemar, ibid, p. 32, 68
573 McNemar, ibid, p. 32
574 See, Synan, *The Holiness-Pentecostal Movement in the United States*, ibid, p. 25

Edward Irving, 1792–1834

The United States was not alone in experiencing a great surge of the supernatural power and presence of the Holy Spirit. God was at work on both sides of the Atlantic.

The Reverend Edward Irving was a highly educated, distinguished pastor of the prestigious Regent Square Presbyterian Church in London. Each Sunday, the church was filled with two thousand of the most prominent citizens of London, including members of Parliament, to hear this powerfully gifted preacher. In 1827, Irving preached a series of sermons on baptism and used as his text Acts 2:38: "Repent, let each of you be baptized in the name of the Lord Jesus Christ for the forgiveness of sins; and you shall receive the gift of the Holy Spirit."

Something had taken place in the life of this young pastor. Rather than following the traditional Presbyterian teaching that the work of the Holy Spirit was deeply personal and that all the manifestations of the gifts of the Spirit, including speaking in tongues had ceased with the apostolic age, Irving broke with the tradition and preached that the New Testament demanded the church to always receive the gifts of the Holy Spirit, just as the early church.[575] His attendance at Albury Park Conferences in 1826 led Irving to seek for and expect the supernatural manifestation of the gifts of the Holy Spirit.[576] By 1829, Irving was convinced that the supernatural powers present in the first century should be possessed by the church as "surely and richly as in the days of the Apostles."[577]

Not only was Irving convinced of the ongoing work of the

---

575 C. Gordon Strachan, *The Pentecostal Theology of Edward Irving*, (London: Darton, Longmann, and Todd, 1973), p.55

576 Albury Conferences were highly influential in the theological development of several significant men during the early 1800s. Many works have been produced concerning the conferences, but one with key insight is Iain Murray's *The Puritan Hope* (Carlisle, PA: The Banner of Truth Trust, 1975).

577 Iain H. Murray, ibid, p. 193

Spirit, his Christology had come to a new understanding. Irving taught his congregation that the power Jesus possessed over sin and Satan was not the result of his deity, but the baptism of the Holy Spirit, which he received at his water baptism.[578] Irving believed Jesus was to be the prototype for each Christian, which meant that a life filled with the power and giftings of the Spirit was intended for each Christian.

While Irving was introducing his new understandings to his London church, a miraculous move of the Holy Spirit was being poured out on the Gareloch and Port Glasgow regions of western Scotland. At Fermicarry in the vicinity of Glasgow, a Christian named Mary Campbell was dying of tuberculosis. During devotions with her sister and a friend on the morning of March 28, 1830, the Holy Spirit fell on her and "constrained her to speak at great length, and with superhuman strength, in an unknown tongue."[579]

Simultaneously, daily prayer meetings were being held at Port Glasgow for the same empowering of the Spirit. In April 1830, James MacDonald experienced what he identified as the "baptism of the Holy Spirit."[580] Immediately, he felt such power and anointing that he departed the prayer meeting to pray over his dying sister Margaret. MacDonald had prayed for his sister on many occasions, but this time of prayer was radically different. Rather than a simple prayer requesting healing, he commanded his sister to rise from her deathbed. When he prayed, she was instantly and miraculously healed. The miracle brought great faith to those gathering to pray, and a week later, on April 18, 1830, James MacDonald and his twin brother, George, both spoke in tongues for the first time. James wrote his friend Mary Campbell, sharing with her of the miraculous healing of his sister Margaret. When Mary read the letter, the Holy Spirit moved upon her, and she too was healed. Later, she wrote of a "power which no words

578 See Chapter One
579 Strachan, ibid, p. 66
580 Hyatt, ibid, p. 120

can describe; it was felt to be indeed the voice of Christ ... I was verily made in a moment to stand upon my feet, leap and walk, sing and rejoice."[581]

These miraculous moves of the Holy Spirit excited the entire region. Soon, the MacDonald house was filled every day with people from all parts of England, Scotland, and Ireland seeking to know and experience the power of the Spirit.[582]

When Edward Irving received word of the miraculous healings and speaking in tongues, he immediately left for Glasgow to investigate.[583] He was amazed to hear this small group of believers speak in tongues and interpret. On April 20, 1830, the first recorded message in tongues and interpretation in modern times occurred as James MacDonald spoke in tongues and George MacDonald interpreted.[584] Irving was convinced.

Upon his return to his church in London, Irving organized prayer meetings for the members of his own church to seek spiritual gifts. The move of the Holy Spirit did not come quickly. After a solid year of praying, teaching, and waiting, on April 31, 1831, a Mrs. Cardale, the wife of a prominent London lawyer and a member of Irving's church, spoke in tongues at a home prayer meeting.[585] Then six months later, on October 30, another woman, Ms. Hall, spoke in tongues in the vestry of Regent Square Church. The following Sunday, several believers publicly spoke in tongues and prophecy during the morning worship service.[586] For three months, similar manifestations occurred.[587]

While most of the congregation supported these activities, several key leaders opposed Irving, which resulted in his being removed from his pastorate of Regent Square Church on May 4,

581 Strachan, ibid, p. 68
582 Eddie L. Hyatt, IBID, p. 120
583 Vinson Synan, *The Century of the Holy Spirit*, (Nashville: Nelson, 2001), p. 22
584 Synan, ibid, p. 22
585 See, Hyatt, ibid, p. 121
586 Strachan, ibid, p. 13
587 Synan, ibid, p. 24

1831, and locked out of his church.[588] A majority of Regent Square Church members left with Irving and formed a new congregation on Newman Street called the Catholic Apostolic Church. Irving and his associates believed God was restoring all the gifts, ministries, and power of the early church. Throughout Great Britain, other likeminded churches and pastors began linking themselves with the Catholic Apostolic Church.[589]

Tongues: The Crowning Act of All

Irving wrote extensively on what he referred to as the baptism of the Holy Spirit and spiritual gifts. He raised speaking in tongues to a high and inclusive place.

> The gift of tongues is the crowning gift of all … It is the proclamation that man is enthroned in heaven, that man is the dwelling-place of God, that all creation if they would know God, must give ear to man's tongue, and know the compass of reason. It is not that we speak, but Christ speaketh.[590]

He saw speaking in tongues as the "standing sign," meaning all other gifts flowed out of speaking in tongues. Irving originated the concept that speaking in tongues was the "outward and visible sign of that inward and invisible grace which the baptism of the Holy Ghost conferred."[591] He also believed deeply in the devotional aspect of singing and praying in tongues.

"Therefore it is nothing to be doubted that tongues are a great

---

588 The presbytery in London convicted him of allowing a woman to speak in his church and heresy concerning some of his Christological teaching and excommunicated him from the ministry of the Church of Scotland March 13, 1833.
589 David Dorries, "Edward Irving and the Standing Sign", *Initial Evidence*, ed. Gary B. McGee, (Peabody, MA: Hendrickson, 1991), p. 46
590 Edward Irving, *Collected Works*, as quoted in Synan, ibid, p. 23
591 Synan, ibid, p. 23

instrument for personal edification, however mysterious it may seem to us; and they are on that account greatly to be desired."[592]

His belief in and commitment to the gifts of the spirit and especially speaking, singing, and praying in tongues cost Irving dearly. He went from being the highly esteemed pastor of the prestigious church to the target of ridicule by those who had once thronged to hear him. Edward Irving did not live to see the fulfillment of his Catholic Apostolic Church. Tragically, he died at age forty-two on December 7, 1834, "a still young, much worn and lonely proclaimer of the place of tongues."[593]

Johann Lutz, b. 1801

Johann Lutz was a Roman Catholic priest in the German town of Karlshuld. Out of his concern for the spiritual life of his parish, he preached his sermon on New Year's Eve of 1827 challenging the people to repent of their sins and seek revival. Later that evening, he was awakened by a group of repentant parishioners wanting to confess. Revival began. For weeks, continuous prayer meetings were held. "On Ash Wednesday, in an all night prayer vigil people suddenly began to speak under inspiration."[594] Individuals were praying in tongues both in the church and in their homes. The people were convinced the Lord would pour out his Spirit as in the early church.

The revival lasted for years with all the gifts of the Spirit, including speaking in tongues, being manifested. During the revival, he became friends with the Irvingites, who encouraged him in the things of the Spirit. Ultimately, he was excommunicated by his Catholic bishop in 1856 and joined the Catholic Apostolic Church.

---

592 Dorries, ibid, p. 36
593 Hamilton, ibid, p. 86
594 Hamilton, ibid, p. 87

Gustav von Below, 1790–1843

Gustav von Below was an aristocratic officer of the Prussian Guard who, along with his brothers Karl and Heinrich, founded a charismatic movement in Germany in 1817 that included speaking in tongues. The three brothers had similar experiences and jointly devoted their estate at Reddenthin to charismatic prayer meetings open to noble and commoner alike. The meetings were dominated by singing in tongues.[595]

The movement spread over Pomerania and ultimately into the United States, where it merged into what is now the Pentecostal movement. Many Prussian officials of high importance were drawn to these meetings at Reddenthin, including the young Otto von Bismarck and the von Gerlach brothers, close friends of the king. The Lutheran Church was somewhat suspicious of these phenomena, until a Lutheran investigatory commission found them to be of God.[596]

The Revival in Cornwall England, 1851 AD

Midway through the nineteenth century, a series of charismatic awakenings occurred that significantly impacted both sides of the Atlantic. The first took place in Cornwall, England, and then spread to the U.S., Wales, Ireland, and then to other parts of England. On Christmas day 1851 at St. Just Church in Cornwall, intercessors met to sing and pray at 3:00 p.m. The Spirit was poured out on them, and they prayed through the night until 9:00 a.m. and regathered that Christmas evening.

Though speaking in tongues was not recorded during this first meeting, there was "fervent prayer, spontaneous shouts of praise, exuberant singing, and joyful testimonies were evidences of transforming spiritual experiences." "In many cases tongues speaking went unreported because observers did not recognize it

---

595 Hamilton, ibid, p. 85
596 Hamilton, ibid, p. 85

or its significance and did not distinguish it from other physical phenomena."[597] The Holy Spirit came with great power. Individuals were slain in the Spirit and lay prostrate while others experienced "very violent" physical manifestations. Healings often accompanied experiences of salvation.[598]

Phoebe Palmer, 1807–1874

Phoebe Worrell was born in New York City and married Walter Palmer, a homeopathic physician in 1827. Her parents were devout Methodists, having experienced a genuine Christian conversion during the Wesleyan Revival in England before immigrating to the United States. Palmer and her husband developed a particular interest in John Wesley's doctrine of Christian perfection. They both experienced what they called "entire sanctification" and felt that they should teach others about the experience.

Along with her friend Sarah Worrall, Palmer launched the Tuesday Meeting in 1836 for the Promotion of Holiness in New York City. At first, only women attended the meetings, but eventually Methodist bishops and other clergy began to attend. Palmer and her husband eventually purchased *The Guide*, and Mrs. Palmer became the editor of the periodical, then called the *Guide to Holiness*. In 1859, she published *The Promise of the Father*, in which she argued in favor of women in ministry. As a result, Palmer quickly became one of the most prominent leaders of the holiness movement.

Ultimately, she began ministering throughout the U.S., Canada, and Great Britain. Thousands became Christians in her protracted meetings that often ran for weeks. There were great supernatural manifestations during her meetings, which was one of the keys to her success.[599] There is no question that

597 Synan, *The Holiness-Pentecostal Movement in the United States,* ibid, p. 25
598 Hamilton, ibid, p. 89–90
599 Phoebe Palmer, *Four Years in the Old World*, (Boston, MA: Foster

speaking in tongues occurred in her meetings. She wrote of one afternoon meeting being "the full baptism of the Holy Spirit as received by the one hundred and twenty disciples on the day of Pentecost."[600]

Oslo, Norway, 1889

In his work *The Phenomenon of Pentecost*, Frank Ewart, 1876–1947, documented a great outpouring of the Holy Ghost that took place in the revival in Norway. He wrote that countless Norwegians were filled with the Holy Ghost and spoke in tongues.[601]

A. J. Gordon, 1836–1895

A. J. Gordon, founder of Gordon College[602] and pastor of Clarendon Street Baptist Church in Boston, Massachusetts, for twenty-five years was a prolific writer and a strong advocate for speaking, praying, and singing in tongues. In his work *The Ministry of Healing*, he demands that prophecy and the gifts of tongues "do not seem to be confined within the first age of the Church."[603]

Revivals and Camp Meetings

Synan presents a condensed excerpt from Barton W. Stone, an eyewitness of the signs and wonders that occurred at early Camp Meetings. Stone described people falling; some having jerks in part of their body; dancing that continued until the dancer was exhausted and fell to the floor; loud, hearty laughing that Stone

& Palmer, 1865), iii
600 Palmer, ibid, p. 107
601 Frank J. Ewart, *The Phenomenon of Pentecost*, (Hazelwood, CA: Word Aflame Press, 2000)
602 Gordon College, in Wenham, Massachusetts, was founded as the Boston Missionary Training School in the basement of Clarendon Street Church in 1889 and continues as an outstanding Christian college.
603 A. J. Gordon, *The Healing Ministry*, (Harrisburg, PA: Christian Publishers, 1961) p. 53

said was indescribable; individuals running until they fell; and singing, which from his description, was singing in tongues.[604]

Throughout the nineteenth century, revivals and camp meetings filled America from Massachusetts to California. Even though speaking in tongues was not singled out as an important characteristic of the meetings, there were many accounts of sporadic outbreaks of tongues associated with the revivals and camp meetings. [605] [606] A great revival swept through the University of Georgia in 1800–1801, and students "shouted and spoke in tongues."[607] During the summer of 1896, a revival was conducted in the Shearer Schoolhouse in Cherokee County, North Carolina. In the revival, one hundred and thirty men and women spoke in tongues and birthed the Church of God of Cleveland, Tennessee.[608]

In other parts of the world, similar experiences occurred. In 1880, reports of speaking in tongues came from a Moravian mission.[609] In 1902, a young Swedish Baptist minister, Lewi Pethrus, spoke in tongues after spending the night in prayer with a group of friends from the Norwegian Holiness Movement. "Tears streamed down my cheeks while I was overflowing with joy. A current of power and sweetness went through my entire being, and I spoke strange words which surprised me a great deal." [610] Synan believes the outpouring of the Spirit was inevitable, "With such a strong emphasis on repentance and free demonstrative worship, it is not surprising that many people received the Holy Spirit and spoke in tongues."[611]

---

604 See Synan, *The Century of the Holy Spirit*, ibid, p. 33
605 Hyatt, ibid, p. 131
606 Hamilton, ibid, p. 95
607 Synan, *The Holiness–Pentecostal Movement in the United States*, ibid, p. 25
608 Stanley Burgess, ed. *Dictionary of Pentecostal and Charismatic Movements*, (Grand Rapids, MI: Zondervan, 1988), p 198
609 Hamilton, ibid, p. 95
610 Hamilton, ibid, p. 96
611 Synan, *The Holiness–Pentecostal Movement in the United States*, ibid, p. 25

Mukti, India, 1905

Pandita Ramabai, 1858–1920, was a well-educated, astute scholar born into the upper caste of India, who spoke seven languages and translated the Bible from Hebrew and Greek into her native Marathi. During a severe famine, Ramabai and her friend Minnie Abrams established a compound for widows and orphan girls in her area near Pune just south of Bombay, or today, Mumbai, which she named *Mukti*, meaning salvation.[612] The compound was quickly home to more than two thousand women and girls.

In January 1905, she began teaching and praying about the need for revival. Soon over five hundred women and girls met twice daily to pray for revival and a genuine outpouring of the Holy Spirit. They met daily to pray for the anointing of the Holy Spirit upon their ministries. On Thursday, June 29, the Spirit moved powerfully on many of the girls. The following day, Friday, June 30, while Ramabai taught from the eighth chapter of the Gospel of John, the Holy Spirit fell on them all suddenly with great power. Each person present began to weep, pray aloud, and cry out to be baptized with the Holy Spirit and fire.[613] Revival spread through their mission and into many surrounding areas. Thirty of the women from the compound began ministering by teams in the surrounding villages. Regular school activities gave way to confession, repentance, and great joy with much praise and dancing. Many spoke in tongues and were filled with zeal for evangelism and social care.

Albert Norton, a missionary to India, wrote of his encounter with the revival:

> I opened my eyes and within three feet of me, on her knees, with closed eyes and raised hands, was a woman whom I had baptized at Kedgaon in 1889, and whom my wife and I had known intimately since as a devoted

---

612 Synan, ibid, p. 84
613 Hyatt, ibid, p. 156

Christian worker. Her mother tongue was Marathi, and she could speak a little Hindustani. But she was unable to speak or understand English such as she was using. But when I heard her speak English idiomatically, distinctly and fluently, I was impressed as I should have been had I seen one, whom I knew to be dead, raised to life. A few other illiterate Marathi women and girls were speaking in English and some were speaking in other languages, which none at Kedgaon understood. This was not gibberish, but it closely resembled the speaking of foreign languages to which I had listened but did not understand.[614]

The Welsh Revival, 1904

The Welsh revival was thoroughly unique. It was a revival in churches among the poor and the outcast. Spontaneity and seeming disorder replaced the normal church life of the small mining towns of South Wales as thousands crowded the churches and chapels of Wales.

The leader, or at least the person through whom God released the revival, was Evan Roberts, 1878–1951, a twenty-six-year-old coal miner and first year theology student. Roberts, who was deeply concerned over the lack of interest in Christianity and the work of the church, had been convicted to spend four hours in prayer each morning before work.[615] In 1904, Roberts experienced what he identified as his "baptism with the Spirit" and became deeply burdened for the young people in his hometown. Determined to obey what he believed to be the direction of the Holy Spirit, he returned home to preach.

With his preaching, a genuine move of the Holy Spirit took place. The people responded overwhelmingly to his humble min-

---

614 S.H. Frodsham, *With Signs Following*, (Springfield, MO: Evangelical Press, 1946) p. 107–108
615 W.T. Stead, "Mr. Evan Roberts," *in The Story of the Welsh Revival Told by Eyewitnesses*, (New York: Fleming H. Revel, 1905) p. 55

istry and broken spirit. Within weeks, many were claiming to be baptized with the Holy Spirit. They were shouting, laughing, dancing, falling down under the power of the Spirit and speaking in tongues.[616] As invitations for his ministry poured in from around Wales, he traveled only as he felt led by the Spirit. Wherever he preached, the revival intensified, but the move of the Spirit was not contained to his ministry alone; others experienced the same outpouring. No one could predict where the revival would manifest.

Roberts emphasized his personal dependence on the Holy Spirit. He claimed to never prepare sermons, rather he insisted, "I leave all that to Him (the Holy Spirit)."[617] Roberts was motivated by a deep sense that the revival was the beginning of a global move of the Holy Spirit, a real outpouring. "The world will be swept by His Spirit as by a rushing, mighty wind," Roberts proclaimed. The great lesson to be learned, he maintained, was "obedience to the voice of the Holy Spirit."[618]

The *Times of London* reported that "people met and poured out their souls in prayer and praise for hours before the preacher came, if he came at all."[619] Public Bible reading and hymn singing usually preceded preaching. However, at any time during the preaching, the people would "burst forth—apparently without lead or concert, but all and at once" into singing. [620] Individuals fell to their knees in prayer or stood to confess sin or give praise.[621] Corporate worship and prayer dominated the meetings. When the excitement of the congregation was "at its highest, the

---

616 Vinson Synan, *The Century of the Holy Spirit*, (Nashville: Thomas Nelson, 2001), p. 41
617 Evan Roberts, "A Message to the World," in *Welsh Revival*, ibid, p. 5
618 Roberts, Message, p. 6
619 "The London Times" February 13, 1905 as quoted by Blumhofer, ibid, p. 150
620 "The London Times" January 3, 1905 as quoted by Blumhofer, ibid, p. 150
621 Edith L. Blumhofer, *Modern Christian Revivals*, (Chicago: University of Illinois Press, 1993), p. 150

outbursts were not successive but literally simultaneous."[622] It was not unusual for the meetings to last eight or nine hours.

The revival was marked by complete freedom of the Spirit with speaking in tongues serving as a major element of the revival. Roberts reported having many supernatural visions from which he drew great inspiration and motivation.[623] What some believed to be the ancient Welsh "hywl," others understood as speaking in tongues.[624] An unusual phenomenon was that "ordinary farm servants, common plough boys and practically unlettered youths spoke classical Welsh."[625] J. Morris Jones, Welsh professor at the University College of North Wales, reported that these individuals spoke with diction, "more chaste and beautiful than anything I can hope to attain."[626] *The London Times* cited the example of a young girl who spontaneously prayed aloud in a congregation of approximately two thousand. In the course of her prayer, she used Scripture and old Welsh hymns as well as her own words "in the purest idiomatic classical Welsh," which "would have done credit to the most scholarly theologian of the Welsh pulpit."[627]

"The revival first set Wales ablaze, then London and then all of England, until people from all over the world were coming to see if this was the new Pentecost."[628]

The incredible effects of the revival assured it press coverage. Alcoholism, a major social problem in southern Wales, was significantly reduced. Miners voluntarily taxed their wages to build libraries and recreation halls, which would provide alternatives

---

622 Blumhofer, ibid, p. 150
623 Robert Owens, "The Azusa Street Revival," *The Century of the Holy Spirit*, ed. Vinson Synan, ibid, p. 41
624 Owens, ibid, p. 41
625 "The London Times" January 31, 1905, as quoted in Blumhofer, p. 151
626 "The London Times" February 4, 1905, as quoted in Blumhofer, p. 151
627 "The London Times" February 4, 1905, as quoted in Blumhofer, p. 151
628 Owens, ibid, p. 41. Also see, Blumhofer, *Modern Christian Revivals*, p. 151

to the saloons. As the numbers of arrests declined drastically, the "magisterial bench" expressed "keen gratification" for the movement.[629] Efforts to conserve its social effectiveness were launched, a popular effort being the creation of institutional churches. Many stories of repentance followed by restitution circulated. The revival manifested itself in sobriety, industry, repaid debts, and healed relationships, as well as in evangelism.[630]

The famed British evangelical, G. Campbell Morgan, briefly visited the Welsh Revival and was overwhelmed by the genuineness of the move of the Spirit. "It is Pentecost continued, without a single moment's doubt. The meetings are absolutely without order, characterized from the first to the last by the orderliness of the Spirit of God."[631]

Morgan challenged the church to learn the lessons of the revival and live in its expectations.

> Let us listen for the Spirit, confess Christ, be absolutely at his disposal. Get things out of the way for God ... your habit that you know is unholy; your method of business that will not bear the light of day; your unforgiving heart towards a church member.[632]

The Welsh revival, with its strong emphasis on the Holy Spirit, occurred just before the Azusa Street Revival, which temporarily made Los Angeles the center of American Pentecostalism. Its direct influence on the religious expectations of American evangelicals can be traced. Many embraced Morgan's view: "I am not at all sure that God is not rebuking our over-organization."[633]

---

629 See Blumhofer, *Modern Christian Revivals*, p. 151
630 Stead, Awakening, p. 62
631 G. Campbell Morgan, "The Lesson of the Revival," in *Welsh Revival*, p. 37
632 Morgan, ibid, p. 50–51
633 Morgan, ibid, p. 50

The Welsh revival was a divine visitation replete with all the gifts and manifestations of the Holy Spirit. It was God's way of saying: "See what I can do without the things you are depending on; see what I can do in answer to a praying people; see what I can do through the simplest who are ready to fall in line and depend wholly and absolutely on Me."[634]

---

634 Morgan, ibid, p. 44

18

Tongues and the Azusa Street Revival

The Preparation

No move of God begins in a vacuum, and that was certainly true of the outpouring of the Holy Spirit at Azusa Street in Los Angeles, California.[635] At the close of the nineteenth century, there was a growing hunger for the genuine move of God in many cities around the world. The same was true in L.A. among a wide variety of Christians.

---

635 Many works have been written regarding the history of the Azusa Street Revival. The most trustworthy are: Vinson Synan, *The Century of the Holy Spirit*, (Nashville: Nelson, 2001); Jack W. Hayford and David S. Moore, *The Charismatic Century*, (New York: Warner Faith, 2006); Cecil M. Robeck, *The Azusa Street Mission and Revival*, (Nashville: Nelson, 2006); Eddie L. Hyatt, *The Azusa Street Revival*, (Lake Mary, FL: Charisma House, 2006); Frank Bartleman, *Another Wave Rolls In*, (Northridge, CA: Voice Publications, 1970)

Joseph Smale, 1792–1834

One of those hungry ones seeking the presence of the Holy Spirit was the pastor of the First Baptist Church of Los Angeles, Joseph Smale. Smale was a brilliant, gifted preacher, a native of England who had studied for the ministry at Spurgeon's College in London. When he heard of the events taking place in the Welsh Revival, he immediately took a leave of absence from his own pulpit and departed for Wales. While at Wales, Smale was so moved by the presence of the Holy Spirit and individuals speaking in tongues, shouting, laughing, and dancing in the Spirit that he fully embraced the outpouring and "actually helped Evan Roberts in conducting services."[636]

Smale was radically impacted by the Welsh Revival. Upon his return to California in 1905, almost a year before the Azusa Street Revival, he devoted himself to intense times of prayer, seeking the presence of the Holy Spirit. Those personal prayer times evolved into home prayer meetings with members of his church crying out for a move of God in L.A. Times of prayer led this changed Baptist pastor to start a series of revival meetings at his own First Baptist Church, hoping to see a duplication of the Welsh Revival. But not everyone was pleased.

Soon the elders of the church challenged Smale and demanded a return to things as usual. Smale resigned. In early 1906, many who agreed with Smale in his desire for the freedom and life of the Holy Spirit followed him and launched the First New Testament Church of Los Angeles, where the nightly revival meetings continued, replete with all the gifts of the Spirit. There was deep spiritual hunger in Los Angeles, so much so that "people were willing to divorce themselves from lifelong commitments in the quest for a new outpouring of the Spirit of God."[637]

---

636 Robert Owens, *The Century of the Holy Spirit*, ed. Vinson Synan, (Nashville: Nelson, 2001), p. 40
637 Owens, ibid, p. 41

Charles Fox Parham, 1873–1929

Charles Fox Parham of Muscatine, Iowa, was a young, itinerant evangelist with Methodist, Holiness, and Quaker influences who is recognized as the person responsible for introducing the defining Pentecostal doctrine that speaking in tongues is the biblical evidence of the "baptism of the Holy Spirit." [638] [639] The baptism of the Spirit was being hotly debated among evangelicals with a plethora of various answers, but none before Parham unequivocally advocated a uniform evidence.[640] Parham was also first to teach that speaking in tongues should be a part of normal Christian worship rather than a curious by-product of religious enthusiasm.

Parham was a seeker. He spent years traveling, interviewing leaders, and longing to find a genuine move of the Spirit. In October of 1900, Parham launched Bethel Bible School and Healing Home near Topeka, Kansas, with forty students, twelve of whom were ministers. "Prayer was the central focus of the school, and the prayer tower atop the mansion was in use twenty-four hours a day with each resident of the school participating in a prayer vigil."[641]

Before leaving the school to preach in Kansas City, Parham had challenged the students to study the Acts of the Apostles and search for the biblical evidence that a person had genuinely been "baptized in the Holy Spirit." Upon his return on New Year's Eve, Parham was astonished to find that each of them agreed that the "indisputable proof was that they spoke in tongues."[642]

Later that New Year's Eve night, Parham and his students

---

638 Eddie Hyatt, ibid, p. 137
639 In the following chapter, I will present my disagreement with the use of the term "the baptism of the Holy Spirit" when speaking of an experience subsequent to salvation.
640 Edith L. Blumhofer, "Restoration as Revival," in *Modern Christian Revivals*, ed. Edith Blumhofer and Randall Balmer, (Chicago: University of Illinois Press, 1993), p. 146
641 Hyatt, ibid, p. 138
642 Sarah Parham, *The Life of Charles F. Parham*, (Baxter Springs, KS: Apostolic Faith, n.d.), p. 32

conducted a Watch Night service to pray in the New Year. In this service, a student named Agnes N. Ozman, a young Holiness preacher, asked Parham to lay his hands on her head and pray for her to be baptized with the Holy Ghost with the evidence of speaking in tongues. Parham recalled, "I laid my hands on her and prayed. I had scarcely repeated three dozen sentences when the glory fell upon her, a halo seemed to surround her head and face, and she began speaking the Chinese language and was unable to speak English for three days."[643]

It was just after midnight and the first day of the twentieth century when Miss Ozman spoke in tongues. Within days, Parham and each of the other students followed Ozman and received the same experience of tongues. "With the restoration of tongue speech, he considered that all the components of the New Testament church were evident in his ministry."[644]

Parham and some of the students from Bethel began conducting evangelistic revivals in surrounding towns, hoping to spread their newfound experience, but with little success. Finally, at Galena, Kansas, Parham experienced the breakthrough in the Spirit with the supernatural gifts of the Holy Spirit and miracle healings he had so desired. Encouraged by the move of the Spirit at Galena, he opened a new Bible school in Houston in 1905 and continued his teaching that speaking in tongues was a sign of the baptism of the Holy Spirit.[645] He began with only twenty-five students, but one was destined to usher in the Azusa Street Revival.[646]

William Joseph Seymour, 1870–1922

William Joseph Seymour was born on May 2, 1870, in Center-

---

643 Eric W. Gritsch, *Born Againism*, (Philadelphia: Fortress Press, 1982), p. 71
644 Blumhofer, ibid, p. 146
645 Blumhofer, ibid, p. 145
646 James R. Goff, Jr. *Fields White Unto Harvest*, (), p. 89

ville, Louisiana, to Simon Seymour and Phyllis Salabarr, both recently freed slaves. Little is known of his early life except that he was raised in poverty and received no formal education. During Seymour's infancy and childhood, his family attended both the Baptist and Catholic churches. On September 4, 1870, young William was baptized in a Catholic ceremony at the Church of the Assumption in Franklin, Louisiana. At age twenty-five, Seymour moved to Indianapolis, and while working as a waiter in upscale restaurants and hotels, he joined the Simpson Chapel Methodist Episcopal Church, which was an African American congregation of the predominately-white Methodist Episcopal church.

In 1900, he moved to Cincinnati, Ohio, where he joined the Church of God Restoration Movement, also called the Evening Light Saints. This group was part of the growing Holiness Movement that embraced faith healing and a belief in the imminent return of Christ. They believed one of the signs of the Second Coming of Jesus would be the integration of races in worship. Seymour fully embraced this idea and remained committed to the integration of the church throughout his ministry.

Received Ordination

While living in Cincinnati, Seymour contracted smallpox, which caused him to lose sight in his left eye. His recovery from this potentially fatal illness compelled him to become a preacher, and in 1902 he was ordained as a minister in the Church of God. For the next three years, he traveled as an evangelist, preaching in Chicago as well as in Georgia, Mississippi, Louisiana, and Texas. In 1905, he settled in Houston, where his family had moved. While there, he was invited by April Lucy Farrow, a niece of black abolitionist Frederick Douglass, to become pastor of her Holiness mission near Houston.[647] Through Farrow, Seymour

---

647 Owens, ibid, p. 46

would ultimately meet the man who would have a strong and strategic impact on his spiritual direction and ministry, Charles Fox Parham.

Lucy Farrow knew of Seymour's great interest in the concept of speaking in tongues and encouraged him to contact Parham. Seymour did so and asked Parham if he could attend the Bible school. Parham agreed, but because of his segregationist tendencies, he would not allow Seymour to sit in the classroom.[648] Instead, Seymour was only allowed to listen to the lessons through an open door or window. Seymour's attendance at the school did not last long, perhaps only a few weeks. He was offended by Parham's racism, especially considering that he believed racial integration in worship was a sign of the Second Coming. But through Parham, Seymour learned a great deal about the concept of "the baptism of the Holy Spirit with the evidence of speaking in tongues."

While attending Parham's school in 1905, Seymour served as interim pastor for a small Holiness Church in Houston. Neely Terry, an African American woman who attended a Holiness church pastored by Julia Hutchins in Los Angeles, was visiting her family in Houston late that year and while in Houston attended Seymour's church. That morning, he preached that baptism in the Holy Spirit was accompanied with speaking in tongues. Terry was impressed both with his character and message. Once home in California, Terry suggested to her pastor, Julia Hutchins, that Seymour be invited to speak at her Santa Fe Holiness mission. After receiving the blessing and financial help from Parham, Seymour accepted the invitation for a one-month visit as a divine call to go to Los Angeles.[649]

On his first Sunday morning in L.A., Seymour preached from Acts 2 and demanded that unless an individual spoke in tongues,

648 There is controversy concerning the extent to which Parham was a racist. See Hyatt, ibid, p. 141
649 Owens, ibid, p. 46

he had not experienced the true "baptism of the Holy Spirit." His teaching on speaking in tongues so upset and offended Pastor Hutchins that when Seymour returned for the evening service, the doors were padlocked.

214 North Bonnie Brae Street

Despite the abrupt end of his work at the Santa Fe mission, Seymour believed he was a man on a divine assignment and was determined to continue. To accommodate those wanting to hear his teaching, Seymour accepted the invitation to move the meetings to the home of Richard and Ruth Asberry at 214 North Bonnie Brae Street. In the beginning, the meetings at the Asberrys were attended by only a few African American washwomen and their husbands.[650] Although he consistently taught the concept of "baptism of the Holy Spirit with the evidence of speaking in tongues," Seymour had not yet received the "baptism" and had not spoken in tongues. This made it very difficult for him to lead others into the experience.

News of these meetings on Bonnie Brea Street spread quickly around central L.A., and soon other pastors and churches were attending to hear and experience Seymour's new teaching concerning the Holy Spirit. By late March of 1906, white believers were joining with African American Christians seeking the presence of the Holy Spirit. In response to the growing numbers and the desire of the people, Seymour reached out to Parham for help. Parham sent two of his students, one of which was April Lucy Farrow, a woman who had spoken in tongues with Parham in Houston. She was a genuine help to Seymour and brought great excitement and anticipation to the meetings with her testimonies.[651]

On April 9, 1906, Seymour was leaving his home for the

650 Owens, ibid, p. 47
651 Owens, ibid, p. 48

nightly meeting when he stopped and prayed for Edward Lee to be healed. In the process, Lee shared with him a vision concerning speaking in tongues and asked Seymour to lay hands on him and pray for him to be baptized in the Holy Spirit with the evidence of speaking in tongues. He did so, and Lee became the first person to speak in tongues as Seymour prayed.

When Seymour arrived at the meeting, he shared what had taken place with Lee. Great faith filled the house, when suddenly "Seymour and seven others fell to the floor in a religious ecstasy, speaking with other tongues."[652]

Pentecost Again: April 9, 1906

Once Seymour began to speak in tongues, it was as though a dam had broken and a torrent of the Spirit broke through. It was unstoppable. The moment Seymour and the others fell to the floor, Willella, the young daughter of the Asberrys, ran out of the house terrified.[653] Within minutes, news of what was taking place inside the house quickly spread throughout the neighborhood, and soon people began gathering outside to see firsthand what was happening.

Those inside came out to the porch and began to preach of the baptism of the Holy Spirit with the evidence of speaking in tongues. One of those who had earlier that evening fallen to the floor speaking in tongues was Jennie Moore, who would ultimately become Seymour's wife. She rose from the floor, moved to the old upright piano, and began to play. "Up to this time she had never played the piano, and although she never took a lesson, she was able to play the instrument for the rest of her life."[654]

The next night the crowds were larger. Synan quotes one eyewitness:

652 Vinson Synan, *The Holiness-Pentecostal Movement*, (Grand Rapids: Eerdmans, 1997), p. 106
653 Owens, ibid, p. 49
654 Owens, ibid, p. 49

> They shouted for three days and nights. The people came from everywhere. By the next morning, there was no way to get close to the house. As people came in, they would fall under God's power...They shouted until the foundation of the house gave way, but no one was hurt.[655]

Individuals came from a broad spectrum of income levels and religious backgrounds. The makeup of the crowd itself was a miracle. African Americans, Whites, Hispanics, and Asians, up to 1,300 at a time, came together from across Los Angeles to worship and seek the outpouring of the Holy Spirit. Even Pastor Hutchins, who had locked Seymour out of her church, eventually came and spoke in tongues herself as her whole congregation began to attend the meetings. Soon the crowds became very large and were full of people speaking in tongues, shouting, singing, and moaning in the Spirit. "This was no quiet demonstration; it was full of noisy manifestations, shouts, speaking in tongues, moaning, and singing in tongues that undoubtedly would have frightened any uninitiated within audible range."[656]

Whatever the exact truth of the night of April 9, 1906, without question, something remarkably supernatural took place on Bonnie Brae Street. The crowds grew so large it was impossible to get close to the house, but that did not halt the move of the Holy Spirit. "People reported falling under the power of God and receiving the baptism with the Holy Spirit with the evidence of speaking in tongues while listening to Seymour preach from across the street."[657] Within a week, the numbers were so overwhelming it became necessary to find a larger location for meetings that were literally lasting around the clock.

---

655 *Pentecostal Evangel*, vol. 6, no. 4 (1946), as quoted in Synan, A Century of the Holy Spirit, p. 49
656 Cecil M. Robeck, *The Azusa Street Mission and Revival*, (Nashville: Nelson, 2006)
657 Owens, ibid, p. 50

The Move to 312 Azusa Street

The decision was made to rent the abandoned Stevens African Methodist Episcopal Church for eight dollars a month. The building was located on Azusa Street in the old downtown industrial district, which was part of the original African American area of Los Angeles. The small two-story structure, which had been used in a variety of ways from a lumberyard to a tombstone shop, was in a state of complete disrepair. Several churches and businesses donated time and materials to replace the windows and doors and remove the trash. Sawdust was placed on the floor. Wooden planks on empty nail kegs served as pews to seat thirty to forty people.[658] Once the building was prepared, Seymour set a box on its end in the center of the room and covered it with a cotton cloth to serve as the pulpit.

While the mainstream media ridiculed the revival at Azusa Street, Frank Bartleman, a Holiness evangelist, kept a diary of what he saw and experienced, and Christian newspapers sent his accounts across the country.[659] The Azusa Street Mission also published a newspaper, *The Apostolic Faith*, which was distributed to fifty thousand people, many of them overseas. By mid-May 1906, up to 1,500 people were attempting to fit into the small building on Azusa Street each day.

This was not a revival restricted to the Holiness movement, but Baptists, Methodists, Quakers, and Presbyterians filled the services. The racial mix, which had started on Bonnie Brae Street, continued. African Americans, Whites, Asians, Hispanics, and other ethnic groups were present and warmly welcomed under the same roof. The openness among the races and the encouragement of women in leadership was remarkable, especially in light of the fact that 1906 was the height of the Jim Crow era of racial

---

658 Owens, ibid, p. 52
659 The Los Angeles Times reports were filled with religious and racial bigotry. See Synan, ibid, p. 56

segregation and fourteen years prior to women receiving suffrage in the U.S.

The Meetings at Azusa Street

The first meeting was held on April 14, 1906.

> Meetings begin at ten o'clock every morning and are continued until near midnight. There are three altar services daily. The altar is a plank on two chairs in the center of the room, and here the Holy Ghost falls on men and women and children in old Pentecostal fashion...and every honest believer has received the wonderful incoming of the Holy Spirit to fill and thrill and melt and energize his physical frame and faculties, and the Spirit has witnessed to his presence by using the vocal organs in the speaking forth of a new tongue.[660]

The meetings were rowdy, spontaneous, unstructured with hand-clapping, foot-stomping, shouting, and an overwhelming anticipation of the supernatural. Meetings normally started with prayer, and then the people began to sing. At first there were no instruments, no hymnals. Singing was sporadic and a cappella and often in tongues. Singing in tongues was a major aspect of each meeting. "It was not something that could be repeated at will, but supernaturally given for each special occasion and was one of the most indisputable evidences of the presence of the power of God."[661]

Seymour did not always preach at the meetings, but when he did, his sermons were focused on the need to repent and receive Jesus. "He did not accentuate tongues or any other manifesta-

---

660 Article in "Way of Faith," October 11, 1906. The article was probably written by Frank Bartleman, a Holiness preacher and participant in the Azusa Revival. As quoted in Synan, ibid, p. 51
661 A.W. Orwig, "Apostolic Faith Restored," *Weekly Evangel*, 18 March 1916, p.4, as quoted by Owens, ibid, p. 57

tion."[662] At times there was spontaneous preaching from others who felt anointed for the moment, and altar calls for salvation, sanctification, and the baptism of the Holy Spirit. At various moments throughout the meetings, the Spirit would spontaneously flow through the room, "knocking people down in ones, twos, and sometimes by the hundreds. Often masses of people would simultaneously rush the altar to seek after God."[663]

There were few periods of silence. Some continually shouted throughout the meetings. Individuals gave testimonies while members of the mission read aloud testimonies sent by mail. There was prayer for the gift of tongues, prayer in tongues for the sick, for missionaries, and whatever requests given by those present or received by mail. Miracles occurred each day. Individuals who spoke foreign languages were being spoken to in their native language by uneducated members of the mission, who translated the languages into English by "supernatural ability."[664]

The Remarkable Impact

The Azusa Street Revival only last three years. The mission never grew to more than fifty to sixty members.[665] Yet hundreds and thousands of people came and stayed temporarily over the years. Following 1909, the mission became a small African American Holiness church, one among many in Los Angeles, and William Seymour, though honored by some, was ignored and scorned by the vast majority of the church. But what came out of the Azusa Revival is staggering in terms of churches planted, denominations birthed, and global missions launched.[666] What began as the

---

662 Owens, ibid, p. 60
663 Owens, ibid, p. 57
664 Richard Newmann and James S. Tinney, *Black Apostles*, (G.K. Hall & Co., 1978)
665 See, Jack W. Hayford and David S. Moore, *The Charismatic Century: The Enduring Impact of the Azusa Street Revival*, (New York: Warner Faith, 2006)
666 See Owens, ibid, p. 65–68

commitment of one young African American man was anointed by the Holy Spirit and changed the world.

19

Releasing Tongues

The numbers are staggering. From a relative handful of marginalized believers at the beginning of the twentieth century has come an eruption of more than 600 million individuals across all denominational lines who speak, pray, and sing in tongues. Today, there is no nation on earth that does not have a body of Christians who speak in tongues. This unprecedented growth makes charismatic Christianity the fastest growing segment of the church in history.

As exciting as the numbers are, they are not adequate. Speaking in tongues is not simply an incidental experience to compete with other Christian experiences in hopes of gaining more followers. Rather, correctly understood, speaking, praying, and singing in tongues is to be a part of each Christian's life on a regular basis. Ultimately, the question is not how many people speak in tongues, but how are tongues released so "that you all speak in tongues?"[667] That answer is discovered by resolving several specific questions regarding tongues.

---

667 1 Corinthians 14:5

The first question concerns the mechanics of tongue speech. What are the dynamics of tongue speech? What actually takes place when an individual speaks in tongues? The Apostle Paul confronted these questions with his First Letter to the Church at Corinth. Fortunately, he was very specific with his answers. He began by describing the mechanics of tongue speech. Paul stated, "One who speaks in tongues does not speak to men, but to God; for no one understands, but in his spirit he speaks mysteries."[668]

He went further and personalized the experience: "For if I pray in a tongue, my spirit prays, but my mind is unfruitful."[669]

The details of the workings of tongue speech are truly remarkable. When a Christian releases his or her voice to speak, pray, or sing in tongues, the Holy Spirit speaks, prays, or sings through the spirit of that Christian. The mechanics are both natural and simultaneously supernatural.

The Apostle Peter helped to clarify the mechanics of tongue speech in his sermon at Pentecost. Reaching back to the Prophet Joel, Peter declared, "I will in those days pour forth of My Spirit."[670] Peter told the gathered crowd at Pentecost that the tongues they heard were the direct result of the work of the Holy Spirit, and it was something they should have expected from the promised Messiah. Later in his sermon he speaks of Jesus and demands, "He has poured forth that which you both see and hear."[671]

Peter's answer was extremely insightful. Jesus died, descended into hell, was born again, raised to be the firstborn from the dead, ascended back to the Father, received His kingdom, and on the day of Pentecost was actively pouring forth the Holy Spirit upon His church. This powerful presence of the Holy Spirit was demonstrated by tongues. As he promised, the Lord Jesus, reigning as King of kings, poured forth the Holy Spirit upon the church, and

---

668 1 Corinthians 14:2
669 1 Corinthians 14:14
670 Acts 2:18
671 Acts 2:33

they spoke in tongues. What happened? The Holy Spirit spoke through their spirits. Thus the pattern was established: When a person speaks, prays, or sings in tongues, it is the Holy Spirit using their spirit and tongue to speak, pray, or sing. It is thoroughly supernatural, yet the instruments being used are the spirit and tongue of the individual Christian.

The second question is also technical: what is tongue speech?

Through the centuries, there has been a wide variety of answers regarding the essence of tongue speech. What is it? Is tongue speech simply mindless utterances, or is it, as some have contended, actual human languages that are simply unknown to the speakers?[672] [673] Several have believed it to be the language of heaven or at least from heaven. [674] [675] Others have declared it to be some ecstatic, unintelligible utterances that require a highly charged emotional moment to experience.[676]

Once again, the Apostle Paul answered this question. By his clear analogy to actual human languages, it is obvious that Paul believed tongue speech was indeed a language, but not a human language.[677] When he wrote of actual human languages, he used the Greek word φωνὴν or *sound*, but when writing of tongues, he used γλώσσαις or *tongue*. The apostle believed tongue speech to be a mystery language of heaven in which a Christian speaks to God, a language that no human understands.

The third question: what are the uses of tongue speech? There are two. One is the personal prayer and devotional tongue

---

672 James D.G. Dunn, *Jesus and the Spirit*, (Grand Rapids, Eerdmans, 1975), 248

673 Siegfreid Grossman, *Charisma: The Gifts of the Spirit*. Trans. Susan Wiesmann, (Wheaton, IL: Key Publishers, 1971) p. 77–78

674 Dunn, *Jesus and the Spirit*, ibid, p. 244

675 Donald Bridge and David Phypers, *Spiritual Gifts and the Church*, (Downers Grove, IL: InterVarsity Press, 1973)

676 Charles Kingsley Barrett, "Commentary on First Corinthians," in *Harper's New Testament Commentaries*, ed. Henry Chadwick, (New York: Harper and Row, 1968), p. 286

677 1 Corinthians 14:10f, 21f

given to each Christian. The Apostle Paul explained speaking in tongues as prayer and worship: "One who speaks in a tongue does not speak to men, but to God."[678] This is the supernatural language of prayer. It is directed to God, who alone can understand. At times, this prayer language is private and deeply personal, but at other times, it can be used in corporate prayer and singing in tongues within the church.

The second use of tongue speech is a ministry gift, and it is designed for and within the congregation. Paul clarified, "God has appointed in the Church ... various kinds of tongues."[679] Think of what is being said. God himself has appointed certain gifts to be present and active in the church of the Lord Jesus Christ, and one of them is various kinds of tongues. There is no word of cessation; no mention that tongues would ever cease being an essential component of the church.

The gift of various kinds of tongues is given to the Church for a critically important ministry for both Christians and non-Christians. If the gift of tongues is allowed to function inside the church, the Lord Jesus will speak to His church through the gift of tongues, and the gift will function as a sign to those who need Jesus as Lord and Savior. When utilized correctly, the gift of tongues should be a part of every public meeting of the church of the Lord Jesus Christ.

The fourth question: should each Christian speak, pray, and sing in tongues? There are two answers: yes and no. Yes, each individual who receives Jesus as Lord and Savior should and can definitely pray and sing in tongues. No exceptions. And no, not every Christian will operate in the gift of tongues to be used in the congregation.

Consider personal prayer and singing in tongues. How can it be stated with certainty that this manifestation of the Holy Spirit should be part of each Christian's life? As far as the Apostle Paul

678 1 Corinthians 14:2
679 1 Corinthians 12:28

was concerned, the answer was crystal clear. First, there was his apostolic desire: "Now I wish that you all spoke in tongues."[680]

θέλω δὲ πάντας ὑμᾶς λαλεῖν γλώσσαις

The Greek here is important. Paul used the postpositive conjunction, δὲ. By doing so, he brought to the verb *I wish*, θέλω, an emphatic sense meaning *indeed, really,* or *in fact.*[681] The verb is first person, present, active, indicative, meaning emphatically, "*Indeed*, I wish that you all speak in tongues." It was the absolute desire of the Apostle Paul that all Christians speak in tongues throughout the history of the church. The wish was followed by a ringing endorsement of tongues: "I thank God, I speak in tongues more than you all."[682] (This is a Pauline pattern. He seldom commanded, even though he reminded his people that he had the right to do so (Philemon 8, 14).)

Ultimately there was the unarguable summation of the Apostle Paul regarding tongues. He stated emphatically, "What is the outcome then? I will pray with the spirit [speaking of the Holy Spirit praying through his spirit]. I will pray with my mind also [speaking of the Holy Spirit praying through his mind]."[683] To this he adds, "Pray at all times in the Spirit."[684]

Saint Jude joined with the Apostle Paul in his expectation of praying in tongues being an aspect of each Christian's life. He exclaimed, "But you, beloved, building yourselves up on your most holy faith, praying in the Holy Spirit."[685]

---

680 1 Corinthians 14:5
681 Brooke Foss Westcott and Fenton John Anthony Hort, *Greek New Testament*, (Peabody, MA: Hendrickson, 1988), p. 244 "This particle has still another use which but very few Greek scholars have expressed; i.e., it is emphatic or intensive at times, and means the equivalent of indeed, really, in fact."
682 1 Corinthians 14:18
683 1 Corinthians 14:15, emphasis added
684 Ephesians 6:18
685 Jude 20

The Apostle Paul emphatically closed his letter to Corinth with a strong Greek imperative, μὴ κωλύετε: "Do not forbid to speak in tongues."[686]

For the Apostle Paul, it was a settled issue. In his walk with the Lord Jesus, and thus in the lives of those he oversaw as an Apostle, they were to follow his example and pray and sing in tongues. In addition to the clear apostolic mandate of Paul, which should be sufficient, there were biblical examples of speaking in tongues that included everyone. First was Pentecost. There were one hundred and twenty people in one room who "with one mind were continually devoting themselves to prayer, along with the women, and Mary the mother of Jesus, and with his brothers."[687] When the day of Pentecost came, "they were all together in one place."[688] Then the violent rushing wind filled the house, tongues of fire came, and "rested upon each one of them."[689] They were each born again as "they were all filled with the Holy Spirit and began to speak in tongues."[690]

So, in one room, one hundred and twenty individuals are all filled with the Holy Spirit, and each one of them spoke in tongues simultaneously. This experience was not reserved for the original disciples or just the men or some chosen ones. In fact, no one was left out. It is imperative to recall what they were doing. The one hundred and twenty were not speaking in tongues for the sake of a crowd. There was no crowd. The crowd did not gather until some time after the followers of Jesus began to speak and praise God in tongues. What took place was a prayer and praise meeting in which each person prayed and praised in tongues. When people heard the sound of prayer and praise coming from the

---

686 1 Corinthians 14:39
687 Acts 1:14
688 Acts 2:1 emphasis added
689 Acts 2:3 emphasis added
690 Acts 2:4 See my chapter two for an understanding of the events of Pentecost.

upper room, a crowed gathered, or as Luke recorded, "When this sound occurred, the multitude came together ...,"[691] not before.

Another example of an all-inclusive tongues experience was at the home of the Roman Cornelius. The Apostle Peter was preaching when "the Holy Spirit fell upon all those who were listening to the message."[692] What did these Gentiles do? Peter and those with him heard "them speaking with tongues and exalting God."[693] Once again, just as took place at Pentecost, each one of them spoke in tongues simultaneously. Obviously, the answer to whether or not each Christian should speak in tongues is settled. To Apostles Peter and Paul, and therefore to every Christian throughout the history of the church, the answer is a resounding Yes! Yes, each Christian should have ongoing prayer and praise experiences in tongues.

While it is true that each Christian should have an active prayer and praise language in tongues, not every Christian will be used to deliver messages in tongues in the meetings of the church. But some will. The Apostle Paul was very precise in speaking of the order of the public congregational meeting. He instructed, "All do not speak in tongues ... all do not interpret."[694]

One of the most important gifts to the church is the message delivered to the congregation in tongues. The Apostle Paul expected each believer at Corinth to seek the gifts of the Spirit, which definitely included both private and public use of speaking in tongues. There was no word of caution, no word of warning; rather, the Apostle added a requirement that would bring order to the public life of the church: "If anyone speaks in a tongue, it should be by two or at the most three, and each in turn, and one must interpret; but if there is no interpreter, he must keep silent in the church; and let him speak to himself and to God."[695]

---

691 Acts 2:6
692 Acts 10:44 emphasis added
693 Acts 10:46
694 1 Corinthians 12:30
695 1 Corinthians 14:27–28

The Apostle Paul drew a parallel between prophecy and interpreted public tongues. He raised prophecy to its rightful place in the congregation and quickly explained his rationale. Once again, this is for the edification of the church congregationally. However, this in no way dampens Paul's commitment to and belief in both private and public tongue speech. He maintains "greater is one who prophesies than one who speaks in tongues, unless he interprets, so that the church may receive edifying."[696]

Obviously, Paul believed God would gift certain ones in the congregation with the ministry of interpretation.[697] If the person giving the message in tongues could not give the interpretation, those individuals were to do so.

There was no doubt that for the Apostle Paul, prophecy in public meetings of the church was more important than the utilization of the gift of tongues, that is, unless the message in tongues is interpreted. Paul established the principle for the church: interpreted tongue speech is equal to prophecy. When public tongue speech was interpreted in the church, it could manifest itself as revelation, knowledge, prophecy, or teaching. "But now, brethren, if I come to you speaking in tongues, what will I profit you unless I speak to you either by way of revelation or of knowledge or of prophecy or of teaching?"[698] Remember, Paul was making his case for the equality of interpreted messages in tongues to the church as he simultaneously argued for the primacy of prophecy. He did so over several verses, decrying the misuse of uninterpreted public tongue speech in the congregation.

"Therefore let one who speaks in a tongue pray that he may interpret."[699]

The great apostle placed a high value on both public and private tongue speech. He believed that when a Christian prays

---

696 1 Corinthians 14:5
697 1 Corinthians 12:10
698 1 Corinthians 14:6
699 1 Corinthians 14:13

in tongues, the Holy Spirit prays through his spirit. Since he believed messages in tongues were equal to prophecy when interpreted, messages in tongues were not to be mishandled or confusing. They must be allowed to fulfill their supernatural role in the life of the church and the Christian. But while placing demands upon the use of tongues, he remained fully committed to its authenticity and irreplaceable standing in the church. "What is the outcome then, brethren? When you assemble, each one has a psalm, has a teaching, has a revelation, has a tongue, has an interpretation. Let all things be done for edification."[700]

Most importantly, the Apostle Paul demanded "let all things be done!" Whatever restrictions he placed were to ensure that messages in tongues to the congregation would continue to take place in the life of the church at Corinth and thereby throughout the history of the church of the Lord Jesus. Specifically, let messages in tongues continue to be a part of the meetings of the church as long as they are interpreted, "for God is not a God of confusion but of peace, as in all the churches of the saints."[701] Remember that the demand of interpretation is only placed on messages in tongues spoken to the congregation, not on corporate prayer or praise given in tongues.

The fifth question: why would a Christian desire to speak in tongues?

First and foremost because Jesus promised that for those who choose to follow him, speaking in tongues was to be a part of their supernatural walk with him. That should settle the issue for every believer. "These signs shall follow those who believe ... they will speak with new tongues."[702]

700 1 Corinthians 14:26
701 1 Corinthians 14:33
702 Mark 16:17 Despite the nearly universal concern that verses 9–20 are a second-century interpolation, they cannot be discounted. First, these verses were known by the church no more than a few decades from the original writing which indicates the words were certainly accepted early as those of the Lord Jesus. Second, if they were an interpolation, it establishes the fact that speaking in tongues was

There are those who resist speaking in tongues and contend it is not for them, but the clear promise of Jesus is that every Christian can and should have a consistent prayer and praise life filled with speaking, praying, and singing in tongues. When a person becomes a Christian, decides to follow Jesus, tongues comes in the salvation package!

Second, "Whatever others (in the world or Church!) may think, when people speak in tongues, they begin to experience in a fresh way the reality of God."[703] When a Christian prays in the Spirit, there comes a moment of awareness both of the presence of the Holy Spirit and that he or she is actually praying the will of God over their life and situation. The more time spent praying in the Spirit, the greater this realization. Many nights I have joined with my pastoral team and prayed for an hour in tongues. The depth of awareness of the Lord is always remarkable, and the supernatural manifestations of the Spirit are very real and powerful.

Third, tongues enable a Christian to reach a new depth of prayer and praise. When Christians begin to pray in tongues, "they find themselves free to praise and thank and adore and glorify their heavenly Father as never before."[704] The Apostle Paul made a clear distinction between praying with the mind and allowing the Holy Spirit to pray through the spirit of a Christian. To pray with the mind is to pray limited to the intellect. This is not bad. Even when praying with the mind, a Christian can be

---

an anticipated aspect of each believer's practice "in both the Jewish and Hellenistic Christians of the first century." Dunn. *Jesus and the Spirit*, p. 246. And third, these verses were ultimately canonized. Searches for interpolations will always continue, but these verses are contested more for their content than dating.

703 J. Rodman Williams, *A Theological Pilgrimage*, chap. 9, retrieved on the World Wide Web, 3.31.09, @ http://www.jrodmanwilliams. net/theological-pilgrimage/tp09.html Parenthesis included

704 Michael Green, *I Believe in the Holy Spirit*, (Grand Rapids, MI: Eerdmans, 1995), p. 198

led by the Spirit by giving visions, words of wisdom, and even words of prophecy.

"When you pray in tongues, your voice is an expression of your spirit,"[705] which is being directed by the Holy Spirit. "Speaking in tongues is not ecstasy; for there is continuing control under the direction of the Holy Spirit. There is joy, elevation—but no irrationality, no lack of conscious control."[706] There is no limit to this remarkable manifestation of the Holy Spirit and the depths of prayer it allows a Christian to experience.

Fourth, speaking, praying, and singing in tongues edifies the individual Christian. "One who speaks in a tongue edifies himself."[707] This is not in any way undesirable. The Greek word for *edifies* is οἰκοδομεῖ; its meaning is to strengthen, to build up, to make more able. The question must be asked as to how tongue speech edifies either the individual or the church. The answer is not difficult.

If tongue speech is truly what it is claimed to be by the Apostle Paul—the Holy Spirit speaking, praying, or singing through a Christian's spirit—then it is the most basic way in which a Christian touches the supernatural presence of God in an ongoing way. Any opportunity to experience the presence of God would be edifying, for it brings confidence in the great love of God for the Christian and the position the Christian holds before God with the ability to allow the Spirit to flow through the Christian at any moment. For instance, when an individual attends a meeting of the church and a message in tongues is spoken and interpreted, this too can be a powerful moment of edification. As the interpretation is released, the Holy Spirit brings to light the will of the Lord Jesus and in doing so speaks a directed word to that person.

---

705 Robert Heidler, *Experiencing the Spirit*, (Ventura, CA: Renew, 1998), p. 162
706 Williams, *A Theological Pilgrimage*, ibid, chap. 9
707 1 Corinthians 14:4

The result is wonderful. Where there was confusion and uncertainty, there is then clarity of purpose and destiny.

This same edification occurs as a Christian joins with the congregation in singing in tongues. Worship words are limited, but tongue speech is limitless, so as the congregation sings in tongues, the Holy Spirit takes them deeper and deeper into the depths of worship and into the very presence of the Lord Jesus. Saints have reported powerful experiences of singing in tongues through the centuries; this was the foremost spiritual release at Azusa Street. Singing in tongues brings great unity to the congregation and takes the individual Christian to a new awareness of the presence of the Lord and the unique place he or she has before the Lord. That is edification!

Arguments have been made and are still being made that a Christian who speaks in tongues is being self-centered and should turn his or her attention away from him or herself and toward the church and the world. That reasoning is absolutely absurd since it is Paul who contended that interpreted tongues was equal to prophecy and insisted that "one who prophesies edifies the Church."[708] So if a Christian speaks, prays, or sings in tongues, he or she edifies him or herself, and if he or she brings a message in tongues and it is interpreted, he or she edifies—strengthens, builds up, or makes more able—the church.

This Pauline insistence on edification appeared in other writings of the apostle. Paul encouraged Christians to edify themselves and others. He stated, "Pursue the things which make for peace and the building up of one another."[709] The word is οἰκοδομῆς; it is from the same root word in the Greek for *edify*. It speaks once again of strengthening and building up. The Christian is to aggressively pursue the activities in the Spirit that builds up his or her spirit and the things that build up his or her brothers

708 1 Corinthians 14:4
709 Romans 14:19. It is doubtful Paul has speaking in tongues in mind, but the principle remains.

and sisters. The apostle again uses the word in his Letter to the Church at Rome, and this time there is a demand attached. "Let each of us please his neighbor for his good, to his edification."[710] *Let each of us* is an imperative. It means do it!

Fifth, the Apostle Paul demanded that speaking, praying, and singing in tongues is desirable because it also allows the Christian to enter into intercession with the aid of the Holy Spirit.

> In the same way the Spirit also helps our weakness; for we do not know how to pray as we should, but the Spirit Himself intercedes for us with groanings too deep for words; and He who searches the hearts knows what the mind of the Spirit is, because He intercedes for the saints according to the will of God.[711]

These are remarkable verses. In the midst of describing the glory the Christian would ultimately enter in eternity, the Apostle Paul turned and demanded that an aspect of eternal glory was to be experienced by the Christian in this life as he or she entered into intercession with the Holy Spirit. This was charismatic prayer, praying in tongues. Paul did not teach that the Holy Spirit was interceding for the Christian apart from the Christian, but that the Spirit was constantly interceding through Christians. "What Paul seems to have in mind is the only form of prayer left to the believer when he comes to the end of himself, frustrated with his own weakness and baffled by his ignorance of God and God's will."[712] Paul declared that at that moment or any moment, the Christian has absolute freedom to pray in tongues and tap into the ever-available intercessory ministry of the Holy Spirit. Great strength and spiritual courage come from knowing the Holy Spirit will intercede with a Christian and pray the will of God in his or her life as he or she seeks direction, does spiritual war-

---

710 Romans 15:2
711 Romans 8:26–27
712 Dunn, *Jesus and the Spirit*, ibid, p. 241

fare, prays for the release of miracles, or any other need of the believer. Timidity, doubt, and fear are replaced with a boldness that no individual could possibly possess in her or his own power or strength.

Sixth, speaking, praying, and singing in tongues usually serves as a catalyst to other gifts and manifestations of the Holy Spirit. Immediately after their experience of speaking in tongues at Pentecost, "many wonders and signs were taking place through the apostles."[713] Peter and John healed the lame man at the Beautiful Gate. [714]

> And all the more believers in the Lord, multitudes of men and women, were constantly added to their number, to such an extent that they even carried the sick out into the streets and laid them on cots and pallets, so that when Peter came by at least his shadow might fall on any one of them. Also the people from the cities in the vicinity of Jerusalem were coming together, bringing people who were sick or afflicted with unclean spirits, and they were all being healed.[715]

Miracles, words of prophecy, words of wisdom, and physical healings flow from the life of those who speak in tongues.

Seventh, Paul stated that speaking, praying, and singing in tongues is a sign to those who have never accepted Jesus as Lord and Savior: "So then tongues are a sign, not to those who believe, but to unbelievers." [716] This is a remarkable statement, especially in light of the fact that the church, at least the American church, has convinced itself of the exact opposite.

Among many of the most wonderful committed leaders there is an aversion to speaking in tongues out of a genuine fear that if

713 Acts 2:43
714 Acts 3:1–8
715 Acts 5:14–16
716 1 Corinthians 14:22

it is allowed in the church, it will cripple the ability of the church to reach the lost. Paul claimed the exact opposite. He stated unequivocally that the release of the supernatural in the church by speaking, praying, and singing in tongues would be a positive sign, not to those who are Christians and do not need a sign, but to those outside Christianity, who desperately need to experience the manifestations of the Spirit as a sign to draw them into salvation. Of course, the Apostle would expect order in the church, but he would override a dead or misguided order to demand *let all things be done*, which calls for tongues.[717] If history is the lesson, once the Church quits being embarrassed and apologizing for the supernatural and releases the gifts, including tongues, those outside the Church will be drawn by the power of the Spirit and His awesome ability to speak to them and meet their needs.

Eighth, the Apostle Paul considered praying in tongues an essential element in the Christian's armor. He stated, "With all prayer and petition pray at all times in the Spirit."[718]

The Greek word for *pray* in this verse is προσευχόμενοι. It is a present, middle participle and carries with it not a demand but an expectation that all Christians would pray in the Spirit and that they would pray in the Spirit in tongues. He voiced this expectation in the midst of itemizing the armor needed by the Christian to do battle with the enemy, Satan, and his demonic forces. "Take up the full armor," he demanded, "that you may be able to stand firm against the schemes of the devil." [719] Obviously, to the Apostle Paul, no Christian was truly prepared for battle without an active prayer life that included praying in the Spirit in tongues. He made his demand as strong as possible when he used the Greek word in the second person, plural, Greek imperative, ἀναλάβετε. It is an all-inclusive command: *You all take up the full armor*, and full armor meant tongues!

717 1 Corinthians 14:26
718 Ephesians 6:18
719 Ephesians 6:13

Paul seemed to include another warfare strategy dealing with tongues. He insisted that when a Christian uses tongue speech, she or he speaks in a heavenly language that "no one understands," then goes even further and contends that "in his spirit he speaks mysteries."[720] Strategically, the Apostle saw tongues as a part of the Christian armor and as a mystery language that no one understands, not even the enemy. Dunn contends that a Christian who is speaking in tongues is "holding a secret conversation with God."[721] It is a conversation not even the forces of hell can decode!

It is very important not to be fooled in this area; it is too important. The expectation of the Apostle was explicit: the full armor included speaking, praying, and singing in tongues. In fact, every critic who desires to deny the validity of tongue speech must develop some scheme to destroy Paul's teaching, for the Apostle was absolute. Praying in tongues was to be a part of every believer's arsenal.

The last question: how does one begin speaking in tongues?

Notice the question. It is not how a Christian receives the baptism of the Holy Spirit with the evidence of speaking in tongues. Hopefully, through the first six chapters of this work, it became clear that the baptism of the Holy Spirit is the salvific moment when the Holy Spirit baptizes an individual into Christ Jesus, and King Jesus baptizes the new Christian with the Holy Spirit. The salvation of Jesus brought with it the full baptism of the Holy Spirit, and the manifestations of the Spirit are to be immediately released in the life of each new believer. There is nothing to receive beyond the Lord Jesus and his salvation. There is no second or third blessing that must be "prayed through" to receive. Each individual Christian has been baptized by the Holy Spirit. That being true, the question should be asked: how does a Christian release tongues?

---

720 1 Corinthians 14:2
721 Dunn, *Jesus and the Spirit*, ibid, p. 244

To begin, it must be stated that if it were not for cultural and ecclesiastical suppression of speaking, praying, and singing in tongues, this question would never be asked. This is not a mild suppression. There are some who hate the very idea of speaking in tongues and are openly hostile toward it and totally distort its biblical validity. Pastors have lost their ministries because they speak in tongues; seminaries are closed to those who speak in tongues; missionaries are fired or told they will be fired if they speak in tongues. The tragedy is that millions of Christians have been reared in churches that teach speaking in tongues as evil and even demonic. If the truth of speaking, praying, and singing in tongues were not so demonized inside and belittled outside the church, each new Christian would emerge from his salvation experience speaking and praising God in tongues. That is the New Testament model! But since this has become an abnormal moment in the life of the church, there are some necessary intellectual and emotional steps that can help to overcome the suppression of the ministry and gifts of the Holy Spirit and release the manifestation of tongues.

First, before anything else, pray and thank the Lord Jesus for His wonderful multifaceted salvation, which includes the baptism of the Holy Spirit. Ask the Lord to take every hindering spirit out of the way. Then ask our precious Savior and Lord for the release of speaking or praying or singing in tongues beyond the limits of the mind.[722] Many times, that is sufficient and a believer will begin to speak in tongues. Remember, in his exalted position as King of kings and Lord of lords, Jesus is the baptizer, and He is the one who wants each Christian to experience the edifying ministry of tongue speech.

Second, it is important, though not necessary, to be convinced that speaking in tongues is a legitimate Christian experience. There must be a degree of confidence and openness that the

---

722 1 Corinthians 14:2

experience is valid. If it is needed, take time to study the history and theology of Christianity until the issue is settled.[723] Find a church where the gifts of the Spirit are in operation. Be careful; many churches claim to be open to speaking in tongues but refuse to or are embarrassed to demonstrate the gift. Those churches will not help a believer to release speaking, praying, or singing in tongues. This does not mean that a Christian must wait until every question has been resolved or that the experience of speaking in tongues is the result of a mental assent to its truth. Although God will not override an individual's will, the supernatural manifestations of the Holy Spirit can override doubt. However, "There is no *compulsion* involved in speaking in tongues. God does not *compel* His people to do things; He *inspires* them."[724] So purposely get fully inspired!

Third, the release of speaking in tongues calls for sensitivity and responsiveness to the Holy Spirit. When a Christian speaks in tongues, it is a supernatural experience. If a Christian is serious about releasing tongues, the Holy Spirit will enable it to happen. Perhaps it will be in prayer or in worship when words of understanding fail, and there is a desire to go on deeper in prayer and praise. It may be a highly charged emotional moment, or it may not be, but at that point, speak! Do not be afraid to speak with syllables and sounds that are unknown. Respond. After all, tongue speech is the Holy Spirit speaking through a human voice, so at some point, a Christian must allow his voice to make sounds he does not understand.

Fourth, refuse to quit or be discouraged. Keep praying. Keep worshipping. Keep singing. Speak whatever, regardless of how unusual or unsophisticated it may seem or sound. Some Christians needlessly struggle with years of questions, faulty theology,

---

723 I have purposely presented this work in a highly structured way to be read again and again.
724 Dennis and Rita Bennett, *The Holy Spirit and You*, (Gainesville, FL: Bridge-Logos, reprint: 2006), p. 61

threats, and fear before releasing tongues, so do not grow weary; do not be discouraged.[725] It will happen! "God indeed keeps His side of the bargain and begins to shape the sound which you continue to give Him into a language of prayer and praise."[726]

Finally, don't be surprised by what occurs. Some Christians release tongues and it is a spontaneous explosion. Others begin with little more than one syllable. Some shake, some mumble, some shout, and some are absolutely calm. None of these matter. Follow the leadership of the Holy Spirit; He will enable the release of supernatural speaking, praying, or singing in tongues.

Remember, as is true in one's entire relationship with the Lord Jesus Christ and His remarkable salvation, speaking, praying, and singing in tongues requires faith. The exciting aspect of faith is that faith itself is a gift of the Holy Spirit. He gifts Christians with the faith to fully obey and receive the will of King Jesus. So as Christians submit to the will of the King and release their tongue speech, there is always an abundance of faith so that all will speak in tongues.[727]

---

725 Some of the greatest Charismatic leaders struggled to release tongues. Read the stories of Seymour, Wigglesworth, Hagan and others.
726 Larry Christenson, *Speaking in Tongues*, (Minneapolis: Bethany House, 1981), p. 127
727 1Corinthians 14:5

Bibliography

A

Alfeyev, Hilarion, *St. Symeon, the New Theologian, and Orthodox Tradition*, Oxford, England: Oxford Press, 2000)

Ambrose, "Of the Spirit," *Nicene and Post-Nicene Fathers*, ed. Philip Schaff and Henry Wace, (Peabody, MA: Hendrickson, 1999)

Ash, James L. Jr., "The Decline of Ecstatic Prophecy" *The Early Church, Theological Studies* (1976)

Athanasius, "Life of Antony," *Nicene and Post-Nicene Fathers*, ed.

Archibald Robertson, (Peabody, MA: 1999)

Augustine, "Homilies on First Epistle of John," *Nicene and Post Nicene Fathers* ed. Philip Schaff, (Peabody, MA: Hendrickson, 1999)

Augustine, "On Baptism Against the Donatists," *Nicene and Post Nicene Fathers*, ed. Philip Schaff, (Peabody, MA: Hendrickson, 1999)

Augustine, "On the Psalms," *Nicene and Post-Nicene Fathers*, ed. Philip Schaff, (Peabody, MA: Hendrickson, 1999)

Augustine, "The City of God," *Nicene and Post-Nicene Fathers*, ed. Philip Schaff, (Peabody, MA.: Henderson, 1999)

Augustine, "The Epistle of Saint John," *Nicene and Post-Nicene Fathers*, ed. Philip Schaff, (Peabody, MA.: Henderson, 1999)

Augustine, "Sermons on New Testament Lessons," *Nicene and Post-Nicene Fathers*, ed. Philip Schaff, (Peabody, MA.: Henderson, 1999)

B

Balfour, David, *Saint Gregory the Sinaite: Discourse on the Transfiguration*, (Athens: 1982)

Barrett, Charles Kingsley, "Commentary on First Corinthians," *Harper's New Testament Commentaries*, ed. Henry Chadwick, (New York: Harper and Row, 1968)

Bartleman, Frank, *Another Wave Rolls In*, (Northridge, CA: Voice Publications, 1970)

Basil, "Letters," *Nicene and Post Nicene Fathers,* ed. Philip Schaff, (Peabody, MA: Hendrickson, 1999)

Bauer, Walter, *Greek-English Lexicon*, ed. Fredrick William Danker, (Chicago: University of Chicago Press, 2000)

Baxter, Ronald E., *Charismatic Gift of Tongues*, (Grand Rapids: Kregel, 1985)

Baxter, George A., "The Great Revival in Kentucky," *The Connecticut Evangelical Magazine*, II. 354, (Hartford: March, 1802)

Beecher, Lyman, *The Autobiography of Lyman Beecher*, (Cambridge, MA: Harvard University Press, 1961)

Bennett, Dennis and Rita, *The Holy Spirit and You*, (Gainesville, FL: Bridge-Logos, 2006)

Bible Knowledge Commentary, John F. Walvoord, and Roy B. Zuck, eds., (US: Victor Books, 1983)

Bloesch, Donald G., *The Holy Spirit* (Downers Grove, IL: InterVarsity Press, 2000)

Blumhofer, Edith L., "Restoration as Revival," *Modern Christian Revivals*, ed. Edith Blumhofer and Randall Balmer, (Chicago: University of Illinois Press, 1993)

Bonaventure, "The Triple Way," *The Works of Bonaventure*, trans. Jose de Vinck (Paterson, N.J.: St. Anthony Guild Press, 1960)

Bovon, Francois, "The Canonical Structure of Gospel and Apostle," *The Canon Debate*, ed. MacDonald, Lee Martin and Sanders,

James A., (Peabody, MA: Hendrickson Publishers, 2002)

Bridge, Donald and Phypers, David, *Spiritual Gifts and the Church*, (Downers Grove, IL: InterVarsity Press, 1973)

Brinton, Crane, *A History of Civilization*, (Englewood Cliffs, NJ: Prentice Hall, 1976)

Brown, Raymond E., *Introduction to the New Testament*, (New York: Doubleday, 1997)

Bruce, F. F., *The Acts of the Apostles*, (Grand Rapids: Eerdmans, 1960)

Bruce, F. F., *The Gospel of John*, (Grand Rapids: Eerdmans Publishing, 1983)

Burgess, Stanley, *The Holy Spirit: Ancient Traditions*, (Peabody, MA: Hendrickson, 1994)

Burgess, Stanley M., *The Holy Spirit: Medieval Roman Catholic and Reformation Traditions*, (Peabody, MA: Hendrickson, 1997)

Burgess, Stanley, *The Holy Spirit: Eastern Christian Traditions*, (Peabody, MA: Hendrickson, 1998)

Burgess, Stanley, ed. *Dictionary of Pentecostal and Charismatic Movements*, (Grand Rapids, MI: Zondervan, 1988)

Butler, Alban, *The Lives of the Saints*, (Baltimore: Murphy & Co., 1889)

Burdick, Donald, W., *Tongues: To Speak or Not to Speak*, (Chicago: Moody Press, 1969)

C

Campenhausen, Hans von, *The Formation of the Christian Bible*, trans. J.A. Baker, (Philadelphia: Fortress, 1972)

Cameron, George G., *Highlights of Our Heritage; Some Landmarks in Our Church's Advance,* (Edinburgh: MacCorquodale & Co., 1953)

Cartwright, Peter, *The Autobiography of Peter Cartwright*, (Nashville:

Abington Press, 1956)

Carwardine, Richard, "The Second Great Awakening in Comparative Perspective: Revivals and Culture in the United States and Britain," *Modern Christian Revivals*, ed. Edith L. Blumhofer and Randall Balmer, (Chicago: University of Illinois Press, 1993)

Chadwick, Henry, *The Early Church*, (London: Pelican Books, 1993)

Chilton, David, *The Days of Vengeance*, (Tyler, TX: Dominion Press, 1987)

Christenson, Larry, *Speaking in Tongues*, (Minneapolis: Bethany House, 1981)

Chrysostom, "Homilies on First Corinthians," *Nicene and Post-Nicene Fathers*, ed. Philip Schaff, (Peabody, MA: Hendrickson, 1999)

Cicero, *In Defense of Manilian Law*, *http://www.uvm.edu/~bsaylor/rome/pompeyoration.html*

Clasen, Claus-Peter, *Anabaptism, a Social History 1525–1618: Switzerland, Austria, Moravia, South and Central Germany* (Ithaca, Cornell University Press, 1972)

Clement, "First Letter to the Corinthians," *Ante-Nicene Fathers*, (Peabody, MA: Hendrickson Pub, 1999)

Cohen, Shaye I.D., *Frontline, Legitimization Under Constantine*, http://www.pbs.org/wgbh/pages/frontline/shows/religion/why/legitimization.html

Cohen, Shaye I.D., *From Maccabees to Mishnah*, (Philadelphia: Westminster, 1987)

Conybeare, W. J. and Howson, J. S., *The Life and Epistles of St. Paul*, (Grand Rapids: Eerdmans, 2004)

Coppes, Leonard, J., *What Happen To Biblical Tongues*, (Phillipsburg, NJ: Pilgrim Press, 1977)

Cox, Harvey Gallagher, *Fire from Heaven the Rise of Pentecostal Spirituality and the Reshaping of Religion in the Twenty-first Century*, (Reading, MA: Addison-Wesley, 1995)

Cutten, George B., *Speaking with Tongues: Historically and Psychologically Considered* (New Haven, CT: Yale University Press, 1927)

Cyril of Jerusalem, "Catechetical Letters," *Nicene and Post-Nicene Fathers*, ed. Philip Schaff, (Peabody, MA: Hendrickson, 1999)

D

Dales, Douglas, "Celtic and Anglo-Saxon Spirituality," *The Story of Christian Spirituality*, ed. Gordon Mursell, (Minneapolis: Fortress Press, 2001)

Daniel-Rops, H., *Cathedrals and Crusades* (New York: Dutton & Co., 1957)

Davies, William R., *Spirit Baptism and Spiritual Gifts in Early Methodism*, (Jacksonville, FL: Cross Fire Ministries, 1974)

DeCenso, Frank, Jr., *Amazed By the Power of God*, (Shippensburg, PA: Destiny Image, 2009)

Deere, John, *Surprised by the Power of the Spirit*, (Grand Rapids, Zondervan, 1993)

Diadochus Of Photike, *On Spiritual Knowledge*, (Peabody MA: Hendrickson, 1999)

Dillow, Joseph, *Speaking in Tongues*, (Grand Rapids: Zondervan, 1975)

Dorries, David, *Edward Irving and the Standing Sign*, *Initial Evidence*, ed. Gary B. McGee, (Peabody, MA: Hendrickson, 1991)

Douglas, J.D., ed., *The New International Dictionary of the Christian Church* (Grand Rapids, MI: Zondervan, 1974)

Dunn, James D.G., *Baptism of the Holy Spirit*, (Philadelphia: Westminster Press, 1970)

Dunn, James G.D., *Jesus and the Spirit* (Grand Rapids: Eerdmans, 1975)

E

Early Christian World, Philip F. Esler, ed. (New York: Routledge, 2000)

Edwards, Jonathan, *Jonathan Edwards on Revival*, (Carlisle, PA: Banner of Truth, 1984)

Ensley, Eddie, *Sound of Wonder*, (New York: Paulist Press, 1977)

Ervin, Howard, *These Are Not Drunken As Ye Suppose* (Plainfield, NJ: Logos International, 1968)

Ervin, Howard *Conversion-Initiation and the Baptism in the Holy Spirit* (Peabody MA: Hendrickson, 1984)

Ervin, Howard M. Ervin, *Spirit Baptism*, (Peabody, MA: Hendrickson, 1987)

Eusebius of Caesarea, *Ecclesiastical History*, (Grand Rapids: Baker Books, 1966)

Eusebius, "The Life of Constantine," *Nicene and Post-Nicene Fathers*, eds. Philip Schaff and Henry Wace, (Peabody, MA: Hendrickson, 1999)

Eusebius of Caesarea, "Church History," *Nicene and Post-Nicene Fathers*, ed. Philip Schaff, (Peabody, MA.: Henderson, 1999)

Evagrius of Pontus, "Chapters on Prayer," Cistercian Studies Series, trans. John Eudes Bamberger, (Kalamazoo: Cistercian Publishers, 1972)

Ewart, Frank J., *The Phenomenon of Pentecost*, (Hazelwood, CA: Word Aflame Press, 2000)

F

Fatula, Mary Ann, *Catherine of Siena's Way*, (London: Darton, Longman, and Todd, 1987)

Fletcher, Richard A., *Who's Who in Roman Britain and Anglo-Saxon*

England, (Chicago: St. James Press, 1989)

Fox, George, *The Works of George Fox*, (New York: AMS Press, 1975)

Foxe, John, *Foxe's Book of Martyrs*, (Peabody, MA: Hendrickson Classics, 2004)

Frend, W.H.C., *The Rise of Christianity*, (Philadelphia: Fortress Press, 1984)

Frodsham, S.H., *With Signs Following*, (Springfield, MO: Evangelical Press, 1946)

G

Gerson, Jean, *Early Works*, (New York: Paulist Press, 1998)

Goff, James Rudolph, Jr., *Fields White Unto Harvest*, (Fayetteville, AK: University of Arkansas Press, 1988)

Goodspeed, Edgar J., *The Apostolic Fathers*, (New York: Harper, 1950)

Gordon, A. J., *The Healing Ministry*, (Harrisburg, PA: Christian Pub. 1961)

Graham, Stephen R., "The Protestant Tradition in America," in *Christian Spirituality*, ed.

Gordon Mursell, (Minneapolis: Fortress Press, 2001)

Gregory the Great, *Morals on Job*, *http://www.lectionarycentral.com/GregoryMoralia/Book08.html*

Gregory the Great, *Forty Gospel Homilies*, trans. Dom David Hurst, (Kalamazoo, MI: Cistercian Pub., 1990)

Green, Michael, *I Believe in the Holy Spirit*, (Grand Rapids: Eerdmans, 1975)

Greenfield, John, *Power From On High*, (London, Marshall & Scott, 1931)

Gritsch, Eric W., *Born Againism*, (Philadelphia: Fortress Press, 1982)

Grossman, Siegfreid, *Charisma: The Gifts of the Spirit*. Trans. Susan Wiesmann, (Wheaton, IL: Key Publishers, 1971)

H

Hamilton, Michael P., *The Charismatic Movement*, (Grand Rapids: Eerdmans, 1975)

Hanna, James a.m., *A History of the Celtic Church from its Inception to 1153*, (Ann Arbor, MI: Edward Brothers, 1963)

Hargrave, Vessie D., "Reformation to 20th Century," *The Glossolalia Phenomenon*, ed. Wade H. Horton, (Cleveland, TN: Pathway Press, 1966)

Hayford, Jack W. and Moore, David S., *The Charismatic Century: The Enduring Impact of the Azusa Street Revival*, (New York: Warner Faith, 2006)

Heidler, Robert, *Experiencing the Spirit*, (Ventura, CA: Renew, 1998)

Hilary of Poitiers, "On the Trinity," *Nicene and Post-Nicene Fathers*, ed. Philip Schaff, (Peabody, MA: Hendrickson, 1999)

Hinnebusch, Paul, *Praise: A Way of Life*, (Ann Arbor, MI: Word of Life Publishers, 1976)

Hinson, E. Glenn, *The Evangelization of the Roman Empire*, (Macon, GA: Mercer Press)

Hogue, Richard, *The End of the Age*, (Cambridge, MA: Phos Books, 2008)

Horsch, John, *The Faith of the Hutterian Brethren*, (Cayley, Alberta: Macmillan, 1974)

Hyatt, Eddie, L., *2000 Years of Charismatic Christianity*, (Lake Mary, FL: Charisma, 2002)

Hyatt, Eddie L., *The Azusa Street Revival*, (Lake Mary, FL: Charisma House, 2006)

I

Ignatius of Antioch, *The Epistles of Saint Ignatius of Antioch*, (Westminster, MD: Newman Press, 1961)

Irving, Edward, *Collected Works*, ed. G. Carlyle, (London: Strahan, 1864)

J

Jerome and Gennadius, "Illustrious Men of the Church," *Nicene and Post-Nicene Fathers*, ed. Philip Schaff, (Peabody, MA: Hendrickson, 1999)

Jerome, "Life of Saint Hilarion," *Nicene and Post-Nicene Fathers*, ed. Philip Schaff, (Peabody, MA: Hendrickson, 1999)

K

Kelsey, Morton, *Tongue Speaking*, (NY: Crossroads, 1981)

Koester, Helmut, *History and Literature of the Early Church*, (New York: Walter D. Gruyter, 2000)

L

Lampe, G.W.H., "The Holy Spirit in the Writings of St. Luke," *Studies in the Gospels*, ed. D.E. Nineham (Oxford: Blackwell, 1955)

Lampe, G.W.H., *The Seal of the Spirit*, (London: S.P.C.K., 1967)

Leadbetter, Bill, "Constantine," *The Early Christian World*, ed. Philip F. Esler, (New York: Routledge, 2000)

Lehner, Francis C., *Saint Dominic: Biographical Documents* (Washington D.C.: Thomist Press, 1964)

Louth, Andrew, *The Origins of the Christian Tradition*, (Oxford: Clarendon, 1981)

Lossky, Vladimir, "The Theology of Light in the Thought of Saint Gregory Palamas," *In the Image and Likeness of God*, (New York: St. Vladimir's Seminary Press, 1947)

Lovejoy, David S., *Religious Enthusiasm and the Great Awakening*, (Englewood Cliffs, NJ: Prentice Hall, 1969)

M

MacLauchlan, Thomas, *The Early Scottish Church: The Ecclesiastical History of Scotland, from the First to the Twelfth Century*, (Edinburgh: T & T Clark, 1864)

Maier, Paul L., *Eusebius, Church History*, (Grand Rapids: Kregel, 1999)

Martyr, Justin, "Dialogue with Trypho," *Ante-Nicene Fathers*, eds. Alexander Roberts and James Donaldson, (Peabody, MA: Hendrickson, 1999)

McDonnell, Kilian, *The Baptism of the Holy Spirit*, (Notre Dame, IN: Charismatic Renewal Services, 1972)

McDonnell, Kilian and Montague, George T., *Christian Initiation and Baptism in the Holy Spirit*, (Collegeville, MN: Liturgical Press, 1991)

McGuckin, John A., "The Early Church Fathers," *The Story of Christian Spirituality*, ed. Gordon Mursell, (Minneapolis: Fortress Press, 2001)

McGuckin, John A., "The Eastern Christian Tradition," *The Story of Christian Spirituality*, ed. Gordon Mursell, (Minneapolis: Fortress Press, 2001)

McDonald, Lee M., *The Formation of the Christian Biblical Canon*, (Peabody, MA: Hendrickson, 1995)

McNemar, Richard, *The History of the Kentucky Revival*, (New York: reprint by E.O. Jenkins, 1846)

McRay, John, *Archaeology and the New Testament* (Grand Rapids: Baker, 1991)

Mennonite Quarterly Review, (Goshen, IN: Mennonite Historic Society)

Meyendorff, John, trans. Adele Fiske, *Saint Gregory Palamas and Orthodox Spirituality*. (New York: St. Vladimir's Seminary Press, 1974)

Moore, Henry, ed., *The Life of Mary Fletcher*, (New York, 1840)

Murray, Iain *The Puritan Hope* (Carlisle, PA: The Banner of Truth Trust, 1975).

Morgan, G. Campbell, "The Lesson of the Revival," *Welsh Revival*, (Boston, Pilgrim Press, 1905)

N

Newmann, Richard and Tinney, James S., *Black Apostles*, (G.K. Hall & Co., 1978)

Nickalls, John L., ed. *The Journal of George Fox*, (Cambridge: University Press, 1952)

Norwich, John Julius, *Byzantium: The Early Centuries*, (New York: Knopf, 1989)

Novatian, "Treatise Concerning the Trinity," *Ante-Nicene Fathers*, eds. Alexander Roberts and James Donaldson, (Peabody, MA: Hendrickson, 1999)

O

Origen, "Against Celsus," *Ante-Nicene Fathers*, ed. Alexander Roberts and James Donaldson (Peabody, MA: Hendrickson, 1999)

Owens, Robert, *The Century of the Holy Spirit*, ed. Vinson Synan, (Nashville: Nelson, 2001)

Oyer, John S., *Lutheran Reformers Against the Anabaptists* (The Hague: Martinus Nijhoff, 1964)

P

Palamas, Gregory, *The Triads*, trans. Nicholas Gendle, ed. John Meyendorff, (Ramsey, NJ: Paulist Press, 1983)

Palmer, Phoebe, *Four Years in the Old World*, (Boston: Foster & Palmer, 1865)

Parham, Sarah, *The Life of Charles F. Parham*, (Baxter Springs, KS: Apostolic Faith, 1985)

Patrick, *Confessions of Saint Patrick*, *http://www.ccel.org/ccel/patrick/*

confession.html

Philo of Alexander, *On Contemplative Life,* trans. David Winston, (New York: Paulist Press, 1981)

The Philokalia, The Complete Text, G.E.H. Palmer, Philip Sherrard, and Bishop Kallistos Ware, eds., (London: Faber and Faber, 1979)

R

Reinhart, A., "St. Vincent Ferrier," *The Catholic Encyclopedia.* (New York: Appleton Company) *http://www.newadvent.org/cathen/15437a.htm*

Robinson, Paschal, "Saint Bonaventure," *The Catholic Encyclopedia.* (New York:

Appleton Company, 1907). *http://www.newadvent.org/cathen/02648c.htm*

Robeck, Cecil M., *The Azusa Street Mission and Revival,* (Nashville: Nelson, 2006)

Robinson, John A.T., *The Redating of the New Testament,* (Philadelphia: Westminster, 1976)

Roche, John, *The Moravian Heresy,* (Dublin: printed for the author, 1751)

Russell, James Stuart, *The Parousia,* (Bradford, PA: Kingdom Publications, 1996)

S

Sanday, William, *Essays on Biblical Criticism and Exegesis,* Craig A. Evans and Stanley Porter eds., with the assistance of Scott N. Dolff, (Sheffield, England, Sheffield Academic Press, 2001)

Schatzmann, Siegfried, *A Pauline Theology of Charismata,* (Peabody, MA: Hendrickson, 1987)

Sellner, Edward C., *Wisdom of the Celtic Saints,* (Notre Dame, IN:

Ave Maria Press, 1993)

Severus, Sulpitius, "The Life of Saint Martin," *Nicene and Post-Nicene Fathers,* eds. Philip Schaff and Henry Wace, (Peabody, MA: Hendrickson, 1999)

Simons, Menno, "Treatise on Christian Baptism," *Collected Works,* trans. and ed. Leonard Verduin, (Scottdale, PA: 1956)

Skinner, William Cumming, *Candida Casa The Apostolic Center of Scotland,* (Dundee, Scotland: David Winter and Son, 1931)

Smith, James, *History of the Christian Church,* (Nashville: Cumberland Presbyterian, 1835)

Smith, T.C., "Acts," *Broadman Commentary,* Clifton J. Allen, ed. (Nashville: Broadman, 1970)

Sproul, R.C., *The Mystery of the Holy Spirit,* (Wheaton, IL: Tyndale House, 1990)

Strachan, C. Gordon, *The Pentecostal Theology of Edward Irving,* (London: Darton, Longmann, and Todd, 1973)

Stanton, Longenecker, Barton, eds. *The Holy Spirit and Christian Origins,* (Grand Rapid: Eerdmans, 2004)

Stark, Rodney, *The Rise of Christianity,* (San Francisco: Harper, 1996)

Stead, W.T., "Mr. Evan Roberts," *The Story of the Welsh Revival Told by Eyewitnesses,* (New York: Fleming H. Revel, 1905)

Stollee, H.J., *Speaking in Tongues,* (Minneapolis: Augsburg Publishing House, 1963)

Sullivan, Francis A., *Charisms and Charismatic Renewal,* (Dublin, Scotland: Gill and Macmillan, 1982)

Sweet, William W., *Religion of the American Frontier,* (New York: Cooper Square, 1964)

Synan, Vinson, *Aspects of Pentecostal-Charismatic Origins,* (Plainfield, NJ: Logos, 1975)

Synan, Vinson, *The Holiness-Pentecostal Movement*, (Grand Rapids: Eerdmans, 1997)

Synan, Vinson, *The Century of the Holy Spirit*, (Nashville: Thomas Nelson, 2001)

T

Tertullian, "Against Marcion," *Ante-Nicene Fathers*, ed. Alexander Roberts and James Donaldson, (Peabody, MA: Hendrickson, 1999)

The New Catholic Encyclopedia, (Detroit: Gale Group, 2001, in cooperation with the American Catholic University.)

Thurston, Herbert and Attwater, Donald, eds. *Butler's Lives of the Saints*, (New York: P.J. Kennedy, 1963)

Torrey, R.A., *The Holy Spirit*, (New York: Fleming Revell, 1927)

Trevett, Christine, "Montanism," *The Early Christian World*, ed. Philip F. Esler, (New York: Routledge, 2000)

Trueblood, Elton, *A People Called Quakers*, (New York: Harper & Row, 1966)

U

Unger, Merrill, F. *New Testament Teaching on Tongues*, (Grand Rapids: Kregel Publishers, 1971)

V

Van Der Meer, Fredrick, *Augustine the Bishop*, (New York: Sheed and Ward, 1961)

W

Bede's Ecclesiastical History of the English People, J.M. Wallace-Hadrill, ed., (New York: Oxford University Press, 1993)

Walsh, Michael, ed., *Butler's Lives of the Saints*, (San Francisco: Harper, 1991)

Wesley, John *The Journal of the Rev. John Wesley*, ed. Nehemiah Curnack, (London: Epworth, 1960)

Wesley, John, *Works*, ed. John Emory (New York, 1856)

Westcott, Brooke Foss and Hort, Fenton John Anthony, *Greek New Testament*, (Peabody, MA: Hendrickson, 1988)

Whitaker, E.C., *Documents of the Baptismal Liturgy*, (London: SPCK, 1970)

White, R.E.O., *The Biblical Doctrine of Initiation*, (Grand Rapids: Eerdmans, 1960)

Wigglesworth, Smith, *The Holy Spirit*, (New Kensington, PA: Whitaker House, 1998)

Williams, J. Rodman, *A Theological Pilgrimage*, *http://www.jrodmanwilliams.net/theological-pilgrimage/tp09.html*

Williams, J. Rodman, *Renewal Theology*, (Grand Rapids, MI: Zondervan, 1990)

Williams, George H. and Waldvogel, Edith, "A History of Speaking in Tongues and Related Gifts," *The Charismatic Movement*, ed. Michael P. Hamilton, (Grand Rapids, MI: Eerdmans, 1975)

Whitfield, George, *George Whitfield's Journal*, (London: The Banner of Truth Trust, 1965)